Desperate Mission

DESPERATE
MISSION

JOEL BRAND'S STORY

as told by

ALEX WEISSBERG

Translated from the German by

Constantine FitzGibbon and

Andrew Foster-Melliar

CRITERION BOOKS

NEW YORK

We dedicate this book to the men of the Waada Ezra we Hazalah.

To those who fought for the destiny of their brothers and to those who died in the struggle.

FOREWORD

THIS book was a cooperative endeavor. The remarkable events with which it deals were described to me by Joel Brand, a leader of the Jewish underground movement in Budapest. He is responsible for the statements contained in it, but wherever his facts seemed to be contradicted by the reports of other participants, I took care to check them against other, independent sources of information.

Research was immensely difficult. The destruction of the European Jews was a rough and ready business that left but faint traces in the official archives. Historical evidence has therefore been limited mainly to the testimony of those who survived. But although it has been hard to verify every detail and statistic, the general outline of these incredible happenings has at least been drawn with sufficient accuracy to enable the discussion of their political significance.

The conversations that Joel Brand had with his companions, with the SS leaders, with the delegates of the Jewish Agency in Constantinople, and with the British officers in Cairo occupy a large part of this book. These I have preferred to render in the form of direct speech. It may be objected that it is impossible to reconstruct a conversation word for word that took place ten years ago. This objection is, of course, valid, but it would also apply to conversations of ten days ago. The dialogue in the book does not pretend to be a verbatim reproduction of the words spoken. It is simply a form chosen for the sake of brevity.

I hope that our joint efforts have succeeded in throwing some light upon this dark and tragic chapter of the history of the Second World War.

Vienna, September 12, 1956   ALEX WEISSBERG

CONTENTS

x   Contents

APPENDIX

PART I

JOEL BRAND'S STORY

ON APRIL 25, 1944, I was taken to the SS headquarters at the Hotel Majestic in Budapest to meet Lieutenant Colonel Eichmann. He stood up to receive me and said:

"I expect you know who I am. I was in charge of the 'actions' in Germany, Poland, and Czechoslovakia. Now it is Hungary's turn. I have got you here so that we can talk business. I have already investigated you and your people of the Joint and the Sochnuth,[1] and I have verified your authority to make a deal. Now then, I am prepared to sell you one million Jews. Not the whole lot—you wouldn't be able to raise enough money for that. But you could manage a million. Blood for money, money for blood. You can take them from any country you like, wherever you can find them. From Hungary, Poland, the eastern provinces, from Terezin, from Oswiecim—wherever you will. Whom do you want to save? Men who can beget children? Women who

---

[1] See footnote page 16.

can bear them? Old people? Children? Sit down and tell me."

The man who said this to me was Himmler's commissioner for the liquidation of the Jews in Europe. He spoke as the representative of his government, at a time when smoke still poured from the chimneys of the gas chambers and crematories of Oswiecim and Treblinka. Five million of my race had already been slaughtered. Now he was proposing to sell the rest, or at any rate a large part of the rest. How did this fantastic offer come to be made?

This murderer was making a serious proposition. If the deal had been concluded, a million people would have been saved from a terrible death. The chance was missed.

Now more than ten years have passed, and passions are cooler. It is time for an accurate account of these events—events in which I took a major role.

JOEL BRAND

Chapter I

I AM JOEL BRAND

I COME of a well-to-do Jewish family from Russian Carpathia (formerly Hungarian Slovakia). My grandfather was the postmaster of Mukachevo. The post office was at that time a private concern, and it was his personal property. He was an energetic man; he exploited the mineral springs in the neighborhood, grew the finest vines in the district, and built whole rows of houses in our home town. Even today a street and a synagogue in Mukachevo bear his name. He invested his money in gold ducats, which he stored in old wine casks. His seven sons had an easy life. When they were out of money, they would dip into the wine casks. My grandfather wanted them to be scribes, but they preferred a more worldly life. He built them a house with seven identical apartments, but when it was finished his sons would not live there, so he left the land of his childhood and went

to the country of his dreams, Erets Israel, where he wanted
to be buried in consecrated ground.

Once arrived in Israel, he began to build again. There
is a whole quarter in Jerusalem called "the Hungarian
houses," and many of these were built by Rebb Joel Brand.
The good people of Jerusalem speak to this day of the great
Nadwan, the benefactor. Again he built a house for his sons,
with seven identical apartments. He waited several years,
but still none of them wished to live there with him. Then
he died.

My father was a contractor and founded the Budapest
telephone company. He was a self-made man, and although
he had never had a college education, he devoted his whole
life to solving technical problems. His hobby was the development of communications. My mother was the daughter of a banker from Nasaud in Transylvania. I myself arrived in this world on April 25, 1906.

When I was four years old, the family moved to Germany. I grew up in Erfurt, took my final examinations
there, and then went to the polytechnic academy in Leip-
zig. I stayed there for a while, but I was nineteen years old
and I wanted to travel.

For a short time I lived with a well-to-do uncle in New
York, and then I went further afield. I tramped across the
United States, working on the roads, in automobile factories, and in the coal mines. I shoveled snow in New York,
washed dishes in Philadelphia and Cincinnati, worked in an
architect's office in Atlanta, and finally went to sea. I
visited Hawaii, the Philippines, Japan, China, and South
America. I changed ships from time to time, and now and
again I spent a few months ashore. I returned to Erfurt in
the summer of 1930. My father had died in the meantime,

and I took over the telephone business that he had founded. Thus began a period of quiet and peaceful work in that little German town.

In public life, however, great decisions were being made. Hitler's Brownshirts and the members of the Red Front jostled each other on the sidewalks. The economic crisis had already thrown seven million people out of work, and in the Reichstag one government after another failed to secure a stable working majority. The crisis endangered the whole political system. My boyhood friends expected a socialist revolution, but instead fascism, in its most murderous form, took over the government of the country.

These matters did not affect me personally until Hitler seized power in 1933. Then I was faced with an entirely new situation. Shortly before the Reichstag fire I was arrested, along with many other Jews and people of leftist views. Two years later I fled from Germany to escape further persecution. I went to Budapest.

I had always been connected with socialist and communist circles at college, but events in Germany and in the Soviet Union forced me to revise my political opinions. I became a Zionist, thus reverting to the traditions of my family and my early youth.

The telephone company in Budapest, which my father had created, offered me a position with excellent prospects. I accepted it; a prosperous future lay open to me. But in my heart I had already finished with Europe. My only desire was to go to Erets Israel and work in a *kibuz*.[1] I was still greatly influenced by the socialist ideas of my student days, and I was filled with ambition to lead a useful and productive life in the land of my fathers. I joined a *hachscharah*,

---

[1] A *kibuz* is a collective farm in Palestine.

the name given to those groups of young Jews who were training themselves for life in Palestine. We lived and ate together, and all our earnings went to the group funds. Even our clothes were common property.

It was in this *hachsharah* that I met Hansi Hartmann. Our struggles and our hopes brought us very close, and toward the end of 1935 we were married.

For business reasons I was forced to leave the collective in the spring of 1936. My mother and three sisters had fled from Germany, and I now had about a dozen people to look after. Even my comparatively high salary in the telephone company was not enough to go round, so I decided to open a workshop with my wife, who was a weaver. We were lucky, and after a few years we were employing more than a hundred workers.

Our plans for an immediate emigration to Erets Israel were abandoned, but I worked all the more enthusiastically in the Zionist movement. I became a committee member of the Poale Zion[2], was elected to the board of the Zionist Land Organization, and became one of the presidents of the Keren Hajesod.[3]

My peaceful work was scarcely disturbed by the outbreak of the Second World War. We did our best to help the refugees, who poured over the frontier in ever increasing numbers, and we enlarged our Zionist activities. But it never entered our heads that Central European Jewry was doomed, and to such a fate!

Before the First World War, Hungary had been one of the European countries best disposed toward the Jews,

[2] Poale Zion (also called Tchud): a socialist splinter group of the Zionist movement.
[3] Keren Hajesod: Zionist building fund.

and in the Hungarian towns the Jews had identified themselves with their hosts more completely than in any other Central European state. They were given every opportunity to prosper in public life, in the civil service, and in the learned professions. In literature, science, and the arts, Hungary owed a great debt to Jewish artists and thinkers. In social life there was practically no anti-Semitic feeling, and Jewish blood often ran in the veins of the aristocracy, who still ruled that semi-feudal country.

All this was altered at one stroke when Nicholas von Horthy, after the fall of the short-lived communist government in 1919, marched into Budapest at the head of his newly awakened Magyars. A period of violent anti-Semitism ensued. Jews were forbidden to participate in the public life of the country, and were often tortured to death by the nationalist Magyar soldiery.

But Europe was still strongly influenced by the humanistic and democratic ideas that had arisen after the defeat of German imperialism by the Western powers, and Hungarian fascism did not prosper. Instead, a form of democracy slowly took its place, and the anti-Semitic laws were often disregarded. The old Hapsburg monarchy used to be described as "absolutism tempered by indolence"; Horthy's Hungary could well have been called "fascism modified by corruption." Indeed, Horthy, who had set out to crush an imaginary Red Jewish domination, found himself in the end opposing Hitler's murderous demands for the liquidation of the Jews.

The outbreak of the Second World War and the acquisition of Transylvania marked a turning point in this development. Many onerous "racial laws" were passed, and the Jews were impressed into a sort of military forced-labor

service. The atrocities that later took place in these labor
gangs were to make them comparable to the camps run by
the Gestapo.

When war broke out with Russia, tens of thousands of
conscripts were sent, insufficiently clothed, to the districts
occupied by the Hungarian troops. Most of them perished.
Hangings, shootings, and cruel beatings were the order of
the day. Often whole companies were forced to crawl on
their hands and knees, with their dinner plates between
their teeth, barking like dogs. Sometimes there were regular mass exterminations. For example, a military hospital
near Korasten, in which five hundred of these conscripts
lay sick with typhoid fever, was ringed with machine guns
one night and set on fire. Those who attempted to flee were
shot down.

Often so-called "shooting parties" would be organized.
The Jews would be forced to climb trees and jump like
monkeys from branch to branch. Woe betide any who
might fall, for the "hunters" would be waiting for them with
their bayonets. If they jumped too slowly, the "beaters"
would deal with them, with whips and sticks. Sometimes
they would be suspended by their tied wrists, and when
they fainted they would be brought round with the help of
a bucket of cold water. If they were drenched often enough,
the Russian cold would turn them into icicles. On other occasions they would be thrown, in chains, onto a campfire
and burned to death.

At first, the worst excesses occurred only in the frontier
districts, where the influence of the German SS was strongest. Hungarian territory proper was still spared these
horrors. Indeed the accounts of forced-labor conditions in
Russia were scarcely believed at home. Only one isolated

incident managed to break the conspiracy of silence in the capital.

In the spring of 1941, the Hungarian government had concluded a treaty of friendship with Yugoslavia, whose government was then on friendly terms with the Axis powers. When this government fell, the Bachka was occupied by Hungarian troops, who instituted a ferocious pogrom on January 6, 1942. In the space of a few hours, some thousands of Jews were savagely done to death. The contradictions within the Hungarian system of government at that time are shown by the fact that the Regent himself now took a hand in the matter. No sooner had the news reached Budapest than he ordered the pogrom stopped. He sent his aide-de-camp to Bachka and had the officers responsible for the slaughter court-martialed. They were found guilty, but their prison gates were left open, and they were allowed to escape to fascist Germany, to return later in the wake of the German SS troops.

I myself took part as an officer cadet in the campaign in Transylvania, but when the labor corps was started, I was expelled from the army with the rest of my Jewish comrades. I should have gone back to Budapest to await conscription into the labor force, but I was determined to avoid this at all costs. With the help of a doctor I knew, I managed to reserve a bed in the St. Istvan Hospital in Budapest. When the messenger arrived at my home with the conscription papers, my wife and our cook, Rozsi Varsoni, refused to accept the summons on my behalf. When my wife told me what had happened, I went immediately to the hospital, where I stayed for some weeks. Fortunately I had mild diabetes, and the doctors repeatedly gave me injections to correct the sugar content of my blood.

After I heard that my company had left Budapest, I went home, thinking I would be left in peace, but much to my surprise I was court-martialed for evading service. However, the Hungarian courts had not yet lost their independence and legality. My defense was simple: that I had never received my papers. The doctors testified that at the time in question I was lying gravely ill, and this was confirmed by my wife.

The judge advocate became angry. "Why didn't you take the conscription papers straight to your husband? Didn't you realize that your action amounted to sabotage?"

"I am sorry, Your Honor; I know nothing about politics. My husband was very ill at the time, and I certainly didn't intend to upset him with matters like that. He wasn't even able to get out of bed. It's bad enough that he has to go through all this now. He's a sick man and this sort of thing won't do him any good at all."

The judge advocate was still furious, but there was nothing he could do. There was no law that compelled wives to perform the duties of army postmen, and I was therefore acquitted.

I now enjoyed almost six months of comparative peace. However, in the summer of 1941, events occurred that tore me away from my unimportant private life and gave me a part to play in the drama of my unhappy race—a part that was really beyond my strength.

On June 22, 1941, German troops marched into Russia, and in their wake followed regiments from Italy, Rumania, and Hungary. The German masters presented their Hungarian vassals with a small strip of land in the Ukraine to administer, and Jewish labor conscripts were immediately sent to this district.

A few weeks after the outbreak of war Lieutenant Colonel Ferenczy, chief of the Hungarian police, struck his first blow. In one night about fifty thousand foreign Jews, most of whom had been settled in Hungary for many years, were imprisoned by the police. They were given no time to collect their possessions, but were herded into railroad cars that had already been prepared for them and were deported to the occupied territories of East Galicia and the Ukraine. Most of these unhappy people were never seen again.

The Jews in Budapest were terrified, but the Jewish community did not dare to protest. Only when the Zionist delegate, Dr. Kahan Nisson, spoke up did the leaders of our community attempt, somewhat timidly, to intervene. This anti-Semitic "action" ceased as quickly as it had begun, although the consequences of it were to be of great importance to me personally and, later, to my work.

Among the Jews who had been deported were my wife's sister and her husband, Lajos Stern. My wife managed to see her sister in the police cage. Next day they were both taken away. But no one knew exactly where they had been sent. The wildest rumors circulated: Hungary was going to annex parts of Poland and settle displaced Jews there; the deportees were going to be handed over to the Germans; they were to be executed; all Budapest Jews were to be deported to Poland; no, only the Polish-speaking ones would be sent, to help with the harvest; and so on and so forth. Nevertheless the truth slowly came out: the deportees were in the neighborhood of Kamenets-Podolski.

My wife was insistent. "Bring my sister back, Joel," she said. "You can do it, if you want to. They will both be killed otherwise. Every day counts. We have got to do something."

I must confess I am very fond of visiting coffee houses. When I am worried, I like to sit at a table and think things over. I nearly always get an idea, or else I meet someone who can help me. And so it happened on this occasion. I had hardly sat down when a man came in whom I knew slightly. But I immediately said to myself, "There's your man."

He was a frivolous young man, who, so rumor had it, worked for the Hungarian secret service. He was notoriously fond of wine, women, and song, and so was always short of cash. We sat down together, and I put my proposition to him. I offered him ten thousand pengös if he would bring my relatives back from the Ukraine. This would not be easy, for I could not even tell him where they were; I could only give him their names and photographs. He said he was willing to try. I, therefore, deposited the ten thousand pengös with a Dr. Kaldi, a lawyer. The young man was willing to do the job, but said he needed five hundred pengös for his expenses. Suspecting he wanted the money to pay a gambling debt, I canceled the deal. But the same evening my wife, without saying a word to me, took him the five hundred pengös. He promised to be back in a week's time, with her relatives hidden in the luggage compartment of his car.

For a whole week we waited in a fever of excitement. Then the telephone rang. It was the young man, calling from one of the suburbs; he told us he would be with us in an hour. But when we met him, he said he had been unable to find my relatives, though he had succeeded in bringing back four Jews from the same district. He promised to set off in a few days' time and try again.

He seemed to enjoy doing this, and the others had

promised him exorbitant sums for their rescue. He impressed on us the need for caution. He said we must hide these people carefully and keep everything very secret. He made several such journeys and always brought one or more people back with him. At last, on his fourth trip, he found my brother-in-law and his wife.

When my wife embraced her sister that evening, we thought that was the end of our problem. In reality, it was only the beginning.

Chapter II

THE JEWISH UNDERGROUND
MOVEMENT

THIS PRIVATE effort to save my brother-in-law led indirectly to the founding of an illegal organization with an ever increasing number of objectives. It was to have its agents in the enemy's secret service; it was able in the end to create a powerful apparatus for smuggling men across the frontiers; and it established a standing and smoothly functioning connection with the Jewish organizations in the Allies' camp. All this happened without any previously prepared plan. We stumbled, so to speak, into world history.

At first my wife and I had means enough to help only isolated individuals in distress. But soon our horizon broadened. Every day new problems arose, and every successful rescue increased the scope of our work.

We were continually forced to compromise. The young man who helped us in the way I have described impressed upon us from the very beginning the extreme secrecy of the work on which we were engaged. If the Hungarian police or the German Gestapo were to get an inkling of what was afoot, we might all be shot out of hand. But good intentions go by the board when men are worried to distraction about the safety and whereabouts of their closest kinsmen. Those who had been rescued told their friends and relatives about their escape, and the latter then made their way to me. My apartment in Buljovsky Street began to resemble a regular headquarters.

At first we wanted to stop this stream of inquirers, for we were afraid of *agents provocateurs*. But the impact of these despairing people who had lost father or son, mother or brother, was too much for us. We began to feel that it was our mission to organize the rescue of these people on a larger scale. As we grew more successful and widened our connections, our anxieties began to disappear. We felt we were no longer alone. The fact that at every stage in our organization we had young men and women working for us who were prepared each day to risk their lives increased our self-confidence and raised our courage.

Those who had been brought back from the Ukraine had terrible stories to tell. The Germans were preparing their large-scale campaign for the physical extermination of European Jewry. Eastern Galicia and the Ukraine were used as experimental fields for the undertaking. Various methods were employed. One night SS troops surrounded a small town and drove all the Jewish inhabitants out into the fields. There they were forced to dig graves and to kneel in front of them until the machine guns shot them down so that their bodies fell straight into the graves. In many towns the Jews were driven into the synagogues, which were then set on fire. These inhuman SS and Ukrainian beasts would even tear the gold teeth out of their victims' mouths before carrying out these mass executions. We had heard before of isolated instances of this kind; yet I must confess we had never really believed them. But the tales brought back from the Ukraine forced every one of us to recognize the grim truth and to face it squarely. From then on we knew that we were living on borrowed time, and that the rescue of the greatest possible number of our people depended entirely on our skill and courage.

After the first Jews had been illegally brought back, I went to see my friend Samu Springmann and told him the whole story. I had got to know Samu Springmann in the *hachscharah,* the socialist community in which I had spent my time when I first came to Budapest. He was a man of slim build and medium height, unusually quick and as sharp as a needle. He was a self-made man with no college education; nevertheless he had an unusual interest in intellectual and spiritual matters. He was a diamond merchant and jeweler by trade, and had managed to work up good connections with the diplomatic corps in Budapest, a fact that was to be of great help to us in the future.

Samu Springmann was fascinated by the possibilities that were open to us. He said at once that it was a matter of the greatest importance to our political party. "But we must get in touch with our members abroad," he said. "When the Sochnuth[1] learns of our potentialities, it will advise and

---

[1] In the Zionist movement every Zionist—that is to say every Jew whose aim is the collection into one sovereign state of the scattered members of his race—is a member of the universal Zionist Land Organization.

help us. We must find homes for the refugees and provide them with new papers. We must try to send them on farther, if possible to Palestine. That's all going to cost a lot of money. We won't be able to raise enough here, but if we can only establish contact with Constantinople, the Sochnuth will help us."

The actual establishment of our organization was simple. The leaders of the Poale Zion called a meeting and empowered Springmann, Kastner, and myself to organize and direct the work.

Dr. Rezsö Kastner was the representative of the Poale Zion in the presidium of the Zionist Land Organization. He was an energetic, vigorous man and had been aware for some time of the danger that threatened his race. He had handed to the Italian ambassador in Budapest a note for Count Ciano, in which he described the terrible plight of the Jews and asked the Italian government to intervene.

This organization, however, is a loose framework, which contains a most varied collection of Zionist parties. On the left wing are the Socialists (called Mapei in Israel); in the center is the liberal group of universal Zionists (called Klal in Israel); on the right wing is the religious orthodox group of the Misrachi. To the left of the Mapei are socialist revolutionary groups, the Schomer Hazaïr and the Achdut Avoda, which used to be known by the name Mapam. Outside the world organizations, and far to the right, is the Revisionist group founded by Wladimir Jabotinsky.

But all the Zionist parties together were only a small minority of the Jewish community in Hungary, at any rate before the time of Hitler and the Second World War. The majority of the Jews were led by men whose ambition was not for a return to Israel, but for the complete assimilation of the Jews with the peoples of the countries where they lived. Also the religious orthodox Jews, of the organization called Agudas Israel, were not Zionists.

At the Zionist Congress in Carlsbad in 1923, the Zionists decided to form a joint committee with the non-Zionist groups and parties, the Jewish Agency. This is known in Israel, and will be referred to in this book, as the Sochnuth. The Jewish Agency was recognized at the Zionist Congress in Zurich in 1929 and later by the British Mandatory Power as the sole legitimate representative of the Jewish people.

The only result of this, however, was that after the Germans had marched into Yugoslavia, the Italians sent forty Jewish children from Slovakia to Budapest in Italian army cars. Kastner tried without success to convene a meeting of all members of the Hungarian parliament who were of Jewish descent.

Rezsö Kastner was a typical Jewish intellectual, with all the good and all the bad qualities of his kind. He had an uncommon facility for discovering the hidden links in a chain of events, and when he really put his mind to something, he was able to achieve the almost impossible. At the same time, Kastner tended to be quick and slapdash rather than reliable; and in illegal work it is accuracy that determines the success or failure of the undertaking. Nevertheless, for all his weaknesses and timidity, Kastner was a courageous man who put his whole heart and soul into the rescue of the Jewish people and who achieved a great deal.

He was not an easy man to work with, and to many people he seemed to be the prototype of the snobbish intellectual who lacked the common touch. He could not be described as a good mixer, and he was especially unpopular with the members of the Chaluzim.[2] Yet as the politician of our triumvirate, he negotiated with the other Zionist parties, with the official Jewish community, with the Hungarian Social Democrats, and with the politicians of other Hungarian groups. After my departure he carried out the negotiations with the Germans.

The three of us constituted ourselves leaders of the organization, which we called Waada Ezra we Hazalah—

---

[2] *Chaluzim:* Pioneers, young people who are engaged in preparing themselves for life in the Israeli agricultural collectives.

Council for Assistance and Rescue, hereafter referred to as Waada.[3] I myself was in charge of the actual rescue work, and consequently was responsible for developing methods of getting the refugees across the frontier from the Ukraine, Poland, and Slovakia. My main concern was to get these people to Budapest, and then to give them legal status by means of false documents and so on.

Samu Springmann had a special task. He acquired the services of Hungarian and German secret agents for our cause, and he also managed to insinuate our own agents into the Hungarian police. He established contact with foreign countries. At critical times he even sent our people to the Jewish centers of Poland and to the ghettos of Cracow, Warsaw, Sosnowiec, and other such places.

In the few weeks after my brother-in-law's return, the work had already reached such proportions that an important member of the Jewish Land Organization heard of it. He was a good and honorable man, but he did not understand the signs of the times. He remonstrated bitterly with me on the grounds that I, as a member of the managing committee, was endangering the stability of the Zionist Organization, and even that of the Jewish community itself, by these illegal activities.

"Do you understand what you're doing, Joel?" he asked. "We are now at war. Do you know what it means to smuggle people across the frontier in time of war? How can you be sure that spies aren't using your escape route? Your actions may bring us all the greatest misfortunes." He

---

[3] I should mention here that there was at the same time an organization of the Sochnuth operating in Israel under the same name, which had representives in Constantinople. Later on we succeeded, through the efforts of Samu Springmann, in establishing an unbroken liaison with this organization.

would have had me brought before a Zionist board of discipline if the president of the Zionist Land Organization, Engineer Otto Komoly, had not taken a hand in the matter.

Otto Komoly came from a peasant family. He was an expert engineer and a man of irreproachable character. The methods used by an illegal organization such as ours were foreign to him, but he saw at once that they were the only ones possible under the conditions imposed by the Hitler terror. It was often necessary for me to go into the enemy camp to rescue men who were in mortal danger, and I then had to join in drinking bouts with the enemy's agents. When my nerves failed, it was always Otto Komoly who reassured and comforted me.

"You must keep going, Joel," he would say. "There are only a few of us who could do this kind of work. It's the dirtiest work but also the holiest, and even though you must wade through filth, you yourself are not defiled by it."

Otto Komoly was wholeheartedly behind us. It was thanks to his influence that the Zionist Organization gave us their support and, so to speak, their full authority to act in their name. At a later date he also undertook direct executive duties. He was to have conducted the negotiations with Eichmann, the SS officer, after I had gone, but he was of too upright a nature to be able to sit at the same table with this murderer. Kastner took his place, and Komoly became our liaison officer with the Hungarian government.

His time came at the end of 1944. All our people had hidden in cellars and bunkers, but he refused to do so. When the Germans sent for him, he obeyed. Since then we have heard nothing more of this good man, but his memory will always be treasured in the hearts of those Hungarian Jews who managed to survive.

The other Jewish organizations did not at first show much interest in us and our labors, and the burden of the work fell exclusively on the Chaluzim. When, however, we began to receive large sums of money from abroad, which then had to be shared, the others began to pay more attention to us. They decided to form a controlling organization to which all the Zionist parties would send their delegates and which would in general supervise the work. The three of us were elected to this committee. This organization, however, never really functioned properly; the party delegates were not energetic, and in practice we found that the work was left in our own hands, as before. Nevertheless, in time more and more representatives of different parties joined our Waada and worked with us on the best of terms.

During the first few weeks we had limited our activities to assisting in the escape of those who had been deported to the Ukraine. But that did not last for long. When the United States of America entered the war on December 8, 1941, the Germans finally dropped all pretenses. The German government decided on a "total" solution of the Jewish question. The operation was given the official title of "Night and Fog," and the German genius for organization now celebrated its most gruesome triumph. From six to seven million people, differing very little from their neighbors, and certainly not distinguishable by the color of their skin, were segregated and murdered by Hitler's people. All this was achieved with a minimum of trouble and expense to the Germans.

In Budapest we watched with bated breath the extermination of our people. Our work was only a drop in the ocean, but we were at least able to save tens of thousands of Jews from Poland and Slovakia.

Poland was the battlefield, and it became of great importance to secure our communications with that country. The police in Kosice were bribed by our Slovakian friends, and thus we learned the times at which certain stretches of the frontier were left unguarded. Most of the refugees made their way across the frontier by themselves, after we had given them detailed instructions. They would arrive in Kosice at dark, go to the synagogue, and on the following night our representative would take them on to Budapest. They had to be constantly on their guard against giving themselves away through their ignorance of the language. They spent their first few days in Budapest in lodgings that we had prepared for them in different parts of the town. If these lodgings were full, then, contrary to all the rules of conspiratorial caution, the refugees would be brought directly to me.

Simon Israel of the Poale Zion and Miklos Moskowitz, a non-Zionist comrade, were responsible for the sheltering of these people. The latter was killed some time later during a revolt against the SS. Our friend Jakubowitz organized the frontier crossings at Mukachevo, on the Hungarian-Polish border. He, too, fell later fighting against the SS.

In spite of there being only one frontier to cross, the direct route from Poland to Hungary was the more dangerous one. The border was more closely guarded, and a keener watch was kept on trains going to Budapest. We often had to swathe the refugees in bandages and pretend that they were sick, so that their ignorance of the Hungarian language would pass unnoticed.

The Waada set up a regular intelligence center in Budapest. Immediately on arrival, the refugees would be

closely questioned so that we could ascertain and record
the situation in the ghettos from which they had come. We
were just as interested in the personalities of the officials
who ran the German extermination apparatus as we were
in the behavior of the various Jewish councils. The experi-
ences of individual refugees on their flight from the ghettos
were used to help those who came after them. The conditions in the various concentration camps, the possibilities of escape, the adventures on the journey and crossing
the frontier—all this information we studied closely, so that
we could test the reliability of our own organization. We
sent hundreds of these records by way of Constantinople
and Switzerland to our head offices abroad.[4]

The Slovakian Chaluzim were the most active fighters
in our movement. All the work in the frontier districts
rested on their shoulders. At the same time, we were not in
a position to refuse the assistance of professional smugglers,
who were often true underworld characters. Cooperation
with these men, however, gave rise to moral questions
that were new to us, since none of us had had much experience in such matters. The Zionist movement had in
the years before the war developed entirely along legal
lines, and the works of Herzl and Nordau told us nothing
about the art of smuggling men from one country to another.

In the mountains on the Slovakian-Hungarian border,

---

[4] It is often said in the press and in books on the subject that the
Allies were informed too late of what was going on in the Polish cities
in 1942 and 1943. We cannot agree with this assertion, and can only say
that the official representatives of the Jewish people were, by means of
hundreds of individual memoranda, fully and immediately informed of
the situation. We also know that our cry of alarm was passed on at once
by the Sochnuth to the Allies.

there lived a "wild" Jew. He was a professional smuggler—
in fact, a bandit. Nevertheless, he took pride in his profes-
sion. He was on the friendliest terms with the Hungarian
and Slovakian frontier guards. He would send his police
friends to the Polish border, where they would bring the
refugees out of Poland and arrest them as Hungarian deserters. They would then take them across the small strip
of Slovakian territory and hand them over to our man. He
next employed very peculiar and doubtful methods. He
forced the refugees to make a declaration of all their possessions, and warned them against concealing any valuable
objects or currency. Many of them told the truth and on
that account got off fairly lightly by paying him a certain
sum as tax. But those who tried to hide their treasures from
him were scandalously robbed. He forced them to strip
naked and went through all their luggage. He was an expert in these matters, and there was no hiding place that he
was not able to discover. Should he find something that had
not been declared, the luckless refugee would have all his
possessions confiscated.

When these people arrived in Budapest, they were
indignant and anxious to put their complaints on record.
The charges against this man increased to such an extent
that we were obliged to make a special investigation. Our
Slovakian friends, however, defended him with all their
might. He was reliable, they said, and he was clever and
courageous. He did not ask for much money, and, above all,
he would bring poor people over the frontier for nothing.
For months we inquired into the matter. Finally we asked
him to come to see us, which he did immediately.

His justification of himself was simple: "I am not a
politician nor a professional philanthropist, but a smug-

gler. That is my business. I bring men and merchandise over the frontier, as another man might make shoes or clothes. You pay me to bring your people over the border, and it is a dangerous business. I risk my neck three times a week. But if you don't happen to have the money, I bring them over to you on credit. If the refugees are poor, and even if they don't come from your people, I still bring them over and I ask for no money. What do you expect of me? If on the other hand I smuggle gold and diamonds as well as people, I must be paid for it. If people try to deceive me and hide things from me, they have only themselves to blame if they lose their money. But even these people I bring over the frontier, and I look after them so that they reach you safe and sound. I have never blackmailed any-one."

The conditions under which we carried on our illegal work made it impossible for us to protest against this logic or against the outrageous methods he employed. Besides, one thing had to be said for him: he had never yet let any-one down. Should danger threaten, he would stand by the refugees and would not leave them until they were safely on their way. We were often attacked for our attitude to-ward this man, but I always defended him. This highway-man and professional criminal was to me a kind of hero, and later events were to prove me right. This Jew from the mountains joined in the revolt of the Slovakian partisans in the autumn of 1944 and fell during their dogged and courageous struggle against the superior might of the Ger-man army.

Every illegal movement must be forever on guard against the infiltration into its ranks of *agents provocateurs*. Our Polish comrades who worked in the enemy camp itself suffered greatly from this danger. On the whole, we were spared this hazard, and only those who have worked in an underground movement can understand how lucky we were. Nothing is more injurious than mistrust, and nothing can be more invigorating than the feeling of confidence in one's fellows. There were, however, some cases in which hard decisions had to be made.

In a village near Beregszasz on the Ukrainian border, two young girls reported for work. They said they were Zionists and members of the Misrachi bnei Akiba, an orthodox Jewish organization, although none of our people actually knew them. They were energetic and brave and brought many refugees over the border. We considered ourselves fortunate to have found two such capable assistants in this godforsaken hole, which controlled an important frontier pass. After a while they asked for more money for their expenses. We saw no objection and gave them everything they wanted. They were very pretty girls, and we assumed that they probably bought clothes with our money.

But one day they came and asked for a very large sum. The frontier guards, with whom they were on friendly terms, had promised of their own accord to bring them Jewish refugees. This pleased us very much, and the scheme had the approval of our head office. The refugees duly arrived, but we soon discovered that they were people who had long been settled in Hungary. The girls had conspired with these swindlers. We were in despair, but matters got still worse. Genuine refugees who came to Beregszasz were shamelessly blackmailed, even those who had been sent by our own people. These two girls and their friends robbed the wretched people of everything they possessed. If any of them resisted, they would threaten to inform the police and have them packed off to Poland. In some cases they held them captive in a barn, until they agreed to their demands.

We bided our time until the day they arrived in Budapest to blackmail us, too. They knew a great deal about our organization, and they knew precise details of our frontier connections. The central office in Budapest was itself endangered. It was not easy for us to reach our decision, but it was a matter of self-defense. The necessary action was carried out by a group of our young comrades.

There were hundreds of such cases in the Polish underground movement, and no mercy could be shown to those who endangered the lives of valuable men. But for us it was the first case of its kind. We had been brought up in a humanitarian movement, and it was not easy for us to obey the hard rules of necessity, which were forced on us in our struggle against German fascist terror.

There often were instances of betrayal, but those were the result of weakness rather than of criminal intention. There was the case of a twenty-year-old girl, who was a leading member of the Slovakian Haschomer Hazaïr, a Zionist socialist youth organization. She was intelligent, well educated, and highly thought of. But even revolutionaries are only men of flesh and blood; it is not given to everyone to stand up to physical torture. This girl fell victim to an informer. She was imprisoned by the Hungarian police and beaten until she divulged the names of her comrades. We had always reckoned with the possibility that those of us who were caught might give way under torture, and we immediately isolated the group in which the girl had been trained and with which she had worked in the movement. All the members of this group had to change their papers and addresses, and they disappeared underground. But there was one fact we had not reckoned with. When this girl was at last forced to betray her friends, she determined that it would not be her own comrades, whom she loved, but a group of the Makabi Hazaïr, with whom she had only a distant connection. Makabi Hazaïr was social democratic in outlook and the girl's friends in Haschomer Hazaïr had left-wing socialist or communist views. So the unexpected came to pass: many members of the Makabi Hazaïr were arrested, but none from the Haschomer Hazaïr. My closest fellow worker and assistant, Perez Revész, was among those imprisoned.

In this instance of betrayal, our decision was easy to make. We told the girl she must leave the country, and we took her to Rumania, where she had to break off all contact with our illegal organization. She lived in Rumania for the rest of the war, and survived.

However, we had a very capable contact in the Hungarian police, Deszö Dán, and he succeeded in obtaining the release of all the prisoners except Perez Revész, against whom the evidence was too grave for the police to be able to let him go. For him we arranged a fictitious deportation to Slovakia, which took place entirely under our control. We knew beforehand when and where the police would bring him over the frontier, and our friends, who were waiting for him on the other side, brought him back to Budapest the same night.

A more dangerous incident of this nature occurred in Budapest after my departure. A stool pigeon of the Hungarian police had insinuated himself into the Chaluzim group. He was not able to discover very much, since we were by this time extremely circumspect, and he was only able to establish close contact with one of our members. He betrayed this man to the police, who imprisoned and tortured him until he disclosed one of our illegal meeting places. The police hid the agent in a place from which he would overlook our street-corner rendezvous, and the results were disastrous. He recognized many of our people and gave their names to the police. Almost all the leaders of the Chaluzim were arrested, and our entire work was temporarily crippled. The situation, however, was correctly analyzed, and the necessary measures were taken.

The secret agent believed himself safe and sought once more to establish contact with our members. A trap was set for him. An athletic young man from the Haschomer Hazaïr, who was nicknamed Pil (the Hebrew for elephant), seized the stool pigeon and shook him as a terrier shakes a rat. He banged his head against the wall until his skull almost cracked. "You criminal," he said, "you filthy traitor. Maybe our people will perish, but no Nazi is ever going to help you again. We're going to kill you here and now, like a dog."

The secret agent thought his last hour had come and, trembling with fear, he stammered, "I couldn't help it. I was blackmailed and had no choice. But if you spare me, I can help you to have them all set free. The trial is to be conducted by a police officer who is a friend of mine. He can be bribed. Let me go, and I will see that it's done."

"And how do we know you won't betray us again?"

"Use your common sense. I'm a Jew, too. Do you think I enjoy getting my brothers into trouble? I was just weak, and after my first betrayal, I was wax in their hands."

"Why didn't you come to us and make a clean breast of it then?"

"I was too ashamed. That's all."

We had no choice but to take the risk. The Waada placed over a million pengös at our disposal. Engineer Biss had raised the money by personal collections and loans. Dr. Breslauer and Zoltán Farkas conducted the negotiations. The Hungarian police were speedily contacted and the exact procedure laid down. A group of our members were to be at an agreed spot at a certain time, dressed in the uniform of the Nyilas, the Hungarian Crossed Arrows party. We found the uniforms, and Raffi Friedel of the Haschomer Hazaïr, one of our most capable men, who later became the Israeli consul in Prague, led the group.

At the head of the spurious Crossed Arrows men, he marched up to the officer of the guard with a forged document in his hand, and said, "Sir! I have orders to take over a group of Jews for execution."

The officer on duty replied, "I know all about it. You are to take away the thirty-nine prisoners immediately."

After a few moments the prison doors were opened and the thirty-nine wretched figures were ordered to climb into a truck. Most of them were friends of the eight disguised Crossed Arrows men, but they had been so fearfully beaten up that they were unrecognizable. Neschka Goldfarb had been tortured with electrodes, a terrible ordeal. But he had remained completely silent, as had all the other prisoners. Half an hour later they were all safe.

By the summer of 1942, the stream of refugees from Poland had become a torrent. We needed more and more money, and for this reason we tried to establish contact with the delegates of the Zionist World Organization in Switzerland and Constantinople. We would not have been able to accomplish this part of our work without the active help of agents of the Hungarian and German secret services.

Samu Springmann, the diamond merchant who was on good terms with the foreign embassies in Budapest, one day got to know a man in the French Embassy called Erich Popescu. Popescu traveled to Constantinople on a number of occasions as an agent of the German intelligence service (the Abwehr). Samu Springmann made him a business proposition: that he should buy diamonds in Constantinople and bring them to Budapest. Actually Springmann had no such business in mind, and only wished to establish closer contact with Erich Popescu.

When the day of Popescu's departure arrived, Springmann gave him a letter addressed to the Sochnuth delegation in Constantinople, and requested Popescu to collect money from the Sochnuth and bring it back to Budapest. A week later Popescu returned and asked Springmann to meet him in the Hotel Metropole. Springman, however, feared a trap and insisted that I come too. I was told to wait at the entrance of the hotel, and if Springmann should not reappear within fifteen minutes, I was to report the matter to a lawyer. However, he came out almost at once and handed me a small parcel, which I took away in a taxi. The parcel contained a letter from Melech Neustadt, at that time one of the delegates of the Sochnuth in Constantinople, together with seven thousand pengös in cash. Melech Neustadt wrote that they were sending only a small sum, since they first wanted to test the reliability of the messenger. Seven thousand pengös was indeed a small sum, but we were glad to have at last established a contact with Constantinople.

But Melech Neustadt, to our annoyance, had also given

instructions as to how the money was to be divided, and these instructions threw the whole work into confusion. Half was to be spent on help for the refugees and the other half on the Hungarian Jews. The Hungarian half was to be divided into three parts, one to be spent in Hungary proper, one in Transylvania, and the third in Russian Carpathia. Nor was that the end of it. Each allocation was to be divided into two, one half going to the Zionist parties and the other to the youth organizations. Each twelfth part thus allocated must then itself be shared among half a dozen parties. The result was that an individual party received one hundred pengös from this consignment. Melech Neustadt had hoped in this way to prevent the money from becoming a further cause of party strife in Budapest. In the event, his over-rigid instructions led to an absurd situation.

Once we received from an elderly Zionist, Dr. Silberschein of Geneva, a gold cigarette box to be sold and divided among his fellow countrymen and friends. The sharing of this cigarette box almost blew the whole organization sky-high. Crowds of people hurried to our residence claiming to be fellow countrymen and bosom friends of Silberschein. It seems comical in retrospect but in view of the secrecy in which we worked it was, at the time, downright dangerous.

In another matter, party rivalry played a momentous role. Up to the time of the German invasion there was still the possibility of a very restricted legal emigration to Palestine. The English government were allowing fifty children from Hungary to enter Israel every month. Although the certificates were only valid for children, it was in fact mostly adults who were sent, and the authorities closed their eyes to this. A murderous battle took place each month over these permits.

We soon succeeded in strengthening our connections abroad. Samu Springmann had a school friend called Bandi Grosz. Of Jewish origin, he had taken the name of André György and was a man of many trades.

He was intelligent and clever and far more adaptable in tricky situations than even our own people, accustomed though they were to illegal work. He was of great value to us in many matters, and I must confess that through his help we were able to enroll in our organization people whose assistance was of inestimable value to us.

When Springmann met him, he needed money as always. This time he asked for an exceptionally large sum. Springmann's task was easy. He offered Grosz the money if he would establish a permanent and efficient means of communication with Constantinople.

Bandi Grosz traveled frequently to Constantinople on his courier's pass, and on the first occasion he punctually brought us back the money and collected his ten per cent share. But his greatest achievement was to put us in touch with the leading agents of the German counterespionage service in Budapest. These people not only restored our contacts with the neutral countries, but also established channels of communication for us with the Jewish communities in Poland, in Czechoslovakia, in Germany proper, and in the other German-occupied territories.

Admiral Canaris's organization was represented in Budapest by a strong group of agents led by a Dr. Schmidt. I first met this man in the somewhat frivolous surroundings of a private room at the Moulin Rouge night club. An agent of the same group, Joseph Winniger, introduced me to his chief, and Schmidt sent the half-naked girls from the room so that we could talk business undisturbed.

"So you are Herr Brand, are you?" he said. "My people have told me a lot about you. You want to help the 'children,' and I am ready to work with you in this. But we'll always refer to them as 'children' and nothing else. You understand?"

Schmidt needed money and was ready to do anything for it. His people also were ready to help us for money. They regarded the whole thing as a business transaction, and paid scant heed to humane considerations.

We kept strictly to our obligations, but we paid only by results. This often led to disagreement.

For example, we were determined to rescue and bring to Budapest a group of people of great value to us who were in the ghetto in Sosnowiec, in Polish Upper Silesia. But Sosnowiec was sealed off from the outside world, and it was almost impossible to pass through the SS lines. We approached Rudi Scholz, who of all the German agents was the most sympathetic toward us. He undertook to smuggle into the ghetto a letter that gave in an easy code the escape route and the password for the contact men. In addition we sent twenty thousand marks. It was our custom never to give the German agents our own money before they set out. They would use their money, and we would refund it and pay their fee when they brought us the consignee's receipt.

The Germans demanded an exorbitant sum for the Sosnowiec operation, but we agreed to pay them what they asked. Scholz came back in a week's time with a terrible story. He had sent an old man, a German, into the ghetto as courier, who had duly handed over the letter and the money to our people there. On his way back, however, he had been caught at the ghetto boundary by the Gestapo. They had stripped him, found the receipt, and then literally beaten him to death.

Scholz had handed over the money, but the twenty thousand marks was only a trifle; the sum due him was several times that amount, and he wanted it now. "We've done our part of the job," he said to Springmann, "and the money and the letter have been given to your friends in Sosnowiec. It's pure bad luck that our man got caught and that we cannot therefore give you the receipt. But you can trust me. I'm not double-crossing you."

Springmann, however, refused to pay unless he got the receipt.

Scholz was furious. "I can't understand your attitude, Herr Springmann. This isn't like a bank transaction in normal times. You've got to give me the money. It's not just that we need to have our expenses refunded, but that we've got to have money to cover up our tracks. The Gestapo is after us, and unless we bribe these people, the whole of our organization will be blown to bits."

We remained adamant: no receipt, no money. Nevertheless we were far from satisfied with the affair.

Then we struck upon an unexpected solution. A week later, on the Day of Atonement in 1943, five of our people, led by Itzbitzki and Liver, arrived in Budapest after a perilous escape from Sosnowiec. The Germans had apparently told the truth and Itzbitzki confirmed the details. "An elderly, grayhaired German brought us your letter and the twenty thousand marks. But he was seen by the Gestapo, and as he left the ghetto they grabbed him near the railroad signalman's house. After they had beaten him for half an hour, they threw him onto a truck, a bloodstained bundle."

Springmann went straight to Rudi Scholz and gave him the money.

Scholz was at first speechless. Then he said, "You've thought better of it?"

"No, but we have had an exact account of what happened, and this report will serve as a voucher for our people in Constantinople. We can therefore pay you the money."

The Germans could hardly believe their ears, but our status as a reliable business partner was in this way considerably strengthened. The very fact that we could receive a detailed report in such a short time contributed a great deal toward the prestige of our communications organization.

Through another Abwehr agent, Dr. Rudi Sedlacek, we were able to establish contact with Cracow. Sedlacek was an intellectual and was ashamed of the colleagues with whom he worked. He wished to appear better than they, and in conversation with our people he always stressed the contempt he felt for the other Abwehr agents. Sedlacek persuaded Herr Schindler, the head of the German industrial workshops in the Cracow ghetto and neighborhood, to visit us in Budapest. Kastner and Springmann met him at the Hotel Hungaria. He gave them a long account of the situation in Galicia, and expressed the opinion that certain Gestapo leaders could be bribed to ease the lot of the Jews there. He added that he himself was ready to help. Later on, when the ghettos were being liquidated, this same Herr Schindler transported a number of his Jewish workmen to Czechoslovakia and even into Germany. He strove at all times to keep them out of the hands of the Gestapo. Sedlacek often took money for us to Cracow, and it was Dr. Hilfstein, I believe, who assured me that this money was always punctually delivered. The Germans also bought food with our money and took it into the ghettos, which were then completely sealed off. As a result the black-market price of bread inside the ghettos fell by twenty-five per cent.

Our efforts to help the Jews living illegally in Vienna were far less successful. A man whom I'd never met before came to me one day from Vienna, bringing a letter and two little Jewish children. A non-Jewish woman, Frau Austern, requested our help. She asked for food, and we were determined to give her all she needed for our starving people in Vienna. However, we had no organization for smuggling goods; in the beginning, Frau Austern, herself arranged this. Every week her messengers brought us children and returned with their rucksacks bulging with food. This went on for months, and Frau Austern, who was a good Catholic, albeit a Social Democrat, sent us a letter on each occasion, praying for the success of the venture.

Our wish to extend this work ended, however, in disaster. Winniger, the Abwehr agent who maintained our contacts with Austria and Slovakia, introduced us to the driver of a delivery truck belonging to the Nazi party newspaper *Völkischer Beobachter*. After he had made three or four journeys, on each of which he took a full truckload of food, all our links with Vienna were suddenly broken.

We had no idea what had happened, so we sent Leon Blatt, one of our most capable men, at once to Vienna. He returned with grave news. Frau Austern was a selfless idealist, and she had divided the food among the starving Jews, without keeping a crumb for herself. A Christian woman,

married to a Jew, had tried to sell her own share of the
food in the black market and had been arrested by the police. When they discovered where the food had come from,
the woman was handed over to the Gestapo, who tortured
her until she told all she knew. Frau Austern was driven
into hiding and our contacts with Vienna were broken.

At last the Gestapo released this woman and used her
as a stool pigeon to uncover the secrets of our illegal organization. We were quite in the dark, for we did not know
whether it was the accident in the black market that had
betrayed us or whether the truck driver was playing a dou-
ble game. Josef Winniger undertook to clear up the matter
in Vienna. The woman who had been released was a terrible danger to our central organization, and it was impera-
tive that something be done at once. So we brought the
woman secretly to Budapest. She freely admitted all that
had happened, and we took care to hide her from the Gestapo. Our connections with Vienna, however, were destroyed, resulting in a great loss to us. We were never more
than partially successful in our attempts to restore them.

Frau Austern later fell into the hands of the Gestapo,
and, in spite of being tortured, she managed to survive. We,
the people of the Waada Ezra we Hazalah, have never forgotten her bravery and self-sacrifice.

Frau Austern was not the only Christian who helped
us. I have already mentioned our cook, Rozsi Varsoni, and
there was also Frau Kövesdi Palne, a weaver in my factory.
In 1941, in anticipation of these events, I had handed the
entire business over to her. Frau Kövesdi never took advantage of her position. On the contrary, she ran the
greatest risks to help us, as did her husband and her niece
Jolenka. She was a plump, elderly woman and a typical pro-

vincial. No one would have believed that it was she who
held our hidden arsenal of guns, and it never entered anyone's head that she was constantly hiding Jewish refugees
from Poland, or that her office and workshop were used by
the refugees as their headquarters. I myself owed my life
on more than one occasion to her courage and determina-
tion.

Remy Mihali, a bank clerk, his pretty young wife, and
their friend, a textile dealer from Pecs, also helped us a
great deal. I had first met these three people in lodgings in
Siofok, and we had become close friends. Remy's apartment was for a long time one of our most important cover
addresses. We gave them money and arms to hide, and they
looked after our illegal printing machines and found lodgings for the refugees.

The janitors of the houses in which we had set up our
illegal offices and lodgings never said a word about our
secret work. The policeman Toth often warned us of impending raids, and the drivers Balasz and Földhazi Giula
undertook the most dangerous journeys on our behalf. I
owe a personal debt of gratitude to the married couple,
Gabor and Vilma Biró, who, after my departure and at a
most dangerous time, cared for my children and saved
them from extermination.

My friend Alois Steger has a special place among the
Christians who helped our movement. Steger was a Sudeten
German, but he lived in Bratislava. He had been brought
up with Jewish children. When Hitler came to power, he
did everything he could to help his Jewish friends, and on
innumerable occasions he drove his car from Bratislava to
Berlin, bringing food for Jewish families there. He helped
many Jews across the frontier and arranged for their pos-

sessions to follow them. When the deportations started in Czechoslovakia, he spent the greater part of his time in his car on the highway between Bratislava and Budapest, smuggling his Jewish friends into Hungary. We kept in touch with him through Perez Revész.

Alois Steger owned a bonded warehouse on the Slovak-Hungarian frontier. He was a wholesale merchant and undertook important contracts, even during the war, for the export of machines from Germany to Hungary. Up to the time the Crossed Arrows party seized power, he was very well thought of by Hungarian government officials. The Customs officers on the frontier regarded themselves almost as his employees, so it was not difficult for him to smuggle men, money, and letters across the border. His great moment came after my departure. He managed to guarantee the delivery of a small number of trucks to the Nazis if they would help save the Budapest ghetto. He was actually able to deliver about twenty trucks, the reward stipulated for the efforts of SS Colonel Becher in rescuing the ghetto. Our friends in Switzerland were not able to give the Germans a trustworthy guarantee of delivery, and Steger's intervention at this critical moment was of great service to our Waada.

Forging documents was an important part of the Waada's work. Refugees had to be provided, according to their needs, with birth certificates, baptismal certificates, certification of domicile, registration forms, and so on. They all needed ration cards. At first we had to rely on very primitive equipment; for example, we used white of egg to erase stamps and signatures. Later on, however, we made arrangements with printers, like Zoltán Gerö's printing company, and the falsification work proceeded on a large scale. We became so efficient that even when the refugees began arriving in hundreds, we were able to furnish them with the necessary documents within twenty-four hours.

These personal papers had a dual purpose. They protected the bearers in the event of a sudden raid, and they gave them the feeling of safety and self-confidence that goes with legitimacy. One is apt to forget how important this can be. A man can often get out of a tricky situation by keeping calm, and he will not lose his head so easily if he has the feeling that his papers are in order. Providing these documents became a routine matter. Eli Kohn had started the work and Menachem Klein and my wife carried it on.

Of more interest was another aspect of our falsification work—the forgery of foreign visas, safe-conducts, and Palestine certificates.

In 1939 Britain decided to limit the number of immigrants into Palestine. In a white paper published at that time, the British government announced their decision to allow only seventy-five thousand more immigrants to enter the country. During the next five years, fifteen thousand immigrants would be given certificates annually, but this figure was to include the illegal immigrants, a proportion of whom had already arrived in the country. This left one thousand certificates a month to cover the whole world, and of those Hungary received fifty. During the first years of the war, and to a lesser extent even after the German occupation, this legal emigration to Palestine was maintained.

The Palestine office in Constantinople sent us the fifty certificates for children every month, but we were determined that these certificates should all be used by people whose lives were really in danger. The Waada succeeded in getting the Hungarian Palestine Office to agree that only refugees should be sent abroad. Those who can grasp the atmosphere of perpetual anxiety in which the Hungarian Jews themselves were living at that time will appreciate the unselfishness of this decision. The presidium of the Palestine Office had four members: Otto Komoly, Mihaly Salomon, Ernö Szilágyi, and Joel Brand. All four were Hungarian Jews, yet they all subordinated their personal interests and the interests of their friends and relatives so that help might be given to those who were most in need of it.

The leaders of the Waada had sworn that they would under no circumstances abandon their posts. For us there was thus no question of emigration to Palestine. In only one instance did we make an exception to this rule. By December, 1943, Samu Springmann, after a short term of imprisonment, had lost his old buoyancy. Years of grinding and dangerous work had left him completely exhausted. The delegation in Constantinople wanted him and we agreed. The Sochnuth delegation there also needed a representative who understood our situation and who would be able to advise the Palestinians on points of detail. We ordered Springmann to remain in Constantinople, but our people there apparently did not appreciate what we wanted and did not succeed in obtaining a residence permit for him. The result was that he had to move on to another country.

The Hungarian police—and later the German police —shut their eyes to all this. On the authority of these permits for children, we sent almost exclusively the vigorous young people of the Chaluzim to Palestine. It even hap-

pened that on the strength of a certificate made out for an
eight-year-old girl we succeeded in having a grown man released from a detention camp. The certificates had the effect of safe-conducts, and whoever possessed one was safe
from deportation. Even people in prisons and camps were
saved by means of these documents.

The Germans wished to be rid of the Jews, and
whether they went abroad or into the gas chambers was
largely a matter of indifference. At the very most only fifty
men could be sent abroad each month, but twelve thousand
could easily be gassed every day. The Germans chose gas
simply because it was the more efficient method of achiev-
ing their ends.

As we saw that these Palestine certificates were the
equivalent of safe-conducts, we began to forge them wholesale.

Foreign passports from neutral countries, of course
—gave the best protection. There was a certain Georges
Mantello who worked in the Geneva consulate of the Republic of San Salvador. In actual fact his name was Georg
Mandel, and he came from my mother's home village of
Nasaud in Transylvania. If anyone wrote to him, sending
his description and photograph, he would be sent a passport as a national of the Republic of San Salvador and thus
would become, as far as the Hungarians and Germans were
concerned, a neutral alien. We sent a courier to see Mantello, and he declared himself ready to give us hundreds of
passports, all duly stamped and signed. We only had to supply him with the names. San Salvador's colony of nationals
in Budapest increased enormously at this time—its numbers exceeded those of all other foreign groups put together.

Since the days of Torquemada there have been practically no Jews in Spain, but after the overthrow of Primo de Rivera's government, the Spanish Republic did its best to make amends to the Jews for the injustices done them at the time of the Inquisition. The Republican government directed its consulates abroad to give entry visas to persecuted Jews who were able to produce evidence of Spanish descent. Later the practice of the Spanish consulates became even more liberal, and Jews who wished to enter Spain in order to prove their descent were also given visas. This practice continued unaltered under General Franco's government. Unfortunately we learned of these possibilities too late. But those few people who were aware of them were able to save their lives.

Toward the end of the war, after the intervention of the Pope and President Roosevelt, the Swedish and Swiss governments decided to give help on a large scale. They issued thousands of passports affording protection, and we forged between thirty and forty thousand more. Holders of all these passports were protected from deportation.

We took special care of a group of refugees whose protection we regarded as a matter of political honor. These were the Allied soldiers, Jews and non-Jews, who had escaped from German prison camps and fled to Hungary. The first one who came to us was a British soldier named Tibor Weinstein. He had been taken prisoner in Crete and had escaped to Budapest, where he found his way to Otto Komoly. Later on many more arrived, mostly British and French soldiers. Komoly supplied these people with safe lodgings, new documents, and all other necessities of life. My friend Wasserberger did a lot for the Frenchmen, in particular.

One day Tibor Weinstein telephoned to say he had something important to tell me. We met, I think, at a corner on Veszelényi Street.

"Joel," he said, "there is a British officer hiding here in Budapest. He is the highest-ranking British officer in the country and therefore my senior commander. He wants to speak with you. I think he has certain complaints and demands to make. Would you like to meet him?"

"Of course, I would," I replied, "and as soon as possible."

The Englishman was hiding in a church, where the Catholics had given him shelter, and Tibor arranged a meeting place near this church. He was punctual to the minute and led me into the nearby presbytery. In a rather dark room he introduced me to his superior, a slim, tall man with attractive features. He asked Tibor to leave us.

"I have heard a lot about you, Herr Brand," he said when Tibor had left. "You are one of the leaders of the Jewish resistance movement in Hungary. I believe we have a common enemy, and therefore I consider it right that we should discuss our common problems."

"I am very glad to meet you, Colonel. You are the first Allied officer I have met. You can be sure that we shall do everything in our power to help you and your soldiers."

"I have two requests to make," he said. "You must help our men to get back to their own countries, and you yourselves must start active military operations."

"I don't understand exactly what you mean, Colonel. We are a weak minority group in this country. How do you imagine we could take any sort of military action?"

"Odd as it may sound," he told me, "you are the strongest underground movement in the country. Yet you

have never so far shown the slightest intention of undertaking real sabotage and diversionary action behind the
enemy's lines."

In the inner circles of the Waada we had often discussed this problem, but we saw no possibility of achiev-
ing anything useful along these lines. There was no real
resistance movement in Hungary. The situation was different from that in Poland or Yugoslavia or Czechoslovakia.
At that period the Hungarian people showed absolutely no
desire to carry on an underground struggle against the Germans. It seemed to me out of the question that a small
minority could take any initiative in such an effort. Nevertheless, Kastner had established contact with the Hungarian Social Democrats, and I myself had taken part in
conversations with Anna Kéthly and Szakasits, who later
became president of the Hungarian Republic. But our proposal that we should embark on active opposition had
evoked no enthusiasm. I personally got in touch with the
Communists, but they only wanted help for their own people. This we gave them. We supplied them with money and
provided them with documents, and we gave them shelter
when they needed it. We suggested to the Hungarians that
armed resistance groups be set up, but this too came to
nothing.

We did arm a number of our Chaluzim, but only for
purposes of defense, since we believed at the time that a
situation might arise in which an attempted mass deportation would have to be resisted by force. In all these efforts
we came up against certain basic difficulties. The Hungarian Jews themselves, if they were capable of bearing
arms, had all been conscripted for forced labor, and only
the women and the refugees remained. The refugees who

had escaped to us from Poland had come straight from hell.
They had been through too much; they had lost wives and
children and had sacrificed everything to save all that was
left to save—their bare lives. Only the very best of them
were prepared once again to risk their lives. There remained the Slovak and Polish Chaluzim. Many of them
were brave young people, but they spoke no Hungarian,
and it was not practicable to form a Hungarian military
resistance movement of Jews who were not natives of the
country. Furthermore, these Chaluzim were already carrying most of the weight of our illegal work, and we could not
burden them further. We would have had to cut down on
our rescue work if we had begun acts of sabotage.

I explained all these objections to the British officer,
but he brushed them aside. "The most important thing of
all is to cripple the enemy's war effort. Sabotage action behind the enemy lines is essential."

"Colonel," I replied, "we ourselves have far more modest ambitions. Our job as we see it is to rescue men whose
lives are in danger. But if you can give us definite tasks, then
you will find among us plenty of young people who are
willing to risk their lives in order to carry them out. We
cannot, however, take the initiative in such actions. If the
Hungarians start such a movement, we will help them and
will even place the apparatus of our organization at their
disposal. But we will never form the cadre of such a movement."

The British officer was not, however, able to give us
any concrete tasks. At a later period our people would
have given much to be able to destroy the lines over which
the deportees were carried to their death in Poland, but

we sought in vain for a Hungarian resistance group willing to help us.

The second question led to a sharp argument between myself and the British colonel.

"Herr Brand, England gives you fifty children's certificates a month for journeys to Palestine. I am informed that most of those you send are, in fact, adults. I must ask you to keep these certificates in reserve, primarily for Allied soldiers, whom I can then send back to rejoin their regiments."

"Colonel, that I cannot do. I have a duty toward those remnants of our people who are still alive. These fifty permits are the connecting link between our community in Central Europe and the community that will exist in Erets Israel. But I am willing to make you a proposal. England can give us more certificates, and we can then share the extra ones. It won't be very difficult for you to convince the British officials, and you can use our organization to send letters to Cairo."

He lost his temper then. "I have no intention of giving orders to my government or of intervening in your immigration politics," he said. "I am demanding that you use the opportunities you now have to send my men back to their countries. This is a matter of military importance."

"Colonel, the immigration limitations laid down in the British white paper date from another age. At that time our people in Europe were not under sentence of death; today more than half of them have already been murdered. I cannot believe that under these circumstances the British government would not be prepared to raise the quota."

"I am not here to discuss these matters. I have definite

orders, and I must insist that you do what I ask. Otherwise you will be answerable after the war for your conduct."

"I am responsible only to my own people and to my conscience, and I am not afraid of your threats. We may perhaps be fighting for a lost cause, but we will nevertheless do our utmost to fulfill our duties. We are ready to help you if you and your government will help us."

None of my arguments had any effect on him, and at last I proposed a compromise.

"Colonel, I am prepared to go a bit farther. I will include Jewish prisoners of war in the monthly emigration quota."

"Herr Brand, you don't seem to understand military procedure. There is only one man who is entitled to decide which soldiers shall go, and that is myself. These people know that I am their commander. I shall forbid them to accept any of these certificates without my permission. I shall select the men who are to go, in accordance with military requirements and regardless of whether they are Jews or not."

He forbade his soldiers to allow themselves to be sent abroad by us and they obeyed his orders. I myself had several meetings with this British officer, but we were never able to come to any agreement.

We tried other means of getting these soldiers abroad. We thought of sending them to Tito's partisans, but the Hungarian-Yugoslav frontier was guarded with unusual care and swarming with informers. In our efforts to contact Tito, we lost some of our best men. The partisans did not particularly care for us, and only reluctantly accepted foreigners into their ranks. They were also afraid that once a route was open, we would send them women and children as well.

The whole question of military resistance was later examined by the delegates of the Sochnuth, and the delegation in Constantinople appointed a man from our ranks to lead the active resistance. He was Dr. Mosche Schweiger.

One day a letter arrived by secret courier, on the envelope of which was written : "This letter is to be handed unopened to our comrade Mosche Schweiger!"

Mosche Schweiger opened the letter in my presence, read it, and passed it to me. It was written in Hebrew and at that time I did not understand a word of our national language.

"What does it say, Mosche?" I asked.

"The people in Constantinople seem to have gone crazy. They want to make me a staff officer. They can't find anyone else, and they've ordered me to organize battle groups. They are going to parachute officers of the Haganah[6] into Yugoslovia and to us here. I've got to send them documents so these people will have some identification when they come to Budapest. They are giving me a separate budget for the military work, and they say that everything I've just told you must be kept absolutely secret."

Mosche Schweiger, one of our most capable men, was fit for any conceivable work except that of an army commander. The people in Constantinople had chosen him because all the political parties[7] had complete confidence in

---

[6] The Jewish underground army from which the official army of Israel evolved, after the foundation of the state.

[7] I must here describe briefly the leading personalities of the Jewish parties, and the manner in which these parties cooperated with each other.

There were plenty of disagreements and political differences among

him. His activities in this matter were, in fact, limited to producing the required documents and sending them to Constantinople. We gave him Menachem Klein as his assistant. The proposed sabotage action came to nothing, and the parachutists who eventually arrived met a tragic fate.

---

us. The root of all our troubles was the attempt to achieve a fair division of assets between the various parties. How was the money to be divided? Should it be spent on *Tiul* (rescue) or for *Ezra* (help, assistance)? A bitter struggle also always took place over the immigration certificates. Even the groups of the Chaluzim suffered from this controversy.

Samu Springmann was deeply involved in these matters. As a fanatical Mapeinik (Jewish Social Democrat), he fought with the other Jewish parties over every trifle. Rezsö Kastner was the foreign minister of the Waada, and he was in charge of its relationship with other Jewish groups, both Zionist and non-Zionist. Friction was inevitable. I had an easier time. I was no politician, and at first my work was confined to the rescue of refugees. My natural sympathies lay with the Chaluzim. Differences of opinion would thus often arise on our committee between myself, Samu Springmann, and Rezsö Kastner. Mosche Schweiger always tried to smooth over these differences, which all originated in the problems connected with our day-to-day work. We never lost sight of our main objective, however, and the work itself welded us into a close group of friends.

There was indeed one contradiction that could never be solved, and that was the relationship between Kastner and Mosche Kraus, the secretary of the Palestine Office. Both men were intelligent, and both were ambitious. Each had his own ideas as to which groups had prior claim to be rescued. Furthermore, after my departure, Mosche Kraus advanced the theory that our people should deal primarily with the Hungarians; Kastner was decidedly in favor of direct discussions with the Germans with a view to ransoming the Jews.

The distribution of the Palestine certificates always led to a bitter struggle between Kastner and Mosche Kraus. Kraus was a Misrachist (the Misrachi is the party of Zionist orthodoxy). He wanted the certificates to be given primarily to distinguished (and well-to-do) orthodox Jews, above all to rabbis. Kastner fought for the principle that the certificates should be shared between the Chaluzim and the foreign refugees.

As a result, grotesque coalitions were formed. Haschomer Hazaïr, a left-wing socialist, almost communist, youth organization, worked closely with us in the Waada and simultaneously supported Mosche Kraus and the Misrachi in the Palestine Office. Their price for this was a few more certificates.

In reality the Chaluzim hated the general secretary of the Palestine Office. There were times when Kraus even forbade members of the Chaluzim who lived illegally in Hungary to use his office, in spite of the excellent shelter it provided for these refugees.

The quarrel between Kastner and Kraus died down during the first few weeks after the German invasion. We scarcely ever saw Mosche Kraus at that time, until one day he came to ask for help when his secretary, Rozsi Binet, had been arrested and he himself was being hunted by the police. Kastner and I succeeded in arranging through SS Captain Wisliceny for the proceedings against Kraus to be dropped, and his secretary was at the same time released from prison. Kraus found a safe refuge in the Swiss consulate. For the first few weeks after the German invasion, he scarcely dared leave the house, but later on he again became Kastner's chief opponent within the movement. I brought this question of their mutual hostility up for discussion in Constantinople, and as a result Kraus was directed to join our Waada and to collaborate with us.

This lack of harmony with the Palestine Office sometimes led to tragedy. In his own sphere Kraus had the final word over life and death. The possession of a Palestine certificate practically guaranteed the safety of the bearer, whereas the illegal transports organized by the Waada offered only a perilous and provisional security. Kraus had unlimited power, and in some cases his policy resulted in real catastrophes. I must here speak of the loss of our comrade Eli Sajo, since it was so painful a matter to me and to our controlling group.

Eli Sajo, a tall, very thin, and sickly youth in his early twenties, was the recognized leader of the Slovak Makabi Hazaïr (Socialist Youth Organization). Physically a weakling, he was mentally a giant—a typical intellectual of the best sort. We all prophesied a great future for him in Erets Israel. His penetrating analysis of the day-to-day situation and the advice he gave us were of great help in our work. Physically, however, he was not strong enough to stand the fatigue and strain of illegal operations, and if he ever took a direct part in activities, the results were invariably tragic. Three times we attempted to bring him from Czechoslovakia to Budapest. We gave him the safest routes and the most reliable frontier crossings, but he was caught every time and terribly beaten, and it was only with the greatest difficulty that we were able to have him set free. At the fourth attempt good luck got him over the frontier. A Palestine certificate was due him, and he was to travel with the last legal transport. But Kraus wanted the place to go to someone else, and the struggle over this one certificate was conducted with unparalleled bitterness. It was all in vain; the other man went, and Eli stayed behind. When the Germans marched in, we tried to send him to Rumania by one of our "safe" routes, but his traditional bad luck followed him and he was caught and tortured. This time we could not save him, and Eli Sajo died a martyr's death. His friends will never forget him.

Cases like this made the relations between the Chaluzim group and Kraus at best unfriendly and at times actively hostile.

Apart, however, from the antagonism between Kraus and Kastner, divergencies of opinion were restricted to objectives and not to personal matters. Personal ambition naturally played its part, but it was never able to endanger our mutual cooperation. In the hour of need, all proved true and staunch.

Chapter III

THE HEROINE, GISI FLEISCHMANN

EVERYTHING WE were able to accomplish at this time was but a drop in the ocean. We had set up a powerful organization, and some hundreds of members took part in our illegal work. Tens of thousands might perhaps be saved, but, meanwhile, millions were being exterminated. We were saddened by the discrepancy between our efforts and the rescues we achieved. We considered ways of taking some kind of large-scale action. Perhaps by direct negotiation with the leading German personalities we might yet avert the fate of those of our people who were still alive. We were not, however, the first to think along these lines.

A courageous woman, Gisi Fleischmann, was head of

the Wizo[1] in Bratislava. She was over thirty years old and married to a well-to-do coffee importer. She had sent both her children to Palestine before the outbreak of war; she herself remained behind and saw to the rescue of other Jewish children. She organized a network of smugglers who brought the children to her. Soon, however, it became unsafe for the children to stay on Slovak soil, and so she sent them over the border into Hungary, mostly on foot, but often in freight cars. Gisi Fleischmann bribed the frontier police, the locomotive engineers, and the smugglers. Her children assembled in Budapest, and in due course we had to provide over twenty homes for them. We succeeded in sending many of these children to Israel, most, of course, after the war.

Toward the end of 1942 it occurred to Gisi to get in direct touch with Captain Dieter von Wisliceny, the head of the SS in Slovakia. The meeting was arranged by Engineer Steiner, who worked with her in the Jewish central office in Slovakia. Gisi spoke directly to the Nazi leader. "What must we do to have the deportations stopped, Captain?" she asked.

He did not mince matters. "Bring me fifty thousand pounds sterling in cash," he replied. "Bring the money here and lay it on my writing table, and I will stop the deportations in Slovakia. Most of your people will have to live in labor camps, but not a hair of their heads will be touched."

At that date fifty thousand Slovakian Jews had already been gassed and twenty-five thousand were still alive. He was thus asking two pounds a life. It was not much, but Gisi did not have the money. "Give me time, Captain. I

---

[1] A Zionist women's organization, occupied with child welfare, among other matters.

must get in touch with our people in Switzerland and Constantinople to obtain the money."

Gisi wrote to Sally Mayer, the Swiss representative of the Joint, and also to the Sochnuth delegation in Istanbul. Sally Mayer refused to help. He was an old man and a professional philanthropist who faithfully administered the funds of the largest American charitable institutions. But he considered it his duty to watch every penny and to put his hand in his pocket only when there was no possible alternative. He would never dream of offering money to these brigands; the whole transaction seemed to him much too speculative, and he would have nothing to do with it. He would readily send food and money to hungry Jews, but not fifty thousand pounds to the Germans.

Gisi had been given only four weeks. Wisliceny had straight away given the order for the deportations to stop and was now waiting for the cash. With the help of our courier, Gisi bombarded the representatives of the Sochnuth in Istanbul. The money did not arrive in time, but Wisliceny gave her a further two weeks' grace. Finally we collected the whole fifty thousand pounds, and sent it by several couriers to Bratislava. All this took up valuable time and the two weeks' period had expired. Wisliceny made it quite plain that he was not to be trifled with by sending three thousand people to the gas chambers. Two days later Gisi had all the money.

"Can we now be sure, Captain, that nothing further will happen to the Jews in Slovakia?"

"A German officer keeps his word," Wisliceny replied. "I have made a definite bargain with you, and I will carry out my part of it."

He did keep his word. Until the partisan revolt in the

autumn of 1944, the Jews in Slovakia were spared, and that at a time when the fires of the crematories were consuming the corpses of Jews from every part of German-occupied Europe.

Six months after this agreement had been made, Wisliceny sent for Gisi Fleischmann.

"We have already done business," he said, "and I am now in a position to make more extensive proposals. If you can bring us two million dollars, we will stop the deportations throughout all Europe."

Gisi could hardly believe her ears. The Slovakian Jews were only a tiny fraction, hardly more than twenty thousand people, but in all Europe there were probably three million Jews still alive.

"In the whole of Europe, Captain? You will let the Jews out of the camps, out of Oswiecim, Treblinka, and Maidanek?"

Wisliceny rose.

"We are determined to free Germany and German-controlled Poland of the Jews. The Jewish question in these lands must be settled once and for all, and so far as that goes I cannot help you. I have already done more for you than I should have dared. The result of my efforts in Berlin is a 'Plan for Europe,' which will apply to all the countries of Europe other than Germany and Poland. In all those lands you can save your people. As I have said, if you bring us two million dollars, you may be certain that the Jews in Bulgaria, Rumania, France, Belgium, Holland, Greece, and Scandinavia will survive this war."

The man had already shown that we could do business with him. Why he should want to do this, we could not tell, but we never doubted that he made his offer seriously.

We sent special couriers to Geneva and Istanbul. The representatives of the Sochnuth in Constantinople were ready to accept the offer immediately, but they had not enough money and without the help of the Joint, the wealthiest Jewish assistance organization, the two million dollars could not be raised.

The Swiss representative of the Joint, Sally Mayer, after much haggling, declared himself ready to guarantee the payment of two million dollars to Wisliceny, but the money would only be paid to Wisliceny in the United States of America, and after the war.

Gisi hardly dared to pass on this offer to the SS leader, and when she did so she made the excuse that it was due to currency restrictions.

Wisliceny did not shout at her, but said, quietly, "Frau Fleischmann, you are an intelligent person. Why do you take me for an idiot?"

"Captain, give us a further two weeks. I hope that we will be able to arrange matters during that time." Wisliceny extended the period as requested. On the first day of the discussions in Berlin, he had already arranged that the deportations throughout the whole of Europe other than in Germany and Poland should be suspended.

Gisi went to see him again.

"I am finding it extremely difficult, Captain, to convince our people abroad that you will keep your word. They are afraid that you will pocket the money and then begin the deportations again."

"Your people are judging others by themselves. Here in Slovakia I kept my word, as you know."

"But it is now a matter of the whole of Europe, Captain. The Joint in America is doubtful whether it is in your power to keep such a promise."

"I will make a counterproposition to you and your people, Frau Fleischmann. Pay me two hundred thousand dollars for every month that passes without deportations. Should there be the smallest movement into the camps during this time, in any of the European countries except Germany and Poland, then you can stop the payments."

We breathed again. We were convinced that our leaders abroad, and the Allies, would at once accept this final offer. Our disappointment was to be boundless.

Sally Mayer was prepared to deposit two hundred thousand dollars a month in a Swiss bank in Wisliceny's name, but the account would be blocked until the end of the war. Not until then would the Nazi leader be able to draw his blood money. Gisi Fleischmann was in despair and did not dare take this reply to the SS leader. The third extension of the time limit had already expired, and she still had not received the money. Nevertheless, she went to see Wisliceny.

"Captain, I must go to Budapest to get the money. Will you let me go?"

Wisliceny gave her the necessary travel permits, and a few days later she came to us.

We were in despair and turned for help to the official Jewish community. Councilor Stern, the president of the All-Hungarian Association of Communes, received Gisi Fleischmann and our delegates.

"I am sorry, gentlemen," he said. "But I am unable to help you. We have no such immense sum as this at our disposal. In addition, I would not be entitled to spend the money on matters that do not concern Hungary alone."

One year later—the Germans had meanwhile occupied Budapest—the same Councilor Stern remarked to us during the course of a private conversation, "I must apologize to you. You chose the right course and I, at that time, decided wrong. Had I been able to see what was going to happen, I would have given the last cent I could find to you and your people, and only to you. You can rely on me now and need only tell me what I should do." Councilor Stern then placed millions at our disposal, and we could hardly get down the stairs for the weight of the money boxes he had given us. He did his best to repair the damage, but by then it was too late.

A certain amount of money arrived from Istanbul, and we gave Gisi our last reserves. She went to Wisliceny with fifty-seven thousand dollars as an advance payment, and begged for a further delay.

"I will wait for two more weeks, Frau Fleischmann," he said. "But this is the last time."

A few days later he intercepted a letter containing Mayer's proposal that the money to be paid him be placed in a blocked account with a Swiss bank. He was furious and sent for Gisi. "The money must be put here, on my desk, in proper bank notes and not in the form of a check postdated to the end of the war. After the war you people won't treat me and my kind as business associates. You know very well how you'll act just as soon as you can lay your hands on us."

The time limit expired and the Joint refused to produce the money. Wisliceny informed Berlin. Once more the apparatus of destruction was started up; once again the trains made their daily journeys to Oswiecim, to Maidanek, and to Treblinka. Because Sally Mayer and the Joint were not prepared to pay two dollars a head until the end of the war, our fellow countrymen had to enter the gas chambers. The Allies' foreign exchange regulations were probably the cause of this.

Nevertheless, Baron Dieter von Wisliceny, commander of the security police in Slovakia, did repay the advance of fifty-seven thousand dollars to the Jewish woman, Gisi Fleischmann, on the day after the agreed time limit had expired. He was apparently untroubled by the German exchange regulations.

So long as Wisliceny remained head of the SS in Slovakia, Gisi Fleischmann and the Slovakian Jews were safe.

In the autumn of 1944, about a year after the talks with Wisliceny had broken down, the Slovak partisans rose in armed revolt. Many young Jews took part in this, and Jewish paratroopers from Israel, with the approval of the Allies, were flown to the aid of the revolutionaries. SS Lieutenant Colonel Brunner, Wisliceny's successor, exacted a terrible revenge on the remaining Jews in Slovakia. Rumors of an imminent deportation began to circulate and many Jews prepared to flee.

Then the new SS leader sent for Gisi Fleischmann and said, "We are now going to put all your people into camps for their own protection. They will thus be able to live peacefully for the rest of the war, though they will have to work. This operation will take place in eight days' time, and I want you to see to it that everything goes smoothly."

This was a bluff the SS had used on many previous occasions. If the Slovak Jews had thought they were going to be sent to Oswiecim, large numbers of them would have fled or, like the fighters of the Warsaw ghetto, would have made a final, desperate stand.

Gisi was not deceived and immediately warned our committee in Budapest. Engineer Biss went to Slovakia with SS Captain Grüson to fetch Gisi back to Budapest, and Kastner sought out Wisliceny and begged him for help. Wisliceny obtained from Berlin special powers, enabling him to take action in Slovakia, and went to Bratislava. In the meantime Gisi had gone to Sered and entered the largest Jewish camp in Slovakia, in order to mobilize the internees and organize a mass escape.

But Lieutenant Colonel Brunner was quicker than Gisi and Wisliceny, and ordered Gisi arrested. A special Swedish file designed to saw through thick iron bars was found in her possession. She always carried it with her and hoped that, if she were ever deported, she would be able to cut through the bars on the windows and jump off the train. This was immediately reported to the SS commander, who gave orders that she was to be handcuffed and placed in a special railroad car, apart from her comrades, and thus deported to Oswiecim. As soon as the train arrived in Oswiecim, she went alone into the gas chamber.

Such was the death of this heroic woman—alone, far from her children, far from that land to which she had dedicated her whole life, and far from the unhappy people who were her comrades in adversity.

When the war was over, I came across her fifteen-year-old child. The child was without money, ill, and alone.

Chapter IV

THE GERMAN SECRET
SERVICES

FOUR MONTHS after the negotiations with Wisliceny
had broken down, I met Josef Winniger, agent of the German Abwehr.

"Our people have something important to tell you,
Brand," he said. "Be here at half past twelve and I'll pick
you up in the car. Dr. Schmidt wants to see you."

I arrived punctually and noticed, as we got into the
car, that two German cars were following us. Winniger
took me to an excellent riverside restaurant on the other
bank of the Danube. As I entered the room, Schmidt rose.

"I am very glad to see you, Herr Brand," he said. "For
the first time I've got some really good news for you. Sit
down. What would you like to drink?"

At first I thought that the Germans wanted more

money and were going to make further business proposi-
tions, but I was wrong.

Schmidt started off gaily, "What I have to tell you
must be passed on to Constantinople just as soon as possible. It's really big stuff. The perpetual struggle between
the SS and the Wehrmacht in matters relating to the Jews
has been decided. We have won the battle and the Jewish
problem has now been handed over to the army for solution."

"How will that affect us, Doctor?" I asked diffidently.

"I'll tell you at once. From now on the Jews are to be
regarded as an important asset to our war economy. They
will be put into work camps and their families will go with
them. These won't be concentration camps, and the people
in them will be well cared for. The Red Cross will be allowed to inspect the camps and to send in extra food. We
are also prepared to let you and your friends send representatives into these camps to supervise the distribution of
the food parcels and other comforts. There will be no more
arbitrary executions, and sentence of death can only be
given by a proper court of justice. The deportations will
cease immediately. All this applies to every European
country, including Germany and Poland, but not Hungary."

I did not understand why he had mentioned Hungary
at all. At that time Hungary was still an independent country and was not under the control of the German police. I
asked, "What is going to happen in Hungary?"

He replied, "There are some special regulations that
are about to be applied to Hungary, but we don't want to
discuss that today."

I was still waiting for him to name his price, but he

had relapsed into silence. I asked, with some hesitation, "What is all this going to cost, Doctor?"

"Absolutely nothing, Herr Brand. It may astonish you to know that we don't want a penny for it. There is, however, one thing we require of you. Here is a list of the people who have been instrumental in bringing about this change of policy. You must forward this list to your people in Constantinople, so that they will know the names of those of us who are trying to fight the war in a civilized manner."

He handed me a paper containing several dozen names, among which I noticed those of Admiral Canaris and many high-ranking German officers.

When the generals revolted against Hitler on July 20, 1944, I found that many of the conspirators were on my list. Also listed, at the end, were the names of *all* Abwehr agents in Budapest.

This list was sent with the next courier, Lieutenant Bagyony, to Constantinople, and no doubt it can still be found in the archives of the Sochnuth.

Schmidt did not ask for money, but he gave us a piece of advice that seemed to us most suspicious. "Herr Brand, if you take my advice you will ask Constantinople to send you a very large sum of money, say about a million dollars, at once. Communications are becoming more difficult every day, and something may well happen in the immediate future that will make it impossible to keep the courier service going. It would be a good thing for you to have a reserve in hand."

I had grown accustomed to hunting for the swindle behind every German suggestion. I thought that Schmidt probably wanted to make a lot of money quickly, but as it turned out there was a very different explanation.

I had no wish to make any decision on my own responsibility, and so we convened a large meeting, which our members from the provinces also attended. The debate continued throughout one whole night, but we could not come to any decision. At last, however, Dr. Kastner, Dr. Ernö Marton, Ernö Szilágyi, and myself were commissioned to sound out the Germans. Winniger, whom we approached, behaved in a very conspiratorial manner, and when I pressed him proved most reluctant to divulge what was in his mind. However, on this same evening, he told me the whole story.

"Listen, Brand, I'll tell you something that would cost me my neck if you gave me away. Next week Budapest is to be occupied by German troops. The decision has been taken. Hungary will cease to be an independent country."

My heart stood still. I hurried back to our people, and the meeting was declared in permanent session. The most improbable proposals were put forward. Dr. Ernö Marton from Cluj suggested that we should immediately mobilize our people for an armed defense of Budapest against the Germans.

"But whom will you mobilize, Ernö?" we asked. "The men, or at any rate those who could carry arms, are all conscripted into the labor service. We haven't any weapons, and in a week we couldn't collect more than a few dozen carving knives. We wouldn't be able to put up the slightest resistance against German machine guns."

My wife sided against me, "We'll pour boiling oil over their heads. They must not be allowed to come."

At last feeling grew cooler and it was decided:

1. To set up small resistance groups, to collect as many hand weapons as possible, and to prepare strong-holds.

2. To inform the leading politicians of the Hungarian opposition parties and to get into touch with the Hungarian secret service; with this purpose Kastner was to seek out Lieutenant Colonel Garcoly immediately.

3. To inform the escaped Allied prisoners of war and their commander.

4. To send a special courier at once to Constantinople with an exact report of the situation so that the Sochnuth would be able to warn the Allies.

Dr. Mosche Schweiger wrote the report for Constantinople in Hebrew, and it was to be signed by all the members of the conference. Dr. Joseph Fischer, the president of the Association of Communes of Transylvania, however, left the conference before it was signed.

On March 19, 1944, German troops marched into Budapest. I was at that time staying at the Hotel Majestic and was in my bath when Winniger, Sedlacek, and Scholz, all three Abwehr agents, burst in on me.

"Brand, get dressed at once. You'll have to disappear. Budapest has been occupied during the night, and the SS are tearing about the city in their cars, arresting everyone of any importance. All the liberal politicians are already under lock and key. Most of the prominent people in business, politics, and the press have been collected into the cellars of the Danube Steamship Company's building. There are crowds of Jews there, including Bandi Grosz. The idiot wouldn't listen to our warnings and was at home when the SS went to find him. Never mind, we'll get him out, but they're after you, Brand, and you've got to disappear. In a few days things will quiet down, and these fellows will remember their manners. At the moment, however, they are dangerous and must be avoided at all costs."

"But this doesn't make any sense, gentlemen. You yourselves told me, only three weeks ago, that the SS had no more say in the Jewish question."

"You mustn't take that too literally, Herr Brand," Winniger replied. "What you were told was true, but the effect of the new administrative decisions hasn't yet reached the lower levels. Besides, Dr. Schmidt told you that the Hungarian Jews were excepted from the new arrangement. But all that is neither here nor there. You've got no time to lose. At the moment the Wehrmacht is quite powerless and the SS are in complete charge."

I tried in vain to get in touch with my wife, but I did manage to speak to Kastner. He already knew everything that had happened. Schweiger had gone. He had left Budapest that day for his native town of Subotica, where he was soon afterward arrested by the Gestapo and eventually taken to Mauthausen. He reappears only toward the end of our story and of the war.

Abwehr agents took me to Dr. Schmidt's office.

"Well, this is certainly a mess," he said. "You must watch out, Brand. The present hysteria won't last long. But in a whirlpool like this, lots of things get shifted around, and nobody gives a damn. We'll take you into protective custody, Brand, and your organization's money and papers too, till the danger is past. Then you can come and collect them."

I had no wish to entrust our funds and documents to the Germans, although I did not at that time believe they

would rob us of them. I answered quietly, "Should I be arrested, Doctor, all our contacts at this critical moment, including those with Constantinople, will be snapped. It is
essential for me to keep in permanent touch with my people. Our funds are not all in one place. For reasons of
secrecy, the money is hidden in many places, and even I
have no idea where they all are. None of us knows what he
does not need to know. We have always avoided burdening
our members with too much knowledge. Then if one of us
gets caught and is tortured, he won't know too much."

"But Herr Brand, I have no intention of letting you be
put in prison. We are simply anxious to look after you. I'll
take you at once to one of our people. His place won't be
raided, but you mustn't leave your room. You can talk to
your friends on the telephone, but you'll have to be very
careful when doing so. This situation won't last more than
a few days. I give you my word for that, Herr Brand."

I accepted the position and they brought me to
Scholz's lodgings, where I lived in one room with him and a
woman friend of his, a Jewish dancer. This woman swore
that Scholz was a respectable person, who had unselfishly
helped her mother and several other Jews.

I asked Winniger to try to find my wife. The Germans
were once again asking for the organization funds. I did not
want to show my mistrust, so I handed over my personal
property for safekeeping.

The next day Bandi Grosz was brought to see me in
Scholz's lodgings. The Abwehr people had removed him
from the SS prison. All the information that I had been
given by the German agents was immediately confirmed
by Grosz.

A few weeks before the entry of the Germans I had

moved out of my Buljovsky Street flat, which had to be fumigated, into the Hotel Majestic. While I was living in Scholz's lodgings, a newspaper article appeared attacking the Jewish clientèle of the Hotel Majestic. One of our colleagues, Engineer Biss, a cousin of mine, who in the final phase of the war was to play an important part in the Waada, read this article. Biss had a very highly developed political sense, and he realized at once that this newspaper campaign was the preliminary to a raid on the Hotel Majestic. He could not get in touch with me, but he hurried to the hotel and persuaded my wife, almost by force, to leave at once. He took her to a house that belonged to him, 15 Semsely Andor Street, which was camouflaged as Aryan property. At midnight on this same day, the SS surrounded the Majestic and rounded up all the Jewish residents. They were sent to the gas chambers, and the hotel became the headquarters of the SS security service.

On the following day the Abwehr agents gave us some very important information. One of the senior SS leaders in Budapest was Dieter von Wisliceny. This news electrified us all. The precedent of Gisi Fleischmann's activities in Bratislava encouraged us to hope that we could buy Wisliceny if we could only get in direct touch with him. We therefore offered the Abwehr agents twenty thousand dollars if they could arrange a personal meeting. This they refused to do. They feared they would lose the profits they were making out of us if we were able to deal with the SS leaders directly. They were prepared only to tell Wisliceny that we wished to meet him, and they had the impertinence to ask twenty thousand dollars just for doing this.

Protracted negotiations ensued. We wanted direct contact and would only hand over the money when that had been obtained. In the meanwhile, Kastner attempted to get in touch with Slovakia. The result was that Gisi Fleischmann, Rabbi Weissmandel, and Dr. Oskar Neumann, one of the bravest of the Slovak underground fighters, each wrote a letter to Wisliceny. These three letters asked Wisliceny to establish contact with our group, with Baroness Edith Weiss (of the Manfred Weiss Works), and with Philipp von Freudiger, the president of the orthodox Jewish community. Wisliceny agreed to this request of our Slovak comrades.

Baroness Weiss had no need of this contact. Through the mediation of Dr. Billitz and Herr Chorin, the general director of the Manfred Weiss Works, the Manfred Weiss family was already in touch with SS Colonel Becher. Becher had far more to offer this small group of very rich Jews than had Wisliceny and Eichmann. Chorin offered the SS a majority holding in the Manfred Weiss Works if they would undertake to bring the entire Manfred Weiss family, together with their near and distant relatives, in a special airplane from Budapest to Lisbon. Becher went to Berlin to discuss this proposal with Reichsführer Himmler, who issued the necessary orders. A few hours later Baroness Weiss and forty-five of her relatives landed in Lisbon.

Wisliceny's discussions with Philipp von Freudiger covered the same ground as our subsequent ones. However, they led to nothing. Freudiger himself left Budapest in mid-August and fled with his family to Bucharest.

We were the last people to be approached by Wisliceny. He had previously visited the Jewish communes, where he had been in the best of spirits.

"You'll be quite safe, children," he had said. "But you must see to it that our orders are carried out and that every-

thing goes smoothly and quietly. From today the responsibility will rest with a Jewish council, and you must bring me
the names of the people whom you would like to have on
this council. The dissolution of all other Jewish organizations and parties is to take effect immediately."

He then produced a list of new regulations concerning
the Jews.

> 1. Every Jew must register with the Jewish council
> and wear the Star of David on the streets.
> 2. Jewish bank accounts were to be blocked, and all
> Jewish fortunes sequestrated. Every Jew must make an
> inventory of all his possessions, down to the last stitch of
> clothing. All money and objects of value were to be
> handed in immediately.
> 3. Jews would not be allowed to use public trans-
> port nor leave their places of residence, even on foot,
> without permission.
> 4. Jews would receive special food cards entitling
> them to "hunger rations." Most of the factories and busi-
> nesses were to dismiss their Jewish employees. And so on.

Every day new regulations were published.

The Abwehr agents advised us to set up the Jewish
council. They would see to it that the people we desired
were nominated to it. This we brusquely refused to do, for
we knew what had happened in Poland. We were well
aware that the Jewish councilors would either have to be
the unwilling tools of the German executioners, or go the
way of Engineer Czerniakow, the president of the Jewish
council in Warsaw, who had put a bullet through his head
rather than carry out the Germans' demand that he hand
over Jewish children.

At this time I had moved to the house in Semsely Andor Street to which Biss had taken my wife just before the

Hotel Majestic was raided. Engineer Biss had placed this house at the disposal of the command staff of the Waada as their secret headquarters. It was the office of his pottery factory, and he lived there as an Aryan. It had a radio and telephone, and beds for more than a dozen people. When I arrived all our leading members and their wives were already in hiding there. Winniger gave us a secret telephone number.

"Should any of you be arrested, ring this number, and we'll come get you out," he said.

We held a full session in this house and after a lengthy debate we finally mapped out a campaign.

"We must pick up the threads where Gisi Fleischmann left them," explained Rezsö Kastner. "The Germans demanded two million dollars in exchange for all the European Jews still alive. We didn't give it to them. It was a fatal mistake, but perhaps some of the damage can still be made good."

After the next meeting we made the following proposal to the Abwehr:

"You must establish direct contact between us and Wisliceny, and we will offer the SS altogether two million dollars, of which they will receive ten per cent when negotiations begin. After that they will be paid two hundred thousand dollars a month until they have received the full two million dollars. All this provided, of course, that the SS carry out their part of the bargain." We offered the Abwehr agents ten per cent of the sum we were paying to the SS, and we gave Winniger a personal tip of two thousand dollars.

At last Dr. Schmidt managed to arrange a meeting with Wisliceny. Kastner and myself were summoned to Winniger's apartment. A few minutes after our arrival, Wisliceny entered the room, accompanied by a ship's captain named Klausnitzer. Wisliceny was, I should say, rather more than forty years old. Tall, very fat, dark-haired, and clad in an exceptionally well-cut uniform, he resembled a Prussian big businessman.

We sat down and Winniger poured drinks, but the brandy remained untouched.

"We were informed, Captain," I began, "about the discussions that took place in Bratislava between yourself and our comrade Frau Gisi Fleischmann. Unfortunately it was not possible at that time to comply with your demands. Now, however, we are in a position to do so, and we are ready to pay the two million dollars for which you asked. We have been authorized to do this and we offer you an immediate advance payment of two hundred thousand dollars. We have only four stipulations to make."

"What are they?" he asked.

"First, that no more ghettos or concentration camps shall be set up. [At that time there were none in Hungary.] Secondly, that there shall be no mass executions or pogroms. Thirdly, that there shall be no deportations. Fourthly, that Jews who hold certificates shall be allowed to emigrate to Palestine."

Wisliceny leaned back in his chair. For over half an hour he spoke slowly, choosing his words carefully. He gave the impression of a professor delivering a scholarly address —only the subjects were murder and blackmail on the one hand, and a last desperate attempt to escape death on the other.

"I accept your first point completely, gentlemen. The Germans have no intention of setting up ghettos in Hungary. I would, however, advise you to agree to the concentration of Jews in communities of about ten thousand. You would then be able to protect your people more efficiently from the actions of irresponsible elements. With regard to the second point I would say that our people want peace and order, and do not wish to start pogroms. But there is a war on, gentlemen, and you can't make an omelette without breaking eggs. I cannot turn our SS troops into protectors of the Jews; that is no business of ours.

"In regard to point three: we can guarantee that there will be no deportations out of Hungary. The Hungarians cannot initiate deportations without us, and we are now the masters of Europe.

"Point four: we must refuse this request. We cannot concur with your view that a small group of people should be allowed to go abroad. This would be far too complicated a business to organize merely for the sake of a few Jews. If it were a question of a wholesale expulsion, we could discuss it."

He often came back to this point. "Except in special cases,[1] there can be no question of individual emigrations. But if you were able to suggest to us some way whereby we could rid ourselves of all the Hungarian Jews at one sweep, that would be something else again. I can imagine that that might be of real interest to the Reichsführer. Think it over. If the Western powers want the Jews, they can have them. Bring your proposals to me; I can't give you a definite answer myself, but I can and will discuss them with my people."

---

[1] This was an allusion to the arrangement that Colonel Becher had made with Baron Manfred Weiss's family whereby fifty-four large industrial establishments of the Manfred Weiss concern passed into the control of the SS.

The talk now turned to more concrete questions.

"I am glad that you have come to a quick decision in this matter of the two million dollars, but I can't promise that this will be enough. In Bratislava we were only dealing with a matter of tens of thousands of Jews, but now it's a question of a good million.[2] In the meantime I'll accept the two hundred thousand dollar advance payment, so that we can get the plan under way. Your people will not be harmed so long as our negotiations are going on. If you find you haven't got enough dollars, we will accept pengös or some other currency. We will, of course, calculate according to the black-market rate of exchange.

"I must warn you of one thing, gentlemen. Be quick and make a deal with us, before the stupid Hungarians in Berlin start raising objections. We don't want to give the impression that our troops have come here to protect the Jews."

Kastner still had one vital request to make.

"Before we complete our discussions, Captain, could you allow us to send a group of some hundred people through Constanta to Constantinople? We have a ship ready at Constanta for this purpose. You will understand, Captain, that the people in Constantinople want to see results. The arrival of such a transport would be a great triumph for us, and this would mean that we could ask for much more money from our people in Constantinople and Jerusalem."

Wisliceny did not refuse this request in so many words.

---

[2] Wisliceny was lying here. He had already received fifty thousand pounds for the Slovak Jews. The two million dollars was for the Jews in the whole of Europe, except Germany and Poland. Hungary had not been occupied at that time.

"That is not easy, gentlemen. We have certain agreements with the Mufti of Jerusalem, which we have to observe. If it were possible to get these people out of Vienna and onto a ship belonging to the Danube Steamship Company, it would have to be done in great secrecy. Here in Budapest, such an action would soon be the talk of the town; so great care must be taken. Nevertheless, I'll consider the matter. Meanwhile, you can prepare a list of the people you want to send."

At this point I had something to say.

"Captain, we have still one wish that lies very near to the hearts of us all. Many of our friends were arrested after the German troops marched in. Could you have them set free?"

"That's asking much too much of me, gentlemen. It would cause an uproar. More Hungarians than Jews have been arrested, and now you want the Hungarians to stay in prison while the Jews go free? That would be going too far. There can be no question of a general release, but I could deal with a few hardship cases. Bring me a list of those prisoners whom you consider most important."

The discussions ended on this note and we agreed to hold a second meeting at the same place.

When we opened these negotiations, our offer was completely theoretical. Neither the Sochnuth delegation in Istanbul, nor the Swiss representative of the Joint, nor the Jewish community in Hungary had given us any authority to offer such sums. It must be realized that while the Hungarian Jews had plenty of money, we Zionists formed only a small part of the Jewish community. The Mapei, our own party, which had built up the underground movement, had only a small say in the councils of the Zionist movement;

yet in the few days that followed the German invasion we became the leaders of Hungarian Jewry. We had a policy. We had analyzed the situation accurately, and had foreseen the events that were now taking place. We knew that we could no longer continue our struggles solely by legal means and that only by a combination of legal and illegal methods would we be able to face the coming storm.

The head of the Jewish Association of Communes in Hungary was Councilor Stern. A financier and a member of the Hungarian upper house, he was a man of aristocratic birth and cultured tastes. He had completely assimilated himself with his Hungarian compatriots and had up to then avoided all social intercourse with Zionists. Illegal methods and the kind of men who built our illegal organization were antipathetic to him. Nevertheless, in his honor it must be said that this man, who stood so far apart from us and from our way of thinking, realized at once what had to be done when the hour struck. He told us later, "You and your friends, alone among us all, were right. I must confess that I deeply regret not having supported you from the very beginning. Much misfortune might have been avoided if I had done so."

With Stern's help and without troubling anyone abroad, we were able to collect the two hundred thousand dollars in less than a fortnight: that same two hundred thousand dollars that Gisi Fleischmann could not produce and for the lack of which she finally died. Councilor Stern invited us to his office and, opening a safe, heaved out notes by the bundle. The box in which we put the money was so heavy that we had difficulty in carrying it.

According to the black market rate of exchange, two hundred thousand dollars was equivalent to over six million five hundred thousand pengös. We took half that sum to our next meeting with the Nazi leaders.

This time Wisliceny was not present. Instead the Nazis sent another man, Lieutenant Colonel Krumey, accompanied by Captain Huntsche.

We were alarmed by this at first, since Wisliceny was already known to us, and after the negotiations in Bratislava we knew what to expect of him. On the other hand the appearance of Krumey showed us that these negotiations were not just Wisliceny's private affair. Krumey's presence stressed the official nature of the proceedings, for the carrying out of which he had received full authority from Berlin.

"Before we begin our discussion, gentlemen, you should know that I am authorized by the head of the SS, Heinrich Himmler, to negotiate in this matter. These negotiations, however, are a state secret with respect to the Hungarians, and this secret must be kept on pain of death. Now, have you brought the money?"

I rose and handed over the box of bank notes.

"So far, Colonel, we have raised only three million pengös," I said.

"What's this, gentlemen! You get me here to receive an advance payment and you produce only an installment!"

I replied, "Since our last meeting a new factor has arisen. The latest regulations order the sequestration of all Jewish property in the country. The Jews have to hand over everything. Anyone who is found with more than one thousand pengös in cash is subject to arrest."

He was furious. "These Hungarians are playing a dirty game. Before we came, they sided with the Jews. Now they

use every trick they can think of to lay their hands on Jewish money."

In actual fact he himself had issued most of the anti-
Jewish regulations, and the German proclamations on the
advertising pillars bore his signature. Nevertheless, so far
as the struggle for loot was concerned, the Germans and the
Hungarian Fascists were keen rivals.

"Another point, Colonel. We are able to collect the
money only if the people believe that something will be
done with it. Herr Wisliceny promised us that there would
be no ghettos in Hungary, but each day we receive alarming
news from Transylvania and Russian Carpathia. Our people there are being herded together with extreme brutality
and forced into ghettos. A large number spent the nights in
the open, without food or water. None of that should have
happened. You have not kept your word."

"That's all atrocity-mongering. We take great pains to
be extremely humane in the border provinces, but Wisliceny himself told you that it would be better to move the
Jews away from the smaller places and put them in big
centers where they can be protected from the activities of
the Hungarians."

We changed the subject. I asked him whether the SS
had accepted the requests we had made at our last meeting.

"I have good news for you on that score," he answered.
"The six hundred people who hold certificates will be allowed to leave German-occupied territory. They must,
however, go to Vienna, and from there they will be brought
secretly by ship to Constanta. We can only dispose of the
Hungarian Jews as merchandise exported from Germany.
Now give us the list."

We had decided not to supply a list right away. It

seemed to us rather sinister that the emigrants should first
be sent to Vienna, and we wanted to gain time.

"We have further prospects to offer you," he continued.
"Wisliceny and I have discussed this matter with Lieutenant Colonel Eichmann, who is responsible for these matters
in the whole of German-occupied territory. In Berlin we
have energetically supported your desire to arrange a
wholesale emigration. I have as yet no authority to make
any concrete promises, but before anything else we must
know whether you are actually in a position to evacuate a
million Jews to places abroad."

He touched us here on our weakest point. We had deliberated this in many an all-night sitting. We knew that
while England gave us fifty Palestine certificates each
month, nothing would induce her to increase this number
by even so much as a dozen. But the forged certificates we
had issued ran into hundreds of thousands. Kastner and I
had been commissioned to tell a story to the Germans that
would win us a little time.

"The British will place at our immediate disposal the
whole of the thirty-five thousand certificates allowed by the
white paper. Each certificate permits the emigration of a
whole family, so we shall be able to resettle a quarter of a
million Jews in this way."

"But what about the remainder? You must move the
lot."

"We cannot decide that by ourselves, Colonel. You
must give us the opportunity of speaking on the telephone
with our people in Istanbul, for it is a matter that will have
to be determined at a higher level."

"I personally have no objection. I will let you know
tomorrow whether it is possible."

The conversation now turned to a matter that lay very close to our hearts. We requested the release of our comrades who had been imprisoned. Rozsi Binet, the secretary of the Palestine Office, was among those whom we wanted set free. She had been arrested outside the Turkish Embassy, where she had gone to obtain a visa. In addition, the general secretary of the Palestine Office, Mosche Kraus, and the leader of the Haschomer Hazaïr, Ernö Szilágyi, had been ordered to appear before the Gestapo.

"I will have your secretary released tomorrow and Szilágyi and Kraus will be told to report to me personally. Nothing will happen to them."

We requested further releases, to which he consented. He kept his word.

Once again we reverted to the question of the ghettos in the border territories.

"Gentlemen, you are being misinformed by malicious people. Nothing is happening to the Jews there. We have given strict instructions that they are to be treated with the utmost humanity. It may be that the Hungarian police, who have also been engaged on such work, are venting their spite on the Jews. If that should come to your notice, you must report it to me at once."

I saw a chance for us here. In the last session of the Waada, Hansi had urged us to request the Germans to issue travel documents enabling us to investigate the ghettos and internment camps in the provinces.

"That, Colonel," I said, "is not an easy thing for us to do. We Jews can scarcely walk the streets of the capital without running the risk of being arrested on some baseless charge. How then could we possibly send our people into the country in order to find out the facts about the situation there? We are constantly receiving terrible reports, but we can never verify their accuracy."

"We can do something about that. I'll issue your people documents that will protect them from being seized on the streets. Give me a list of names, and tell me in particular whom you want to send to the provinces. I will give you and Herr Kastner documents authorizing you to call on me at the Hotel Majestic."

(We were overjoyed at this outcome of our talks. The provision of such documents for our officials—whatever the grounds on which the Germans supplied them—would be of inestimable value to our movement. Our insecurity in the streets crippled the whole of our organization both in its legal and, to a far greater extent, in its illegal work.

(At first we hoped, by using these documents, to establish contact with the provincial communities, but in this we were too optimistic. It transpired that we would need further special permits to use the railroad, so it was only possible for us to visit the camps in the vicinity of Budapest. Our complaints to Krumey fell on deaf ears, for he himself had realized in the meantime what dangerous tools he had placed at our disposal for our illegal work. Our freedom of movement was, in consequence, considerably restricted. On one occasion when our comrades, Engineer Andor Biss and Sulem Offenbach, entered the Rök-Szillard Street camp they found that during the whole of their visit they were at all times under SS supervision. It was impossible for them to fulfill the important commissions we had given them. They were supposed to have warned the inmates to organize and prepare for flight. These permits were, however, very useful in Budapest itself. Dr. Kastner, accompanied, of course, by the Abwehr agent Dr. Sedlacek, twice succeeded, with the help of these permits, in reaching Cluj. On the return journey he brought my sister back to us in Budapest.

(A fierce struggle took place at one meeting of the Waada over who should receive the permits. The party representatives wanted the decision to be in accordance with party strengths, as in the case of the Palestine certificates. Engineer Komoly, who was chairman of the meeting, sharply rejected this proposal. The permits would be given only to those whose work made it absolutely essential that they have them. A single exception was made to this rule. Dr. Ladislaus Gottesmann, the leader of the revisionists, complained that his party was always unfairly treated and so one of these permits was given to him. Besides those received by Dr. Gottesmann, Rezsö Kastner, and myself, permits were also given to Engineer Komoly, Ernö Szilágyi, Sulom Offenbach, and, if I remember rightly, Menachem Klein.)

Krumey observed our satisfaction and immediately increased his demands.

"You see, gentlemen, I am able to appreciate the needs of the Jewish people. But you can't expect me to do everything unless you are prepared to meet me halfway. Your failure to pay the whole of the advance due today creates a thoroughly bad impression. This must be straightened out before we can go any further."

We promised to bring him the rest of the money in the near future. However, at our next meeting we again brought him only two million pengös, instead of the three million five hundred thousand we had promised.

He now shouted at us, "How can we believe that you will pay millions of dollars when you can't even raise this beggarly sum? I'll let you in on a secret: we're engaged in private negotiations for moving a few rich Jews abroad. It's only a question of a couple of dozen, not hundreds of thousands. Nevertheless, the sum they are offering us is so vast you wouldn't even be able to write it down. The reason we are continuing to negotiate with you and to make a few modest demands is that we have other, very important inducements for doing so, and these have nothing to do with you. I can only say this to you now: if the money is not all here the next time we meet, then we'll break off the negotiations and you can go and whistle for your Jews."

I tried to make excuses. "In spite of your permission, Colonel, we have not been able to establish telephone communication with Istanbul, and this is the sole reason for the delay. As a result of the occupation of Budapest, none of our couriers has so far returned, and we are waiting daily for the money to arrive from abroad."

"Don't talk nonsense; that's all so much hot air. You can easily raise the money in Budapest. The fact is you are not taking the matter seriously enough; otherwise you would at least have checked the bundles of notes you handed to me. One of them was short a hundred-pengö note. That's your crookedness. If I hadn't checked them myself, I would have had to make the loss good out of my own pocket."

Without a word I took a hundred-pengö note out of my wallet and laid it on the table. He picked it up, also without speaking, and then left the room with his companion.

Schmidt and Winniger remained and were full of reproaches.

Schmidt said, "You just don't understand what's happening. Your behavior is ridiculous and incompetent. Unless you act quickly the SS will strike and the Budapest Jews will be sent to Oswiecim. Yet here we are, waiting for two weeks for a mere one million five hundred thousand pengös. I have put you in touch with the highest circles of the SS, and now I have to watch you muff your chances through gross inefficiency."

The lack of contact with Istanbul was indeed hampering our work. On the day after our first conversation with Krumey, Sedlacek brought us the news that permission had been given for us to telephone Constantinople. I did not want to make the call from my lodgings, which were then being used for our secret work, and so I went to my abandoned apartment in Buljovsky Street. I waited there for hours, but the call did not come through. That evening I went to my new lodgings, but left a man to watch my old flat from the outside. Toward midnight I was told by this man that Hungarian detectives had searched the building. Next morning I explained to Sedlacek what had happened. He went there with me and concealed himself in the bedroom. I put the call through again. Half an hour later there was a hammering on the door and four members of the Hungarian secret police poured into the flat.

"Who are you and who gave you permission to telephone to Turkey?" one of them shouted. "And who are you trying to speak to there?"

I was about to produce my authorization when Sedlacek entered the room. "Take it easy, gentlemen. German criminal police. This matter is no concern of yours."

He took the leader of the Hungarians aside, spoke a few words into his ear, and then they both went to the telephone. The Hungarian called the number that Sedlacek had given him, and I could see from the expression on his face that he was mentally standing at attention. Without a word the Hungarians thereupon left my flat. We were still unable to get through, but whether this was due to sabotage on the part of the Germans or the Hungarians, I never knew.

About a week later we brought Krumey the rest of the money. He was satisfied now. "We cannot proceed much further at present, since we haven't received the necessary authority from Berlin, but I will be able to let you have some information within the next few days."

We lived in a perpetual state of nervous tension. The negotiations with the Germans were a very great strain, but nevertheless our normal work had to be much intensified. We were feverishly constructing strongholds. We moved people to neighboring countries, particularly to Rumania and Slovakia, for Hungary was no longer safe. The people whom we sent back to Slovakia did not go there simply for a place of refuge for themselves. They took an active part in the preparations for the great partisan revolt, which was to break out in the mountains and forests of Slovakia in the autumn of 1944. We hurriedly set up in Budapest several illegal printing presses and produced great numbers of forged documents. We copied the official stamps of the security service and of other German and Hungarian departments. We bought as many weapons as we could. We worked ceaselessly, but without confusion. Though our efforts were intense, we did not neglect precautions for our own safety, and we took care that others would be able to take our place should we be arrested. I always drove through the streets followed by another car in which sat my bodyguard, the loyal Chaluz Perez Revész. He kept a watch on my car from a distance and had been given all necessary instructions about the steps to be taken should I be seized by our enemies. In addition, he carried out small jobs for me that turned up in the course of my day's work.

I almost always slept in my clothes, between jobs, and I found it an effort to keep going without recourse to alcohol. My wife looked after us and forced us all to eat as much as we could. At this time my wife became an official member of our Waada, to which for all practical purposes she had belonged since its foundation. She took over the department that dealt with the supply of false documents as well as with the boarding out and welfare of the refugees. Later other fields of work were added, such as the welfare of children who had lost their parents.

The organization we had built up proved itself equal to the heavy demands that were made upon it. For reasons of security we decentralized our work as much as possible. The rank and file of our fellow workers, especially the Chaluzim, acted increasingly on their own initiative, and were thus able to reduce their demands on the central office. Despite this, however, the burden placed on the shoulders of the leaders was far too heavy.

So the days passed until the events occurred that are my reason for writing this book.

Chapter V

MONEY FOR BLOOD

ON APRIL 25, 1944, my birthday, I met Winniger at 8 A.M. in the Café Opera.

"Brand, I have important news for you. Matters are reaching a critical stage, and you're to meet Eichmann today. You know who Eichmann is, don't you?"

We had known his name for a long time. Lieutenant Colonel Adolf Eichmann was the head of Department 4B in the head office of the Reich security service in Berlin. Department 4B was concerned with the Jewish problem, and Eichmann had been Himmler's representative in this field since about 1934. When war broke out his sphere of work was extended, as were his powers. He was the man who implemented the decisions of his government. He organized the concentration of the Jews in the German-occupied territories and in Germany itself, and their subse-

quent extermination. When America entered the war, the
German government, on Hitler's and Goebbels's initiative,
decided to go ahead with Operation Night and Fog. That
meant the physical liquidation of the European Jews. Eichmann was commissioned to carry out this action, with maximum secrecy. The reason for secrecy was twofold: to prevent foreign countries from learning about it, and to keep
the Jews themselves in the dark lest they offer a last desperate resistance. Eichmann completely justified the trust
that Hitler had placed in him. He brought into action the
system of gas chambers and crematories by which he was
able, quietly, to murder five million Jews.

The policy of the Nazis in this matter was contradictory, and they constantly fluctuated from one view to another. Before the war Eichmann had favored the wholesale
emigration of the Jews. He had an unshakable faith in
Hitler's racial theories. He believed in the fairy tales of the
Protocols of the Elders of Zion. In addition he regarded the
Jews as persons who were mentally sick, with an infectious
malady that made them a public danger. A mass emigration
would cleanse Germany of Jews and at the same time would
spread the "Jewish infection" among Germany's enemies.
Before the war, Eichmann negotiated with the Zionist
leaders toward the acceleration of such a mass emigration.

When war broke out, he conceived the plan of founding a Jewish state in Poland, in the Lublin district, in
which all the Jews driven out of Germany would be concentrated. He ordered the Jewish communities to draw
up lists of their people who were then to be deported. Only
one such transport, however, actually took place, and the
idea was soon abandoned when the plans for a Russian campaign were seriously considered.

At this period Eichmann was still in favor of the emigration of the Jews to the Western nations. But by this time, in the early years of the war, emigration could take place only on a very limited scale. Although the threat of extermination hung over the heads of the Jews, England would still allow only a few hundred to enter Palestine each month.

Illegal emigration from countries within the German sphere of influence had to contend throughout the world with the opposition of the British consulates. The British tried, and succeeded, in insuring that the Jews waiting at Constanta did not obtain passage on ships going to Palestine. After the entry of Russia and America into the war, the Nazis believed they had a free hand to carry out organized, wholesale murder. In the middle of the war and in spite of the protests of the Wehrmacht, thousands of railroad cars and trucks were set aside for the deportation of the Jews. Whole regiments of men capable of bearing arms were sent not to the front but to spend their time murdering unarmed people. For two horrible years the slaughter went on. During this period four fifths of European Jewry was exterminated.

Now it appeared that Eichmann wished to revert to his original idea of a wholesale emigration. Had he already seen the handwriting on the wall? Was he trying to secure a general pardon for himself and his friends? He believed the myth of a Jewish domination of the world. Did he see in the poor, impotent Jews of Budapest representatives of this mighty world power? At the time I was at a loss to understand what his motives might be.

When Winniger told me that in an hour's time I would be face to face with Eichmann, my knees trembled. I did not believe I would ever return from this meeting, and I decided to explain the situation to my comrades at once. There was no time to call a meeting, so I talked to Kastner, Komoly, and my wife on the telephone. They all said the same thing: this was no time for caution, and I must go into the lion's den. There was nothing further to discuss among ourselves; our policy was set. I must lay our four-point program before Eichmann.

Winniger told me to stay in the café and wait for an SS car, which would pick me up on the opposite side of the street at nine o'clock. A black Mercedes drew up punctually at the appointed time, and an SS sergeant sprang out.

"You are Herr Brand?"

"I am."

"Please get into the car."

We drove very fast up the Schwabenberg and drew up in front of the Hotel Majestic, where I had so recently been living. The SS guards saluted. I waited in the hall for a minute or two and was then led to Eichmann. He received me with the words that open this book:

"I expect you know who I am. I was in charge of the 'actions' in Germany, Poland, and Czechoslovakia. Now it is Hungary's turn. I have got you here so that we can talk business. I have already investigated you and your people of the Joint and the Sochnuth, and I have verified your ability to make a deal. Now then, I am prepared to sell you one million Jews. Not the whole lot—you wouldn't be able to raise enough money for that. But you could manage a million. Blood for money: money for blood. You can take them from any country you like, wherever you can find them. From Hungary, Poland, the eastern provinces, from Terezin, from Oswiecim—wherever you will. Whom do you want to save? Men who can beget children? Women who can bear them? Old people? Children? Sit down and tell me."

He spoke in short, sharp, clipped sentences. I took a close look at the man.

He was about forty years old, of medium height and slim build, with fair hair. He might have been an office clerk in a business firm. Only his eyes were unusual. Steely blue, hard and sharp, they seemed to bore through me. I shall never forget those eyes. It was only later that one noticed his small face, his thin lips, and his sharp nose, and my gaze was continually drawn back to his eyes. He wore a well-cut uniform and moved quickly but rather awkwardly. His manner of speech was also unusual. He would rap out a few words and then pause. When he spoke, it reminded me of the clatter of a machine gun. He spoke without an accent, but occasionally used words incorrectly.

A stenographer sat behind me, and during the whole of our talk a tall, smartly dressed civilian stood beside Eichmann.

I was no longer frightened. As he spoke, it grew clear to me that this time we were talking real business. I forgot that a nod from this man could send me to the gas chambers of Oswiecim.

"Colonel, you are putting me in a most difficult position. You are asking me to decide who shall survive and who shall be murdered. I cannot agree to do that. I do not want a single one of my people to lose his life."

I was afraid I had gone too far, but Eichmann reacted with a smile, as though I had paid him a compliment.

"I am a German idealist, Herr Brand, and I regard you as an idealistic Jew. Today I am able to sit at a table with you and discuss business. Tomorrow, maybe, I shall have to talk in a different tone."

Dealing as I was with a mass-murderer, I found this light conversational tone quite intolerable, and I wanted to get down to business as quickly as possible. I replied: "I am no idealist but only an ordinary Jew, like dozens of others in the streets of Budapest. I have come to ransom my people and to save them from extermination. I do not know what goods I can offer you, for all our Jewish factories and businesses are closed and all our property has been seized. But I can offer you money. How much do you want?"

"I cannot sell you all the Jews in Europe—not even if you were able to collect that amount of money or goods. At any rate not yet, although it might one day be possible. But I can let a million Jews go. We want goods, however, not money—at least I have no authority at present to discuss a money transaction with you. I go to Berlin day after tomorrow, and I'll discuss the matter again with our leaders. In the meantime you must decide what kind of goods you would be in a position to offer us."

"But I cannot offer you any goods that would be of interest to you. In any event you can commandeer whatever you want."

"I appreciate that, of course, and as a matter of fact I am not interested in Hungarian goods. I realize that the sort of agreement I have in mind would be impossible if you were limited to the resources available to you in this country. I have had you brought here to make you a proposition that, I believe, will achieve our mutual objective."

I listened attentively.

He continued, "I want you to go abroad and get in direct touch with your people and with representatives of the Allied powers. Then come back to me with a concrete proposal. When we have reached an agreement, you can rely on us to perform our part of the bargain with our usual German thoroughness. Tell me where you want to go, and we will give you the necessary documents for your journey."

There was a pause while I thought this over. Sally Mayer of the Joint was in Switzerland. My Zionist comrades, however, were in Constantinople, and they would understand the situation much better. They had direct links with the Allies in Jerusalem and Cairo. But even more important, our comrades in Constantinople were flesh of our flesh and blood of our blood. We had maintained an unbroken connection with them, and they knew me well personally. I decided on Constantinople.

"I shall have to go to Istanbul, Colonel. What kind of goods do you want?"

"I shall have to think that over, Herr Brand. You too must consider what you have to offer me."

After a pause, he went on, "Yes, you shall go, Herr Brand. But your wife, your mother, and your children will stay here, in my hands and under my protection, until your return. I will keep an eye on them and will guarantee that no harm comes to them, but they must stay here. Then I can be sure that you will come back.

"And there is another thing that I must make clear to you, Herr Brand. These negotiations are top secret and no one in Budapest must know about them. It could cost lives."

"But Colonel, I shall certainly have to discuss your proposition with my people. I don't even know whether the leaders of our group will entrust me with this mission."

"You can talk the matter over with your closest friends,

but you'll pay for it with your life if any Hungarian should get an inkling of what's going on." He rose. "Get everything ready for your journey. I will be back in a few days and will be in touch with you on my return."

I left the hotel completely stunned.

The whole Waada was waiting for me in my illegal apartment, and I repeated the conversation I had had with Eichmann, word for word. Our meeting was conducted in an atmosphere of suppressed excitement. We all felt that here at last lay a chance of saving the rest of our people in Europe. They approved of what I had done and began to consider who should go to Istanbul.

Kastner proposed his father-in-law, Dr. Joseph Fischer. Dr. Fischer was a lawyer and a professional politician. For many years he had been a member of the Rumanian parliament and was president of the Zionist Provincial Association of Transylvania. He was without doubt better qualified to conduct diplomatic negotiations than I. Kastner emphasized this fact and at the same time pointed out that my presence in Budapest was indispensable.

Kastner's proposal was rather coolly received, and he then made the alternative suggestion that Dr. Ernö Marton, the editor of the Zionist daily paper *Uj Kelet*, be sent.

The representatives of the Chaluzim organization, Perez Revész and Ernö Szilágyi, next rose to their feet. "In a matter such as this we do not want diplomats, but rather a man in whom we have confidence. Joel knows exactly what is going on here. He will go to Constantinople and explain the situation. He will say what we want him to say and will then come back. Joel is the man to send."

The overwhelming majority agreed with the Chaluzim.

Only my wife protested. "Joel must stay," she said. "He is needed here. Besides, there are his two small children to think of. You cannot expect him to leave us at a time like this, and give his children to the Germans as hostages." But her interruption was not taken seriously.

Otto Komoly spoke next. "I think we all feel that Joel Brand is the best man for the job. We shall have to send him."

Everyone was of one mind now, and Kastner also agreed.

That afternoon we met the representatives of the German Abwehr. Dr. Schmidt, the chief of this group, was not present, and we dealt with Winniger and Dr. Sedlacek. And now a remarkable state of affairs arose. These German espionage agents, who had hitherto organized our courier service and who had finally arranged direct contact between us and the leaders of the SS in Budapest, objected strongly to my journey.

"We won't allow you to go," said Dr. Sedlacek frankly. "We will protest to SS supreme headquarters. The people in Berlin will stop it, even though it is on orders issued by Eichmann here in Budapest."

"But why do you now want to harm us? You've always helped us before. And this is our best chance in years."

"We started this business and we intend to see it through to the end. It is a matter that comes within the competence of the Abwehr. Negotiations abroad are no concern of the SS. We ourselves can carry out the necessary conversations in Constantinople for you."

It began to dawn on me that this was a question of professional jealousy. The Abwehr people were afraid that they would be completely eliminated and unable to earn any more money if our group were to bargain direct with the security service of the SS and with Istanbul. It was a ticklish business. We did not want to offend the Abwehr, for they were in a position to do us great harm. They had been blackmailing us mercilessly. In the recent negotiations with Krumey and Wisliceny, they had behaved worse than the SS men. They would have to be calmed down.

"I'll make you a proposition," I said to Dr. Sedlacek. "Why don't you send your own representative to Constantinople with me? He would be a great help to me there."

My suggestion seemed to impress them, and they retired to discuss it among themselves.

"We will consider it, Brand, but there is one snag. The Turks have become rather tricky during these last few weeks, and they won't give our people visas. You must cable Constantinople and ask Venia to obtain a visa for Josef," said Dr. Sedlacek. (Venia Pomeranz was the man who always received the German couriers on behalf of the Sochnuth in Constantinople.)

"I can't promise anything definite as yet, Brand," he continued. "I shall have to talk to Dr. Schmidt. But if he agrees, you and Josef can travel together. Otherwise Winniger will go alone."

His hectoring manner had by now ceased to impress me. I knew that there was no real power behind his words, and that it was the SS who controlled the course of events. Nevertheless this Abwehr group had helped us build up our connections with foreign countries and in other matters had been of inestimable value to us. We did not want to break with them completely.

During the next few days there occurred a number of events, inexplicable to me. I was not able to unravel the tangled network of relationships that existed between the various German power groups. All I knew was that we were not dealing with a monolithic authority, but that each group was intriguing against the others and that strangely enough we were of use to them in their tactical maneuvers, despite our weakness and helplessness. I will only describe what occurred, without attempting an exhaustive explanation of the causes.

Bandi Grosz, the agent of the Hungarian secret service, had hitherto been at the disposal of the German Abwehr. Now, however, he realized that a more powerful force was in command in Budapest, and he at once turned his coat and tried to establish close connections with the SS security service. He was not at all worried that the price of his new allegiance was a complete break with his former friends in the Abwehr.

Two days after my talk with Eichmann, Grosz asked me to meet him in the Café Biarritz. He was accompanied by Klausnitzer, the Danube Steamship Company captain whom I have previously mentioned. This Klausnitzer had played an obscure part on the night of the German occupation. Indeed, even before the German troops entered Budapest, he had formed a body of shock troops from the German parachutists who had landed in the capital. He had then proceeded, in accordance with a list prepared long beforehand, to arrest all those who were of any importance in political and commercial circles in Budapest, including many Jews. These were the people who had been herded into the Danube Steamship Company's warehouses. I had been included on his list, but had been saved by the timely warning given me by the Canaris group. Later on, during our negotiations with Wisliceny, Klausnitzer was present, but I am still not clear as to the exact part he then played. Now, however, he was posing as a man of liberal outlook and a friend of the Jews.

The conversation was opened by Bandi Grosz, who said, "Joel, I now have a contact that is much more important than any we have had so far. The Schmidt group has been superseded, and there is no point in having anything more to do with them. This afternoon we are going to meet Herr von Klages's representative. Herr von Klages is a very important person who is often directly employed by the highest authorities in Berlin. No one must have an inkling of this meeting, least of all Kastner. Herr Klausnitzer will pick you up in the car."

Naturally I took no heed of this warning, and immediately told Kastner all about it.

After Klausnitzer picked me up, we drove for about thirty kilometers and stopped in front of an isolated farmhouse. At that time many Jews were fleeing the city, and the police were searching all cars at the city boundary. The policeman who stopped our car knew me, and before Klausnitzer could produce his papers, he waved us on with a smile. He apparently was under the impression that he was helping me to escape.

When we arrived at our destination I was introduced to a very tall, dark-haired man, in the prime of life, called Laufer.[1] His wife, who said at once that she herself was

---

[1] Laufer was a Jew and a notorious man. Originally a waiter in Prague, he later became an agent of the SS security service. Shortly before the departure of the Germans, Laufer proposed to the SS that they kill off the leaders of the Waada. Apparently he wanted to eliminate witnesses. It did not help him, however, for he was shot before the end of the war, though whether by Germans or by the advancing Allied soldiers is not known.

half Jewish, had already prepared a meal for us. When Laufer began to speak, I recognized who he was. For many years he had had an office in the Vörös-Marty Square in Budapest, under the name of Schröder. One of our couriers had brought us a letter from Constantinople addressed to this Herr von Schröder and had asked us to forward it to him unopened. My wife had undertaken to do so, but could not, as he had already gone away. I had no idea what sort of relationship this man had with our Constantinople delegation. When I inquired after the war, I was told that this letter had been sent by the British.

We drank a lot. Klausnitzer could be described as a professional drunkard, and I needed alcohol at that time to soothe my nerves. The Laufer couple, alias Schröder, boasted loudly of all they had done to help the Jews. Then the conversation turned to the Schmidt group.

"There's one thing you must understand, Herr Brand. It is true that these people have done a lot for you, but don't forget they asked a heavy price for doing it. The fate of the Jews themselves was a matter of complete indifference to these bandits. Now, however, the situation is different, and a new policy has been laid down. The leaders of the SS themselves are taking a different line on the Jewish question, and this constitutes your last and only chance. You must throw the Schmidt group overboard. Anyhow they have simply been blackmailing you for some time, as Herr Grosz has told me. We want to collect evidence against these criminals so that they can be arrested. I have all the necessary information, it's true, but it is important that my facts should be confirmed. These people are troublemakers, and once they are out of the way, it will be much easier for you to come to an agreement with Eichmann."

He then talked a lot of rubbish about Himmler's having a far more humane attitude toward the Jews than Hitler.

I did not bother to protest at his attempt to whitewash that bloodstained criminal, but concentrated all my efforts on considering what my attitude should be to his proposal. One fact was obvious to me. These people wanted the Abwehr agents arrested so the field would be clear for them to do business. But as Jews we had not the slightest reason for becoming involved in the internal affairs of the Germans. It was true that the Abwehr agents had often betrayed and blackmailed us, but at the same time we had managed through their help to save many of our people. The gas chambers of Treblinka, Maidanek, and Oswiecim, however, were controlled by the SS, and not by the Abwehr. It was not, therefore, to our interest to furnish the SS with weapons to use against their competitors.

On the other hand, we had to move very carefully if we were to use these rivalries within the German camp for our own purposes. Laufer was right in one respect. The Schmidt group was certainly making trouble. Because of their envy of the SS, they wanted to prevent my journey to Constantinople and to stop me from coming to an agreement with Eichmann, an agreement that might result in the rescue of several hundred thousand of our people.

"Herr Laufer," I said, "we are weak and helpless. We want to save our people and to do all in our power to stop the extermination. But you cannot expect me to take sides in a dispute within your own ranks."

"Herr Brand, I speak with the authority of Captain von Klages. He has always had a soft spot in his heart for you Jews and has helped you as much as he could. In your interest he now wants to eliminate the Schmidt group. He believes that the German Abwehr here in Budapest consists of criminal elements who are harming Germany's good name. I advise you to give us the material evidence required, together with a full statement about your relations with the Schmidt group. It is true that Herr Grosz had already given us all the information we need, but nevertheless we want you to confirm what he says."

"I cannot make a decision in this matter without first consulting our committee," I replied.

"But I cannot allow you to do that, Herr Brand, for Kastner must not hear of it. Kastner is in league with the Hungarians. Your life would be in danger if the Hungarian secret service were to learn of these negotiations."

"You must give me time to think it over. I can't make a quick decision in a matter like this."

Klausnitzer drove me home. I gave him plenty to drink in the hope that it would loosen his tongue, but he fell fast asleep before I could find out what was behind this odd episode.

That evening I discussed the affair with Kastner. "Can you explain, Rezsö," I asked, "exactly what these people want of me? If they want to arrest Schmidt and his gang, why do they need our help? If they want evidence from us, they have only to arrest us and torture us till we speak."

"But don't you understand what's happened, Joel? Eichmann really does need us to make a deal with the Sochnuth or the Allies, or whatever it is he's after. He can't therefore arrest us all just now, because if he did who would believe him after that? But at the same time he wants to eliminate the Schmidt group. And you mustn't think that is easy. They can't simply be killed off, as if they were Jews.

So he needs some incriminating evidence against them that is really watertight. You don't really think that Admiral Canaris would allow the SS security service to arrest his agents abroad unless there was a very good reason for it?" He also said I was wrong to have let myself get involved in these matters.

A few days later I was summoned once more to Eichmann. Next to Eichmann on this occasion there sat a high-ranking officer of the SS whom I had not met before. I was to learn later that this officer was Herr von Klages. Eichmann spoke first.

"Herr Brand, we have intercepted a parcel addressed to you from Switzerland. It contains two hundred and seventy Swiss francs and over fifty thousand dollars. The money is stated to be for the purpose of helping Jewish children. Here is your money. You must acknowledge its receipt to your principals at once."

He leaned across his desk and handed me the parcel. I was astounded. Was this a trick that they were playing on me? We had never before received so large a sum in a single consignment.

"There are also letters for you here. A great pile of them, mostly in Hebrew or Jewish or Polish. We can't be bothered with them, but you must read them. They are presumably connected with your children's welfare work, but if they contain anything else you must tell me at once."

I could not make out what was happening. Eichmann seemed to be appointing me as a German censor. Was it a trap? Had Eichmann had photostatic copies made of the letters and did he now want to test my honesty? I was completely at sea. He began to speak again, in his short, clipped sentences.

"I got back yesterday from Berlin. I have obtained assent from the highest levels to these negotiations. Have you now considered what you can offer me in the way of goods? Are you ready to go to Constantinople?"

"I am ready to leave at once. But I am not at present able to offer you any kind of merchandise. We can, however, offer you a very large amount of foreign currency."

"That is of little interest to me, Herr Brand. What I really want are army trucks. Would you care to have one million Jews?"

"I want all the Jews who are still alive."

"We'll talk about that some other time, perhaps. At present we are concerned only with one million. I'll make you a fair offer. You deliver me one army truck for every hundred Jews. That's not a steep price."

I did not reply.

"That makes a total of ten thousand trucks. They must be brand-new, complete with spare parts, and equipped for winter conditions. If you want to make a further deal on the side, fill the trucks with a few thousand tons of tea, coffee, soap, and similar commodities. You can rest assured we'll give you a decent price for them."

"Tea, coffee, chocolate, and such like, Colonel, should not prove too difficult. But trucks—that's another matter. They're war material."

"I can give your Allies a definite assurance, on my word of honor, that these trucks will never be used in the West. They are required exclusively for the Eastern Front."

I had by now recovered from my first surprise, and I began earnestly to consider how to go on from here. I did not for one moment believe that the Allies would send me ten thousand trucks to save the rest of the Jews from destruction, but I was convinced that an alternative solution would present itself during the course of these negotiations.

"Colonel, I personally believe that you will keep your word," I replied. "But I do not possess ten thousand trucks. The people with whom I shall have to deal in Constantinople will ask for guarantees. No one will hand over ten thousand trucks without some security. What kind of guarantee would you be able to give that these million Jews will really be set free?"

Eichmann replied in words that convinced me we still had a chance of saving the European Jews. He said, "You judge us by yourselves, and you think we are all swindlers. Well, I'll show you now that I've more trust in you than you have in me. If you return from Constantinople and tell me that the offer has been accepted, I will close Oswiecim and bring ten per cent of the promised million to the frontier. You can take one hundred thousand Jews away, and afterward bring me one thousand trucks. We'll go on like that. A thousand trucks for every hundred thousand Jews. You can't ask for anything more reasonable than that."

When I heard these words, I could scarcely conceal my excitement. For the first time I saw a door open through which some of my people might escape to freedom.

I was silent for a few minutes, but the SS men did not guess what was passing through my mind. At last I rose and said, "I am convinced, Colonel, that this latest offer will be accepted. When may I start on my journey?"

"Within the next few days."

I left the hotel in a dream. With the parcel of money and letters under my arm, I went at once to our office, where all our leading members were assembled.

Every one of them was shaken by the news I brought.

No one could tell exactly how matters would work out, but each felt this was the turning point.

Some, it is true, doubted whether the Allies would give us any goods at all.

Eli Sajo from Bratislava—who was killed two weeks later while he was crossing the Rumanian frontier—objected on principle. "Comrades," he said, "are we justified in supplying war material to the Germans? Can we go to Constantinople and make such a suggestion?"

I took strong exception to his line of thought. "Comrades, it is not a question of supplying the Germans with trucks or any other sort of war material. You don't really understand what this is all about. An entirely new element in the situation has appeared. The Germans are willing to give us one hundred thousand Jews in advance of payment. Do you realize what that means? They are prepared to send one hundred thousand men abroad in the middle of the war. They'll have to go to Spain. The Germans won't evacuate them through Bulgaria and Turkey because of their agreement with the Mufti of Jerusalem. Switzerland is out of the question, since the emigrants would have to go on, which would mean crossing German-controlled territory again. Spain is therefore the only country left. When we've got the Allies to agree, we shall then have to negotiate with the Spanish government. Can you imagine how long all that is likely to take? And even then arrangements will have to be made with the countries who will ultimately receive our people. After which the question of transport will arise, and shipping space will have to be found. All this will take months, perhaps as much as half a year. In the meantime the Germans will have collapsed, and we won't have delivered a single truck. And there's something else, comrades, that you haven't taken into account. Eichmann has promised that once his proposal has been accepted he will blow up the Oswiecim chambers. Do you imagine that after six to eight months of negotiations with Spain and with the Allies, he will rebuild them and start gassing our people again? Can't you picture what the German situation will be in half a year's time? They are already badly shaken, and the only reason they want to bargain with us is because they know the end is in sight."

Ernö Szilágyi backed me up. "Comrades, it is an historical fact that in the final stages before defeat, terrorism breaks down. Perhaps the leaders may still give orders for slaughter, but the executioners are no longer to be found. For these men are beginning to bargain with their victims. Joel is right. If we are in a position to stop the extermination for half a year, then we are saved. Oswiecim won't be built again."

My wife, who was normally a very quiet person, now joined in with great excitement. "You're all talking high politics, and you don't see what is happening under your noses. While you are bargaining with the Germans, the murders go on in the provinces. In Russian Carpathia and Transylvania, tens of thousands are being herded together in the open, without bread or water. They will be deported and gassed before Joel ever gets to Constantinople. But that doesn't even enter into your discussions. I consider it a great mistake that Joel didn't request Eichmann to have all that stopped at once."

My wife was supported by Kastner. It was decided that I be deputized to submit some immediate demands to Eichmann.

We then opened the parcel that Eichmann had handed

to me and shared the money out between the different groups. Most of the letters from Switzerland were addressed to private individuals, largely refugees who lived among us, and they were of no particular interest. But we found two letters that made our hair stand on end as we read them.

Nathan Schwalb, one of the few Zionist delegates remaining in Switzerland, had written to us in Hebrew saying that we should join forces with the Hungarian opposition, the Liberals and the Social Democrats, and organize a joint resistance movement. We were to set up partisan groups and carry out acts of sabotage behind the enemy lines. He sent us a list of Hungarian politicians on whom we could rely, and he said that if we undertook these tasks he would be able to send us an unlimited amount of Allied money.

He did not give us a single name with which we were not already familiar. A great number of these people had been arrested on the day the Germans marched into the country, and the rest were living illegally in hiding places that we had prepared for them. Nathan Schwalb evidently had no idea of what had taken place in Budapest, in spite of the dozens of factual reports we had sent abroad. He believed that through his mediation we would be able to obtain help from the Hungarian politicians he had named, whereas in fact it was these politicians who were now coming to us for assistance.

We did not yet know how these letters had come into Eichmann's possession. He had handed them over to us with a sum of more than a hundred and twenty thousand dollars. Was this a trap? Did he want to test our good faith? Had he already read the letters? Even if he had not, he might still have had photostatic copies made, so that he could at his leisure study the lines of strategy laid down for us by Nathan Schwalb. I was almost too frightened to examine the full significance of all this.

In addition there was a letter from Sally Mayer. He wrote, on or around May 4, 1944: "I am not impressed by your reproaches in the Wisliceny affair. . . . The Germans must first of all produce clear evidence of a change of heart."

We almost tore our hair out. Were these people living on the moon? Had they no idea of the danger we were in? Didn't they know that five million people had already taken the road that has no turning? But we had no time to get into all this.

The news that was coming in from the provinces was in fact extremely serious. While we were bargaining here, our people out there were being exterminated. We resolved to intensify our work of building shelters and strongholds, and during these days we issued large numbers of Aryan documents. On the Hungarian frontiers we prepared escape routes into Slovakia and Rumania. Hungary had now become the focus of German interest, and the situation in the neighboring states had improved to a point where the refugees were already considering going back to their old homes.

A few days later Laufer met me in the Café Biarritz. "Herr Brand," he said, "I have some confidential information for you. Everything has been arranged, and Schmidt and his people are to be arrested today. You needn't be in the least upset; they were real criminals, and were only out to rob you. Nothing whatever will happen to you or your people, except that Kastner will be taken into protective custody for one day."

I had rarely felt more exasperated. "Herr Laufer, I have absolutely no interest in these matters. They are no concern of mine. Furthermore, I do not intend to have any further relations of any kind with you."

I simply left him standing there and hurried to a telephone booth, from which I called Kastner. Laufer ran after me, and as I was dialing the number told me I was too late. He said I would not be able to get hold of Kastner. Nevertheless, Kastner answered immediately, and reassured me when I gave him my warning. Detectives were already with him, he said, but they had confirmed that he would soon be released. I took a taxi and drove to Kastner's apartment, but he had already gone.

Laufer was still dogging my footsteps. "Herr Brand, you are getting excited about nothing. Kastner will be all right. I have spoken to Herr von Klages about it. We only want to stop him from rushing to the Hungarians when the action against the Schmidt people starts."

I went home, dead tired, and a few minutes later Bandi Grosz arrived. He was followed by Winniger and Scholz, whom Grosz had apparently asked to call on me. I was not able to warn them while Bandi was there. Perez Revész posted himself outside the building to prevent any members of the Waada from coming up.

Bandi Grosz was in the best of humors. He was pouring out brandy when the bell rang. I opened the door and found a man in civilian clothes pointing a gun at me. More than a dozen armed men rushed into the room. Winniger's glass fell from his hand. We all sprang to our feet.

"We are German criminal police," said the two Abwehr agents. "Here are our identification cards." It availed them nothing, and their revolvers were taken from their pockets. Four private cars took us all to the Hotel Pannonia. Winniger, Scholz, and Bandi Grosz were immediately led off by SS detectives. My wife and I were kept under guard for a few minutes and then released, with instructions that I was to report to Captain von Klages at ten o'clock on the following morning. That same night Dr. Schmidt, Sedlacek, and other Abwehr agents were also arrested.

Bandi Grosz was soon released and came up to me beaming all over his face. "It was I who put the administration up to this," he said. "Everything went splendidly."

"Have you considered what this means, Bandi? Who's going to take our letters abroad now? These people are certainly bandits, but they did help us. You shouldn't have done it."

"The Schmidt people are of no more use, and they won't be given any more visas for abroad. Everything will go much better from now on. You can rely on me, for I'm now operating right at the center."

I left him and went to bed. That night I slept the sleep of the dead, and it was already late when I awoke. I had to go to see Klages at once.

I took a taxi to the Schwabenberg, and in Klages's ante-room I found Bandi Grosz. I had started to talk to him when an SS sergeant shouted, "Shut your mouth! Who do you think you are? This isn't a mothers' meeting."

My courage deserted me. I decided I had been sent for in order to be arrested. Ten minutes later I was taken in to the chief.

Herr von Klages, the head of the SS security service, was a tall, imposing man with an attractive face. I now

recognized him as the man who had stood near Eichmann
when the latter had handed me the money from Switzerland. The strangest things were rumored about this man.
Many maintained that he was a friend of the Jews, and it is
certain that after my departure he always assisted my wife
or other members of the Waada when they turned to him
for help. Kastner and my wife afterward told me that he
had never asked for, or taken, any money. There were people who asserted that he sympathized with the group of
men who planned the July 20 revolt against Hitler. Against
that must be weighed the part he played in the arrest of
Horthy's son.

On this occasion he received me courteously. "You are
Herr Brand? We have called you here so that you can cor-
roborate your statement."

I did not understand what he meant. I had not made
any statement.

"Well, what is it that you have deposed against Dr.
Schmidt and his people?"

"Captain, I have made no statement of any sort in the
matter."

"You haven't made any statement, Herr Brand?"

"No, sir, no one has interrogated me."

"You really haven't made any statement, Herr Brand?"
he repeated several times.

I insisted that I had said nothing. At this moment Laufer came into the room and spoke a few words to the chief,
who at once realized his mistake.

"Yes, you are quite right, Herr Brand. I had mistaken
you for Herr Grosz. There is, however, another matter that
I want you to explain. Shortly before the occupation of
Budapest by our troops, you gave Lieutenant Bagyony a

letter for Constantinople. What were the contents of that letter?"

I began to wonder how I was going to get myself out of this mess. It was the letter in which we had informed Constantinople of the policy changes toward the Jews of which Dr. Schmidt had told us, and of the forthcoming occupation of Budapest. Mosche Schweiger had written the letter in Hebrew.

"I have not read the letter in question, sir. My chief, Dr. Schweiger, wrote it in Hebrew and I cannot read Hebrew. Dr. Schweiger is in prison, but if you will allow me to visit him I will be able to answer all your questions. You could, in any case, ask him yourself."

Mosche Schweiger had been arrested on the day after the German occupation, and all our efforts to have him set free had proved unavailing. The Germans accused him of having incited people to murder Hitler. Some years previously he had, in fact, published a pamphlet that contained a couple of sentences that could be so interpreted. In addition, he was supposed to have cooperated with the Yugoslavian partisans in setting the Bachka grain fields on fire. One had only to know Schweiger, a scholarly man who would not hurt a fly, to realize that he was by no means a terrorist. The Germans, however, never troubled to inquire into the facts, and took him to Mauthausen, where by a miracle he survived the war. Meanwhile, at the moment, I was trying to exaggerate the part Schweiger played in our group, so that I might obtain his freedom.

Klages began to speak again, in his usual calm manner. "Well, Herr Brand, you really don't remember what was in the letter?"

"I never read it, sir."

"That is quite incomprehensible. I must have this matter cleared up. Go into the anteroom and wait there, Herr Brand."

It was a different room that I went into this time, and I already felt as though I had been set free. Laufer came in and told me not to worry as everything was going well. Kastner, he said, had already been released. After we had talked together for a few minutes, I was summoned again into Klages's office. Sitting in an easy chair beside Klages, and contentedly smoking a cigar, was Dr. Schmidt.

"Herr Brand," he said, "why don't you tell my friend the Colonel the whole truth? We have nothing to hide in this affair. I told you the sort of letter I wanted you to write and send abroad, so surely you know what was in it? Eh?"

I stuttered, so great was my confusion.

"You needn't be afraid, Herr Brand. Just tell the whole truth. The letter contained the news we had given you on that same day, didn't it? We told you at the time, didn't we, that Berlin had decreed that the Jewish question was to be dealt with in future by the Wehrmacht?"

I was dumbfounded. After I had seen how the SS in Budapest had assumed full powers over the Jews, I had naturally taken this information of Schmidt's as pure trickery. But now Schmidt was repeating it in front of Klages. I felt there must be something behind it all. In retrospect, I remember how, up to that moment, the policy of the Germans had been to free their own territory of Jews, and in this they were almost completely successful. From then on, however, they had been dispatching Jews in ever increasing numbers from the camps to work in the German armament factories. They were of course still lodged in camps when they got to Germany.

Schmidt was making it easy for me. I told Klages all I knew, and I saw that he was satisfied. Soon afterward I was allowed to go. I found Kastner at my lodgings. He had spent the whole night in conversation with Klages and was convinced that he would be a useful man for our purposes. The conversation had been conducted partly on the roof of the house, from which the SS leader chose to watch an air raid on Budapest that was truly spectacular. Next day we learned that Dr. Schmidt and all his agents had been set free and taken to Vienna. Budapest was no longer a happy hunting ground for the German Abwehr.

Our members in Constantinople were informed by cable of my imminent arrival, and we received the reply: "Joel must come. Chaim awaits him."

We assumed from this that Chaim Weizmann, the president of the Executive, was going to handle the business himself, and we were therefore convinced that our people in Constantinople understood the importance of my business.

On receipt of this telegram I went to see Eichmann. "I am now ready to go, Colonel. The president of our organization is awaiting me in Constantinople."

"Then why are you hanging around here, Herr Brand?"

"So far I haven't received any permits or travel documents."

"Of course. Get in touch with Lieutenant Colonel Krumey. He'll give you all you want. You may go now."

"Colonel, I have one more important request to make. While we are bargaining here, my people in the provinces are being hounded to death. Every day we get alarming reports of this. If you want Constantinople to take your offer seriously, you will have to do something at once to stop the slaughter."

"That's all atrocity propaganda, Herr Brand. I have traveled back and forth throughout the country, and where-ever I go I see nothing but trucks laden with food for your camps. Stop plaguing me with stories like that."

He was extremely irritated, and seeing that I could make no impression on him, I changed the subject.

"We have been promised, sir, that we shall be allowed to send eight hundred prople abroad immediately. If that could be done, it would be a very good start for my nego-tiations with Constantinople."

"You've been talking about this for the last three weeks. We have agreed and have asked you to give us lists of the people whom you want to go. But you have never produced these lists."

This was true. We were afraid to give these names to the Gestapo, and we were holding them back until the de-portations started again, when we would have no alterna-tive.

"You bring me the lists," he said. "The people will go from here to Vienna, whence they will be sent down the Danube to Constanta. You must arrange for a steamer to take them on from there."

In the beginning we had spoken only of six hundred people. Krumey had then agreed to a further two hundred and Eichmann had talked of one thousand or over twelve hundred. In the end it was almost seventeen hundred. These people did in fact eventually go abroad, not via Con-stanta and Turkey, but via Bergen-Belsen and Switzerland. It was one of our greatest achievements that we were able to save these seventeen hundred, and it was only made possible by the courageous efforts of my fellow workers after I had left the country.

We had furnished these seventeen hundred with false certificates, and we had never worried our heads over what would happen to them when they reached Palestine. We could not bring ourselves to believe that any world power would prevent these people, who had so recently escaped from the jaws of hell, from landing in their own country.

Herr von Klages and Colonel Becher were present during the whole of this conversation with Eichmann. Klages did not speak a word, or give any indication that he was interested in the matter. When we had finished, Eichmann told me to go to see Krumey and, as I left, called after me, "You'll have to be quick, Herr Brand. Go at once and return as soon as possible, or it will be the end of your people here. Do you understand? Also, as I think I've told you, Herr Grosz travels with you. He'll be able to give me an exact report of what goes on."

Krumey received me in a matter-of-fact manner. "Everything is ready, Herr Brand, and you'll be able to get away this week."

I ventured to make a personal request. "I must leave my old mother, my wife, and my two children behind. While I have been here, you have given me a security pass to prevent anything from happening to me. Would it be possible for you to give my family a similar pass during my absence, to protect them against seizure by the Hungarian police?"

"Let me have your pass and give me the names of your relatives," he said. I did so, and he immediately added their names to it. "Now you can get your people to make photograph copies of it, so that nothing will happen to them on the streets."

The situation in Hungary was steadily deteriorating. I myself was preparing for my journey and could no longer engage in the routine work of our organization. During the last session of the Waada that I attended, my duties were transferred to other members. My wife undertook our increasing share of the work, especially in connection with the refugees and the forging of documents. Perez Revész and Sulem Offenbach, together with my wife, took over the organization's accounts. Otto Komoly should have carried on my negotiations with the Germans, but he was not psychologically fitted for this, and his duties were later taken over by Kastner.

New members were enlisted into the central executive, among them Mosche Rosenberg, Menachem Klein, and Raffi Friedel. Wilhelm Karoly, on behalf of Councilor Stern, worked closely with us at that time as the representative of the Association of Communes.

I was given full authority to represent all the Zionist groups. Councilor Stern and Philipp von Freudiger presented me with the following document[2] in the name of the official Jewish community and of the orthodox community.

THE CENTRAL COUNCIL OF HUNGARIAN JEWS BUDAPEST VII,
SIP-UTCA 12

BUDAPEST, MAY 16, 1944

LETTER OF CREDENCE
*The Central Council of Hungarian Jews hereby con-
firms that Herr Joel Brand from Budapest is undertaking*

---

[2] See photostatic copy in the documentary appendix.

his foreign journey in the interests of the whole of Hungarian Jewry, and we hereby request all qualified Jewish people and institutions to give him all the support within their power in his undertakings.

In view of the vital importance of the business that Herr Brand has to accomplish and that he personally will execute, we urgently request that he be given all possible assistance.

We wish to emphasize that Herr Brand through his unfailing loyalty and unselfish participation in Jewish relief work deserves well of Jewry, and as he now starts on his journey in pursuance of the task that has been given him, we wish emphatically to affirm that on the result of his mission the existence and fate of our community depends.

[The seal of the Central
Council for Hungarian Jews]

Councilor Samuel Stern
President
Philipp von Freudiger
Member of the Central Council

On May 15 I was summoned to see Eichmann for the last time.

"Herr Brand, you must leave as soon as you can. A courier plane will be placed at your disposal within the next few days. You must complete this business as quickly as possible. I cannot wait any longer. The deportations are being resumed as of today. Twelve thousand Jews will be transported daily, but I am prepared to send them to Austria and not to Oswiecim. I will keep part of them in Slovakia. The transports will wait there until you come back, and they can then easily be rerouted to the Spanish frontier. If you don't return or if you aren't back in good time, these people will go to Oswiecim."

A cold shiver ran down my spine.

"Colonel, if you must start the deportations again now, you will completely ruin my chances of arranging a deal. No one in Constantinople will believe then that your offer is meant seriously."

"You leave that to me, Herr Brand. I know my own business. I must get tough with you Jews. If I behave like a softy now, your people will think that they're safe anyway, and we'll never reach any agreement."

"Colonel, you have proved often enough that you can destroy our people if you wish. But if you really want to make a bargain, then you will have to show yourself to be humane, at least while the negotiations are in progress."

I begged him to reconsider what he had said, but it was no use. He would not yield an inch.

"It is up to you, Herr Brand, to get the matter settled with all speed and thus avert this danger. If you come back in a week's time, or shall we say at the latest in two weeks' time, and bring me a definite decision, then I'll blow up Oswiecim and the people I am deporting today will be sent to the Spanish frontier as the first consignment of those I have promised you. But I warn you, Herr Brand, that you must not stay away too long. I can't just put your Jews on ice. Those who are able to work can, it is true, be given some casual labor, but the women and children and the old people must be got rid of. So it is in your own interest to come back as speedily as possible."

"It is true that our president awaits me in Constantinople, sir, but it may be that we shall have to get the approval of the Allies to these negotiations."

"If, when you arrive in Constantinople, you find that it is necessary to go on, in order to achieve your purpose, to Jerusalem or London or even to New York, then you must take the first available plane and go. Your people must arrange all that for you. But first send me a cable and I will put the brakes on."

I must have made it plain that at this time I was absolutely determined to bring the Germans a positive decision, even if I should find that the leaders of the Sochnuth could not make a definite agreement. I was counting on time as our most reliable ally, and so I was not frightened by his threats. My only fear was for those who were now being deported.

I tried once more to make him change his mind, but he bluntly refused to do so. I fell silent and my eyes moved casually to the revolver holster that lay on his table. He noticed my glance and must have guessed my thoughts. He laid his hand on the revolver.

"Do you know, Brand, I often think how glad some of your people would be to bump me off." He leaned back, and smiled sarcastically. "But don't be too optimistic, Herr Brand. It may be that times will change, it may be that we shall lose the war, but you won't catch me or my family—I have a wife and two children, you know—no, I have made all arrangements against that eventuality."

He spoke the truth. At the end of the war, Wisliceny was hanged in Slovakia, and Krumey, who was acquitted by the courts, now lives in Germany. But Eichmann, with millions of victims on his conscience, vanished without a trace.

"Well, Herr Brand, you travel tomorrow. Lieutenant Colonel Krumey will take you in his car to Vienna, where you will receive your documents and board the courier plane for Constantinople."

I rose and started to leave. As I reached the door he called after me, "Hurry up, Herr Brand, and come back quickly. I haven't been joking."

Krumey had already got everything ready. He told me to bring my suitcase and meet him in the Café Opera on the following day. Bandi Grosz had already been informed. I must bring photographs with me.

When I got home I immediately called our members together. We first discussed the terrible news concerning the new deportations, which had already begun, and we agreed to send messengers out into the provincial ghettos once again, to persuade the people there to flee to Budapest and central Hungary. Although at that time we were convinced that we would be able to save our people through our agreement with the Germans, we did not rely solely on this. We decided to issue warnings to all our people, to hand out false papers in great numbers, and to build strongholds and shelters. We called upon our people to make a stand against the new deportations, and we hoped that the Germans would recoil from the prospect of a blood bath at this time. We determined to buy weapons from any source.[3]

---

[3] We were often later reproached for not doing enough to warn the people in the provinces of the dangers that threatened them. Because the provinces were sealed off, our chances of doing so were limited. Even so, we did the best we could. However, our difficulty in making our warnings effective in the provinces was principally because those in peril of death would simply not listen to us. The following story bears witness to this. Zsiga Léb, an old Klal-Zionist, resident of the Cluj orthodox community, had the right as a severely disabled and much decorated officer to move to Budapest. He told us this tale.

We then passed to the second point on the agenda, namely my journey to Constantinople.

Kastner said, "We must be on our guard against the English. They won't want to deliver any trucks. What you must try to obtain, Joel, is some kind of counterproposal. Don't deal direct with the Allies, but with Weizmann and the delegates alone. The Sochnuth will surely find a way out. The important thing is that the negotiations with Eichmann should continue. You, Joel, must bring back some useful proposal as quickly as possible. We will be on tenterhooks here."

Komoly said, "We must also try to establish direct contact with the Allies. Steinhardt is the American ambassador in Ankara, and he is a Jew. Joel ought to go to him and tell him everything. He will send a report to Roosevelt and will be able to put our case before him in the best possible light. If you see Steinhardt, ask him to be utterly discreet. I have high hopes that he will be able to work out some feasible solution with President Roosevelt."

"The worst part is that the people simply won't believe what is hanging over their heads. I told everyone I could reach to get away from the ghetto and to flee to Rumania, or to go underground with false papers. One out of a hundred followed my advice. The rest, in spite of all warnings, obediently went into the ghettos. I have no hope that they will finally find the strength or the will to resist being deported. It is impossible to discuss armed resistance with them. Anyhow, in most cases it would be madness, since no preliminary arrangements have as yet been made. The most difficult task is to convince the orthodox Jews of the danger that hangs over them. These people simply cannot bring themselves to contemplate the possibility of their extermination. A typical example of this is my uncle, Anselm Grünfeld, the chairman of the burial community Chevrat-Chadischa. When I urged him to go underground, he assembled a number of aged Jews and, pointing at me, cried; 'Don't listen to him. The president of our devout community is a blasphemer. He says that God will allow it to come to pass that our very devout community, which has done so much good and has helped so many of the poor, will be exterminated. Do not listen to him and his schemes. May the will of the Almighty be done. Pray to God, for He alone is our protection.' "

My instructions were clear. I was to bring back *some*, indeed *any*, counterproposal. We were convinced that Eichmann would in the last resort take food or money.

They all urged me to break the conspiracy of silence abroad about the fate of European Jewry. I was to try to get the important Allied newspapers to understand the true situation.

After the session was over, Kastner took me aside. "I cannot understand, Joel, why you are allowing Bandi Grosz to travel with you."

"Do you imagine it's my choice, Rezsö? Eichmann insists on sending someone to watch me."

"If I had been there, it wouldn't have happened, but you have pushed me aside time and again."

"How can you say such a thing, Rezsö? I can't help it if Eichmann has arranged for a watchdog to go with me. Whenever it has been possible, you and I have always gone to see these people together; to Wisliceny, and to Krumey. Bandi Grosz and Laufer are responsible. They put the idea into Eichmann's head that you are on the side of the Hungarians. I denied that at once, but without effect."

"So it was all Bandi Grosz's fault. On that account alone you should have stood up against him. Bandi is only going in order to save his own skin. You shouldn't have let yourself become involved with so irresponsible a fellow. We two should be going together."

At that moment, however, I had other things to worry about. I was certainly not overjoyed to have a man like Bandi Grosz for a companion, but it would have been far more unpleasant if the Germans had ordered that a Nazi go with me.

On the following afternoon I said good-by to my children. The elder was five and a half years old. Both of them felt that I was abandoning them, and they stood in front of the car and tried to prevent it from driving off. My wife came with me to the Café Opera, where Komoly, Szilágyi, and Kastner were already waiting. After about an hour a car appeared, driven by Krumey. Bandi Grosz sat beside him. I embraced my wife and my comrades and got in the back.

We crossed the frontier without incident and arrived at Vienna in the evening. Krumey took us to the Hotel Metropole, the Gestapo headquarters, and obtained a room for us with six beds. We were allowed to go out, but not for longer than one hour. Krumey took my identification particulars, but Grosz had a Hungarian service pass.

On the following afternoon Krumey brought me my passport. It was a normal German passport, made out in the name of Eugen Band, an engineer from Erfurt. The date of birth was the same as mine. He introduced me to the SS commandant of Vienna, Lieutenant Colonel Adolf Ebert. He then told me I must pay for the airplane tickets for Grosz and myself, in dollars. I had over two thousand dollars on me. Despite the German exchange regulations, this did not apparently seem odd to Krumey.

At five o'clock next morning Krumey took us in the car to the airport. The formalities were a farce. Neither my suitcase nor my pockets were searched. I was asked if I had any money and on Krumey's instructions I said I had none.

Shortly before we took off, Krumey led me aside and asked me not to forget him during my negotiations in Turkey. I was to let them know that the SS did not consist entirely of people like Eichmann but that it also contained honorable officers such as himself and Wisliceny. He for his part would do everything in his power to save the Jews.

In his tone, I could sense his anxiety over the impending collapse of the Nazi régime.

"Come back soon, Herr Brand, with everything settled. We here will keep our word; you can rely on that. The courier plane flies every week from Constantinople to Vienna, and two seats are permanently reserved for your use."

We then boarded the plane.

Chapter VI

TILTING AGAINST WINDMILLS

THE AIRPLANE made two intermediate stops in the Balkans. Grosz at once exhibited his cunning. He knew every petty official on the airfields. He had already made the same journey a dozen times, and he had a small gift, or at least a few friendly words, for everyone he met.

He spent the flight itself studying a letter many pages long with the deepest concentration. "These are my secret instructions," he explained importantly. "I have to learn them by heart and then destroy them."

He did not wish to tell me what the letter contained, and I had no interest in it myself. I was thinking of my own mission. Then he tore the letter into small pieces in a most ostentatious way.

Early that afternoon we landed in Constantinople.

When we disembarked, Bandi let the others go ahead, while he peered around.

"Do you see that car standing by the railings, Brand? Those two men are Barlasz and Brod." Chaim Barlasz was the chief delegate of the Jewish Agency in Constantinople. Grosz knew them both from his previous visits here.

As Bandi spoke, both men looked in our direction, then immediately got into the car and drove off.[1]

I imagined I would meet them shortly in the waiting room, but time went by and no one arrived to meet me. I grew anxious. I could not understand why no one had come, for we had exchanged telegrams.

And now a most peculiar chain of events took place. It was pointed out at the Customs barrier that no visa had been deposited for me. Grosz spoke to the officials and inquired again whether there was not a visa in the name of Eugen Band. But there was no visa and therefore no permission to land. I was dumbfounded. We had received several telegrams in Budapest from Constantinople, telling us that an entry permit was ready for me, and I had sent a cable from Vienna with my pseudonym. I was certain that Chaim Weizmann, together with the chief officials of the Constantinople Sochnuth, would be at the airport to meet me, but not a single delegate was there. The Turkish officials told me that I could not go into the town, and must remain at the airport. The plane would take me back to Vienna early next morning.

I was in despair. What would happen in Budapest? Eichmann had negotiated with us because in his Nazi mind we represented a secret world power. Now he would be-

---

[1] Chaim Barlasz now maintains that he drove into the town to get me a visa.

lieve that my contacts were not even capable of producing a Turkish visa for me. It was obvious the Germans would at once arrest me and the whole Waada and dispatch us to Oswiecim while the Hungarian Jews, left leaderless, would soon be massacred.

I would undoubtedly have been sent back to German territory without more ado if that Hungarian secret agent, that man who was so alien to us, that Bandi Grosz fellow, had not now intervened. His connections were apparently better than ours. Later on, I was convinced that Bandi Grosz had arranged with the Germans to accompany me with the firm intention of never returning. He had already obtained a Turkish visa for his wife and had sent her to Constantinople before the German occupation. She was now waiting for him. He telephoned her from the airport and told her to go at once to Machmed Bey. Machmed Bey was the president of the Turkish Transport Company, a seminationalized concern, and was on very good terms with Bandi Grosz, who always posed in Constantinople as a director of the Hungarian Transport Company. Machmed Bey had great influence in government circles in Constantinople, and he now stood surety for me with the Ministry of the Interior. Half an hour later the Turks stamped my pass, and Bandi Grosz took me to the Hotel Palace Pera. He himself stayed at his wife's flat. The Pera Hotel was the headquarters of the Jewish delegation.

Two minutes after my arrival, when I was just going to have a bath, the door of my room was flung violently open by a slim young man who ran in and threw his arms around me.

"You're Joel. I'm Venia. When did you leave Budapest? What sort of a journey did you have? Did you travel with Bandi Grosz? How's Otto Komoly? What's Kastner doing now? And Perez? And Zwi Goldfarb? Is it true that they've begun the deportations?"

A few minutes later Benjamin Griffel, the representative of the Agudas Israel, entered the room. My background is a socialist one, and I have not much sympathy with the followers of this orthodox religious party, but Griffel made a good impression on me. He was particularly well informed on how matters stood with us, and he did not question the accuracy of our reports. What I noticed most about him, however, was a certain tendency toward emotionalism. In Budapest we always kept cool heads, even in times of panic, and made a point of discussing our daily tasks objectively, even when great heroism was needed to carry them out. But this Benjamin Griffel seemed to live permanently in a kind of ecstasy.

I unpacked some cakes that my wife had put into my suitcase, and I offered them each one. Griffel said, "I never eat with a stranger, for I am afraid the food might not be strictly kosher. But from your hands I would accept anything, for they are holy hands."

I was rather embarrassed by this compliment, and turned away.

They both explained to me that the whole Waada was assembled and awaiting me with the greatest excitement. I washed quickly and went with them to Chaim Barlasz's office, which was on the same floor.

About a dozen people had collected there, and I handed my letter of authority to the representatives of the various parties and groups. I was then asked to speak.

I spoke for several hours. I am not a good speaker and I was excited, but on this occasion I spoke well. The magnitude of the task on which I was engaged inspired me, even as it did my listeners. I spoke of the misery and want and of the daily terror. I told of our hopes, and I described in detail every twist in our negotiations with the Nazi leaders. Soon everyone was deeply stirred, and many wept. At last I came to my own actual mission.

"Comrades, I do not understand what you have done up to now. Three weeks ago we cabled you, and you replied that I should come, that Chaim expected me. I was convinced that this meant Chaim Weizmann. Is one single member of the Executive here today? With whom am I expected to deal? Have you the authority to make decisions in this matter, decisions on which the fate of millions of people will depend? How are we to proceed? It is a question of days, of hours. Eichmann will not wait. Every day twelve thousand people are being driven into cattle cars. Eichmann has promised to keep them in Austria until I come back, but what guarantee have I that they will not go straight to the gas chambers? Are you prepared to accept the responsibility for the slaughter of even a thousand more Jews, just because no one with the authority of the Executive has turned up at the right time in Constantinople? Have you really considered all the implications of this matter?"

They did not answer. Instead, as southerners will, they began to gesticulate wildly and argue with each other in Hebrew. I could not understand one word of this and began to lose my temper.

I waited for some minutes and then said, "Comrades, I do not understand Hebrew. You can speak German or English or Yiddish, if you like, but I must be able to follow every word. And I will tell you one thing. I will not be satisfied with any kind of majority decision. I am conscious of my responsibility toward the hundreds of thousands who have sent me here. Their very lives are at stake. I expected that someone from the Executive would be here. You must arrange by cable for someone to come at once.

"I myself am certain that it will not be possible to reach a hard and fast decision in so short a time. We do not believe the English will give the Germans army trucks in the middle of the war. But that is a minor point. We must make some serious counterproposal, so that the negotiations can proceed. Tomorrow I will cable Eichmann and tell him that all goes well and that his offer is accepted in principle, provided the deportations are stopped immediately. If Eichmann does that, representatives of the Germans and of the Sochnuth can meet in some neutral country to work out the details. We must not give them trucks, but we can propose food. If worse comes to worst, we can offer them money. Do you see what the basic problem is, comrades? Things are getting tricky for the Germans. They feel that the catastrophe is approaching, and they want to strike a bargain. Eichmann has offered us one hundred thousand Jews in advance. Do you understand what that means? One hundred thousand Jews evacuated to the Spanish frontier. Think of the shipping that will have to be arranged to bring them overseas. Think of the discussions that will have to take place with the countries that are to receive them. It will all take at least six months. As things are going now, we can expect that in half a year the Germans will already have met their fate. But even assuming that they are still there, can you believe that once Eichmann has blown up the gas chambers of Oswiecim, has started official negotiations with the Sochnuth and has sent one hundred thousand Jews abroad who will inform the world about what has happened in Poland, can you then believe that after half a year he will once more start gassing our people, just because we cannot give him a thousand trucks? And even if everything miscarries and we make promises to the Germans that we cannot keep, we will at least have saved one hundred thousand lives. Is that nothing? Furthermore, we will be able to carry on our normal work. We can incite the people; we can build strongholds. Many will join the partisans. We will be giving them precious time, comrades. Every hour means five hundred saved from death."

The assembled company remained silent. Then Barlasz rose to his feet and tried to reassure me. "Joel, we all feel as you do. We are only wondering what is the best course to follow."

I said that someone ought to cable Jerusalem. Weizmann or Mosche Shertok, at that time head of the political department of the Sochnuth, ought to come here.

"I insist, comrades, that someone should come whose name is known to the world. The Germans are sure to keep a watch on us here, and their secret service will know at once of Weizmann's or Shertok's arrival. If we find we can't come to any concrete arrangement with the Allies during my short stay here, I can then at least go back to Eichmann and tell him that the Sochnuth has accepted his offer. Then Oswiecim will be blown up, and the emigration of the hundred thousand will begin. Negotiations can be started later —those of the Sochnuth with the Allies and those of the Sochnuth with the Germans. Perhaps Allied representatives will even meet German representatives, who knows? We shall offer them other sorts of goods, or maybe only money. But we shall have won time. Events are developing fast. We have got to stop the deportations. I have a suspicion, comrades, that our people are not being sent to Austria but into the gas chambers. However, I am absolutely convinced that this offer of the Germans is a serious one. If we accept it, or if we pretend to accept it, then our people will live. It may be that I shall have to bluff these Germans, but I cannot bluff if I don't see someone here who has real authority. The Germans will know if anyone has been here who has power to make a deal."

Menachem Bader spoke next. "Joel, this cannot be settled in five minutes, as you suggest. We cannot make these arrangements by telegram. We can never know if our telegrams have arrived on time or even whether the wording won't be garbled."

I buried my head in my hands. "I completely fail to understand. In the underground movement in Budapest we managed to establish communication with enemy countries across the frontier. Yet here in Turkey you cannot even send a telegram to Jerusalem, which is under British control, that is to say the control of people who are now the allies of the Turks."

This remark of mine was brushed aside, and now, for the first time, I began to feel that something was going on behind the scenes, something of which I was being kept in ignorance. At this moment I recalled the instructions that our Waada in Budapest had given me at their last session.

"Comrades," I added, "there is one thing I must ask of you. Do not for the present let the British know the details of the German offer. If they were to refuse these trucks outright and officially, I should no longer be able to play Eichmann along. And there is something else I must ask of you. We in Budapest have decided to get in touch with the

American ambassador, Steinhardt, and tell him the whole story. Steinhardt is said to be a good Jew, and above all a fine man. He can win his government over to our side and then we are saved."

I saw from the faces of my audience that they were electrified by this suggestion. It was agreed to at once, and unanimously.

Barlasz declared, "That's an excellent idea. I will telephone Steinhardt tomorrow and ask him for an appointment for us both. Steinhardt can do a lot for us."

Finally it was decided to cable Jerusalem and to urge Mosche Shertok to come here to Constantinople.

Echud Avriel then joined in the discussion. "It is not enough just to send a cable to Jerusalem. We must send a messenger. There is a train leaving the day after tomorrow. Venia himself ought to go and bring Shertok back with him. He will be able to give him all the facts during their return journey."

"But that would mean a week lost, comrades. Why doesn't Venia take a plane, if possible, tonight?"

They all smiled. "You make it all sound so easy, Joel, but we can't arrange an air passage in a flash, just like that."

They were all speaking at once. Then I said, "I can't understand you. I was able to get the Germans to provide me with a courier plane and now you say you can't even arrange for a flight to Jerusalem?"

There was nothing to be done, however. It was apparent that we in Budapest had greatly overestimated the influence of our Constantinople delegates.

The next day was spent in individual discussions. Almost a dozen parties and groups were represented in Constantinople. Each one of them had its own particular line of policy and often several alternative ones too. What shocked me most was the inability of these people to see the forest for the trees. Each of them took me aside and made derogatory remarks about all the others. If the policy of the others was followed, our people would certainly be destroyed. Of course, we had our own party squabbles in Budapest, but for some time now we had forgotten our differences in the face of the common peril. But here everyone was fighting everyone else for the respective positions of the party groups that they represented.

They often spoke of Alijah Beth, which was the code word for the illegal immigration into Palestine. After the publication of the British white paper which so severely limited immigration, our members in Jerusalem had set up an organization for the purpose of bringing people into the country against the decree of the mandatory power. I was taken aside by Echud Avriel, Zeev Szind, and Mosche Averbuch, who explained that the most important undertaking now was illegally to charter ships that would bring refugees from Constanta to Haifa. But this would, at the most, amount to about a hundred a month, whereas no fewer than five hundred Jews were being sent into the gas chambers every hour.

Menachem Bader and others referred again to the question of Haganah, of military resistance. I was familiar with conditions in Hungary, and I knew that we of the Jewish underground movement were quite unable to take any action that would harm the Germans militarily. It was my opinion that any acts of sabotage could only be in the nature of gestures. I requested, however, that if we were to devote part of our energies to this, then the objectives for such acts of sabotage should be selected in accordance with our

own interests. I supplied the members with an exact ground
plan of the Oswiecim concentration camp. I demanded the
bombing, so far as that was technically possible, of the gas
chambers and crematories, and I asked for diversionary actions and for aerial bombardment of the railway junctions
on lines leading to Oswiecim. I gave them detailed de-
scriptions of the places where Jewish parachutists could
land, and also a list of the documents and other necessities
that the parachutists must have with them if they were to
get through. I also gave them the addresses of reliable people who would help them on the roads to Budapest.

Chaim Barlasz, the head of the delegation, was pre-
occupied with questions concerning legal emigration. The
representatives of the Agudas requested that the legal certificates be given only to orthodox rabbis and to the recognized heads of the orthodox communities. In Budapest we
had long since forgotten the distinction between legal and
illegal certificates. For us everything was half legal and
half illegal. I showed one of our forged certificates to the
representative of the Palestine Office in Constantinople,
whose job it was to draw up and sign these certificates. He
was flabbergasted. He was quite unable to distinguish between his own genuine and the forged signature.

All these secondary conversations, however, did not
distract me from my primary mission. It was, indeed, an
idée fixe with me. The others noticed my obsession and
gradually became infected by it themselves. At noon Barlasz told me that the American ambassador was willing to
see us, and asked me to come to Ankara as quickly as possible. We at once got everything ready for the journey.

There was one other matter to which I devoted considerable attention: the settling of accounts with Mena-

chem Bader, who was the financial representative of the
delegation. If I had thought for a moment in Budapest that
I would get to Vienna, and later abroad, without having my
luggage searched, I would have brought the original accounts with me. As it was, I had to rely on my memory.
Later on, after a perusal of all the documents, I was able to
verify that I had not been far out in my figures. I accounted
not only for the money that we had received from Constantinople and from the Joint in Switzerland, but also for that
which we ourselves had raised in Budapest. Bader expressed himself as satisfied.

In the afternoon I had a futile conversation with Erie
Jabotinsky. He was obsessed with the idea of forming a
Jewish Legion, and he showed me the proclamations that
he had had inserted in several American newspapers. "This
one cost three thousand dollars," he declared. "And for this
one here we had to pay five thousand dollars." But he
showed not the slightest understanding of the critical nature of our present situation.

After all these private discussions, I was left with a
stale taste in my mouth. They were, without doubt, worthy
men. They lived modestly, and they conscientiously carried
out the tasks that Jerusalem allotted them. But they lacked
any awareness of how critical a period of history this was.
They had not looked death in the face day after day as we
had done in Budapest, and they had not, like us, lived dan-
gerously. In Budapest we had left the frontier of legality far
behind us. We knew the risks we ran, but we were determined to play for the highest stakes. Here in Turkey,
however, I was with people who still preserved the attitude
of Sally Mayer, who was prepared to offer the murderers

blocked Swiss bank accounts in exchange for Jewish lives, but nothing more.

Another thing depressed me. In Budapest we had ceased to play Zionist party politics. The fact that a man like Councilor Stern listened to us and helped us made us feel that we represented the interests of our entire race. But the people in Constantinople thought only of the Alijah (immigration) to Erets Israel. As Zionists they wanted to lead their race back to the land of their fathers; they did not notice that their followers were being massacred en route.

On the next day we accompanied Venia Pomeranz to the station. He was to return with Mosche Shertok as soon as possible, and during the long journey from Jerusalem to Constantinople, he was to give him a full account of the situation.

I spent the following day making courtesy calls on various people. Bandi Grosz asked me to go with him on a visit to Machmed Bey, the director of the Turkish Transport Company who had helped us with the airport police. Barlasz agreed to this. That afternoon I met a rich Turkish Jew called Simon Brod, who had done everything he could to help the Zionist delegates in Constantinople. He had considerable influence with the Turkish authorities and made full use of this to help the oppressed members of his race. Constantinople was at that time an assembly place for refugees from all the countries under Hitler's control. It was from Constanta that the transports of emigrants, both legal and illegal, set out, and it depended on the Turks whether the illegal emigrants were allowed to stay temporarily in the country while they obtained from some legation terminal visas in exchange for their false certificates. Brod was indefatigable in his efforts to help these people.

Meanwhile since Barlasz had heard from the American ambassador in Ankara that he was awaiting our arrival with impatience, I wished to set off at once. Again, however, we found that no aircraft was available, and we had to resign ourselves to the long and arduous journey by train. Next morning all the delegates accompanied Barlasz and myself to the Haider Pasha station, on the Asiatic side of the Bosphorus.

A strange thing now happened. We had already bought our tickets when Brod arrived and led a group of the delegates aside. They conversed with great excitement, and I could see expressions of consternation on their faces. They then came across to me and told me I must leave the station at once as the Turkish police had issued a warrant for my arrest. My permit was only valid for Istanbul and did not entitle me to travel to Ankara. Brod had learned that a warrant had been issued, but had used his influence to arrange that I be allowed to return to my hotel. Barlasz decided to go on to Steinhardt alone. Akiba Levinski brought me back to my hotel.

We had scarcely arrived when the telephone rang, and the porter informed me that two detectives of the foreign department of the police wished to see me in the foyer.

For the first time I began to panic. I said hastily to Akiba Levinski, "You must get me out of this hotel somehow or other and hide me. If I am arrested all is lost. The Germans will hear of it through their agents at once, and that will mean the end of our pretense of power. They will realize how small our influence is in this country. That must be prevented at all costs."

Akiba was willing to help, but there was little he could do except try to get the others by telephone. Bandi Grosz had also stayed at this hotel but, being cleverer than I, had managed to disappear without leaving a trace. The delegates promised by telephone to use all their resources to have me set free immediately, and while we were still speaking, the detectives entered the room.

They took me to the foreign control police station. I was not put in a cell, but was left in an office through which members of the public were constantly coming and going. A policeman accompanied me to the washroom and searched me for arms.

The competent official at last arrived and explained. "They're going to send you off to Svilengrad today. Have you got all your luggage with you?"

"Mr. Commissioner," I said, "this whole business must be based on a misunderstanding. You can't seriously mean to expel me suddenly like this. Will you please telephone the Palestine Office and ask them about me?"

"We already know all about you. The expulsion order is irrevocable and there is no appeal against it."

I was in despair. I feared the worst; I was not even sure that I should reach Budapest alive. As a Jew with a German passport, I would probably be arrested by the SS when I reached German-controlled territory and be immediately liquidated, as had often happened to people before now in Svilengrad. It was true that I was on a secret state mission, but the SS frontier guards would not know about that. No one would believe my fantastic story, and I would be killed before any inquiries were made. Even if I did manage to reach Budapest, Eichmann would be convinced that we were completely useless and helpless and without any influence at all with the Allies. He would have nothing more to do with us and would at once order the deportation and gassing of the remaining eight hundred thousand Hungarian Jews.

I begged and I threatened, but all to no avail. At last the policeman said to me. "You arrived without an entry permit, so you cannot expect me to let you stay here any longer. The only advice I can give you is to go to the Turkish consulate when you arrive in Vienna and obtain a proper visa."

He spoke good sense, but he had no idea who I was or what was at stake. Or did he perhaps know more than he was allowed to say?

I now had a little time to think things over. There was obviously something curious about the whole affair. Weeks ago we had cabled from Budapest and Barlasz had answered: "Joel must come. Chaim awaits him." But Weizmann was not here, and there was no entry permit ready. "Chaim" referred to Barlasz, and not to Weizmann. We had decided to go to the American ambassador in Ankara, but suddenly the Turkish police had heard of this and issued a warrant for my arrest. Thereupon Brod mysteriously turned up at the station, prevented my arrest, and got me back to my hotel. And all this time the delegates had left me severely alone. What was going on? What unseen hand was pulling the strings? In my last conversations with various delegates, I had got the impression that some of them were in regular touch with the British mission in Constantinople. Could it be the British who were back of all this?

Once more Bandi Grosz came to my aid. Not in person this time, but by his disappearance. The Turkish police searched for him all that day, but he was nowhere to be found. In the afternoon I was told that my expulsion would be postponed until the following day, since Bandi Grosz was to be expelled with me, and so far they had not been able to find him. I would have to spend the night at that police station, but I would not be imprisoned, only detained.

This was an eye opener. It was true that in my case there had been a breach of the passport regulations, but Bandi Grosz held a proper visa and, as a director of the Hungarian Transport Company, had been to Constantinople more than a dozen times on business with the head of the Turkish Transport Company. What did they have against him? Even if the Turkish government had learned of my mission, they had no interest in either furthering it or hindering it. In any case how could they have learned about it? The only possible explanation was that someone had told the British, and that they were now pulling the strings. All these thoughts passed through my head, but at the time I could only speculate as to what lay behind it all. Again and again I dismissed my suspicions. It was unbelievable that Britain, who had fought on alone after all the rest of Europe had surrendered to despotism, that Britain, whom we had praised as the stubborn champion of freedom, should now wish to sacrifice us, the weakest and the most pitiful of the oppressed.

By evening the Turks had succeeded in finding Bandi Grosz. He was beside himself with fury. "These friends of yours!" he said. "They must all be either idiots or cynics. Just look at the mess they've got us into now. If we're sent to Germany, we shall be shot like dogs as soon as we cross the frontier." He was trembling like an aspen leaf. He begged me to get my friends to do everything possible to prevent our expulsion.

I was already becoming resigned to the situation. "You know, Bandi, we may manage to jump off the train. If worse comes to worst, I can tell Eichmann that the Zionist delegation has accepted his offer completely, but that we would have had to inform the Turks of the purpose of our mission to get our permits extended. I can tell him that we did not want to do that until we had received instructions from Jerusalem and Cairo. The negotiations would then proceed, and the Allies would send their authorized representatives to meet the German delegates in Switzerland."

Bandi then said something to me that at the time I took for complete humbug. "Joel, you're as blind as a bat, and you simply do not understand what is going on behind the scenes. Do you really believe that Eichmann wants to free a million Jews in order to get dollars or trucks? I have talked a lot with Herr von Klages and I know which way the wind is blowing. The Nazis realize they've lost the war, and they know that no peace will be made with Hitler. But Himmler wants to make use of all possible contacts in order to start conversations with the Allies. Do you remember my telling you of my secret mission? I had to tear up the instructions on the airplane, but seeing the situation we are in, I can tell you something about it now. I was given the task of establishing contact with the English and the Americans so that negotiations for a separate peace can be begun. The whole of your Jewish business was just a side issue. We might have saved the Jews, but that would have been only an incidental result of my own mission, although for us, of course, the most important."

At that time I did not believe a word he said, but now,

after the lapse of a decade, I see many things in a different light.

He argued with me incessantly. "Don't fool yourself, Joel. We shall be lost if we are sent back into German-controlled territory. The Nazis will realize that we have no connections worth mentioning, and they will throw us aside like squeezed lemons. I don't expect any mercy from them."

He abused the Zionist delegates roundly. "What can your Sochnuth be thinking of, putting such an impotent bunch of people here? Constantinople is the crossroads of world diplomacy. Your people must be either fools or knaves, and probably both."

I began to grow angrier and angrier, particularly when I saw Bandi receiving visitor after visitor, while no one bothered about me at all. Bandi's wife came, and then some Turkish business friends of his, who were going to try to help him. But no one came to see me, and I sat in my corner resigned to my fate.

Bandi tried to stir me up. "It'll be plain suicide, Joel, if you give up now. We shall all be lost. You don't understand how important my secret mission is to the Germans. Himmler believes he can drive a wedge between the West and Russia. He knows that a separate peace with Hitler is not possible, but he may well sacrifice Hitler without hesitation, should it help him to achieve his ends. And he is clever enough to know that he will have to disentangle himself from Hitler's Jewish policy. So the two go hand in hand. The Nazis believe that we are the right people to establish contact. If we are now thrown out of the country as troublesome foreigners, the game will be up, and we'll be eliminated without anyone's caring a red cent. You just can't let that happen, Joel. You must move heaven and hell to prevent it. I'll tell you one thing: whatever you may decide, I won't allow these Turks to put me across the frontier. Unless I can complete my mission, Budapest will never see me again."

"But what can I do, Bandi? There are no avenues left open to me. I can't get hold of anyone, and no one comes to see me."

The office was now closed to the public and the officials had left. The detective on duty explained that we would not be taken to prison, but would have to spend the night there.

Bandi started to argue with him. "How do you propose we should do that, Mr. Commissioner? Where do you expect us to sleep? On the floor?"

The Turk advised us to put a couple of tables together, but at this suggestion Bandi immediately took umbrage. Waving his arms violently and speaking a mixture of Turkish, French, and German, he declared to the detective that he must be immediately allowed to inform his wife. The Turk at last gave in and Bandi telephoned. In half an hour his wife arrived with blankets, bedclothes, and so on. We settled ourselves down for the night, and the detective left us, locking the door after him.

The man had scarcely left the room when Bandi hurried across to the telephone. In a quarter of an hour he held about a dozen conversations. I have no idea who all the people were with whom he spoke, but he did seem to be soliciting the most improbable help. When at last he had finished, he urged me—I must admit against my will—to get on the telephone. I rang up Menachem Bader, and he was almost struck dumb when he heard my voice.

"What's happened? Have you been released?"

"No."

"Have you escaped then, Joel? This isn't Budapest. You'll get us all into trouble if you do things like that. The Turks might deport the whole delegation."

"Don't upset yourself, Menachem. I am locked up here, not in a cell but in an office. The official on duty locked us in and went away, so I simply sat down at his table and telephoned you."

He calmed down at last and I told him to come to see me in the morning. He still couldn't understand the situation. "How can I come to see you, Joel, when you're in prison? We will do everything we can to get you out."

"Menachem, I'm not in prison, as you assume. I'm simply sitting here in an office, which is used by the public. Bandi Grosz is also here and has already had a dozen visitors. It is vital that someone should visit me, but not one person has come. I just cannot understand your behavior."

In the end he promised to come and to let the others know what had happened.

Bandi Grosz, however, was still not satisfied. He kept banging on the door and making fresh demands. I felt sure the Turkish official would start getting tough with him. But as it happened it all turned out differently. Bandi inquired after the Turk's family and soon discovered that the poor man had many children and very little money. Bandi had no need to hear more. He at once offered him a small bribe if he would take us to the Hotel Pera. The Turk hesitated.

"But don't you see, Mr. Commissioner? We have to sleep here on the hard table, and you have to sit outside and guard us. It would be much better if you agreed to my suggestion. We can all three take a room at the Hotel Palace

Pera, have a good supper, and sleep in decent beds. You can
lock the door, and then in the morning you can bring us
back here before anyone arrives."

The Turk appreciated the logic of this, and perhaps
even more our good Turkish pounds. We drove to the hotel, where our friendship became firmly cemented. We ate
and drank well; finally the Turk was so completely oblivi-
ous of his duty that I was allowed to move about the hotel
as I pleased.

I saw that this was my chance, and I telephoned Menachem Bader, Zeev Szind, Echud Avriel, and Mosche Averbuch. I begged these people to come to the hotel as soon as
possible. My friends displayed an anxiety incomprehensible
to me. Those young people, although of great personal
courage, apparently did not understand why I had to side-
step the law.

One of them informed me on the telephone, "You have
no right to make off like that and put the whole delegation in jeopardy. If the police hear of it, they will expel us
all."

I shouted at him, "If you were all expelled it would be
the least of our misfortunes. Others would soon take your
place. But if I am sent back to Germany tomorrow, a million Jews will end up in Oswiecim and not in Israel."

They promised to come, and around midnight we began our session. I had managed to calm down in the meantime, and I explained the situation to them all with great
urgency. I asked them to use every means in their power to
prevent my expulsion. They were, however, convinced that
they would not be successful in this.

Menachem Bader said, "We have made every effort today, but the order for your expulsion has come from the

highest level, and I must tell you that I am pessimistic. I do not myself believe that we shall be able to have it canceled."

"In that case we shall leave the hotel tonight and you can hide me somewhere."

"It's not so easy as you think, Joel; Turkey is a police state and we cannot risk that sort of thing."

I was growing exasperated. "Budapest is under the control of the German Gestapo, but when we have to, we can hide a thousand people there. Yet you say you can't conceal me, illegally, for just one week?"

There was no reply.

I went on, "Every day we are risking our lives in Hungary, but we are used to it, and no one thinks twice about it these days. But we also run the risk of being tortured in the most fearful manner, and this is something each of us thinks about the whole time, for woe betide anyone who falls into the hands of those butchers. Nevertheless we carry out our duty to our people. But you people here, living in a free country where no real harm can come to you, you tremble at the prospect of being expelled."

They remained silent. I did not upbraid them any more, for I was already considering another solution.

"If it were possible to arrange for me to leave this country freely, on the German courier plane, then all would not be lost. I would be able to bluff the Germans and say that you, representing the Sochnuth, had in principle accepted the Eichmann proposals. The details would have to be discussed with the Allies, and delegates would have to be sent to some neutral country to conduct the actual negotiations."

They were impressed with this idea, and Menachem

Bader was especially attracted by it. Someone proposed
that we should draw up a provisional agreement for me to
lay before the Germans. We discussed this for hours and
eventually agreed on the following draft:[2]

PROTOCOL

*At a meeting held today between the authorized rep-
resentatives of the Jewish Agency and Herr Joel Brand,
the representative of the Central Council of Hungarian
Jews, it was determined that the representatives of the
Jewish Agency empower Herr Joel Brand in his aforesaid
capacity to transmit the following:*

*1. The condition precedent for a concrete agreement
is the immediate cessation of deportations.*

*2. Special delegates of the executive of the Jewish
Agency are on their way here. The Jewish side expects
the opposite side to send their authorized representatives
to Constantinople. If it is so desired, this meeting can take
place in another country.*

*3. The supply and delivery of the goods requested
by the opposite side present very great practical difficulties. A way, however, will be found to overcome these
difficulties as soon as the Jewish side, during the course
of negotiations, becomes convinced that the opposite side
is in earnest over the proposed plan.*

*4. Until the conclusion of a definite agreement, the
Constantinople representatives of the Jewish Agency propose to the opposite side the immediate conclusion of an*

---

[2] I cite here only the sense of this document and not the actual words,
although I have it in front of me as I write. It is everywhere interspersed
with Hebrew words and drawn up in a very complicated manner. It is
more practicable to reproduce it here in a form that is easily understood.

interim agreement, which shall contain the following conditions:

(a) *The deportations shall cease forthwith, for which the opposite side shall be paid one million Swiss francs a month.*

(b) *The emigration to Israel shall be permitted. For this the opposite side shall be paid four hundred thousand dollars for every transport that brings to Erets Israel one thousand persons selected by us.*

(c) *The emigration to overseas countries through neutral countries, as for example Spain, will be allowed. For this the opposite side shall be paid one million dollars for each transport of ten thousand persons.*

(d) *It will be permitted to send food, clothes, shoes, and medical supplies to the ghettos and concentration camps. For this the opposite side shall be paid fifty per cent of the value of the goods sent.*

5. *Until an agreement has been finally reached on the arrangements referred to in point number two of this protocol, Herr Joel Brand is hereby authorized to conduct negotiations and enter into binding obligations.*

The representative of the Central Council of Hungarian Jews JOEL BRAND	*The authorized representatives of the Jewish Agency* CHAIM BARLASZ, ECHUD AVRIEL, MENACHEM BADER

I then asked for a large sum of money for our illegal work, and Menachem Bader promised to raise at least one hundred thousand dollars, and probably much more, before my departure on the following day. I noticed the relief with which he agreed to this request, and he did in the end go a long way toward meeting my financial demands.

The next day Bandi Grosz warned the delegates against giving me money to take with me, as the Nazis would be sure to confiscate everything at the frontier.

It was already morning, and I did not try to sleep. In the early hours we accompanied the detective back to the police station, Bandi having, I believe, spent the night not in the hotel at all, but with his wife. On this day everything was conducted in the most formal manner, and through the German consulate, the Turks obtained for me a transit visa valid for Bulgaria, Yugoslavia, and Hungary. At about noon Menachem Bader arrived with the good news. My expulsion order had been postponed for a few days; all that was required was that I report to the police every day. In the meantime Mosche Shertok would have arrived, and I would be able to return to Hungary with an authenticated agreement.

A heavy weight had been lifted from my heart. An hour later we were both allowed, this time officially, to return to the hotel. On the following day I was visited by an American correspondent called Levy. We waited hour after hour for Shertok, but still he did not arrive. I sent cables to Budapest, some of them open and some in code, and as I received only the gloomiest replies I decided to report, also by cable, that a provisional agreement had been concluded. I cabled that special delegates were already on the way here. I could not understand at the time why I received no reply, but I learned later that my wife and several other leaders of the Waada were at that time held under arrest by the Hungarian police. My wife was tortured to make her reveal where I had gone and the nature of my mission, but she endured it all without uttering a word. Some days later she was freed by the Germans, who feared that she might betray to the Hungarian authorities the state secret of my mission.

My permit to remain in the country was renewed by the Turks from day to day. We awaited Shertok's arrival. Still he did not come. When I complained to the delegates, they placated me with encouraging words.

Meanwhile Barlasz was back from Ankara. He had spoken with Steinhardt, who was deeply impressed by our news. Steinhardt advised Barlasz not to let me travel to Jerusalem before he received a definite assurance from the British that I would be allowed to return. Barlasz also cabled Jerusalem to this effect. As I learned at a much later date, Mosche Shertok replied that he was making every effort to get to Istanbul, but that up to that time he had been unable to obtain the necessary papers. He said that Barlasz must try to get my residence permit extended until his arrival, but that if this were impossible, *I was not to go to Jerusalem in the present circumstances, but to return to Hungary*. Steinhardt also promised to send a report to his government in Washington at once. Later I discovered that he had done so, and that Roosevelt, after discussing the problem with Stettinius, had instructed the latter to send a special plenipotentiary to Constantinople. This plenipotentiary was Ira A. Hirschmann,[3] who arrived a few

---

[3] This was the second time Ira Hirschmann had come to Constantinople. On January 22, 1944, Roosevelt, as the result of energetic representations from Jewish circles in the U.S.A., had founded the War Refugees Board. In connection with this, Ira Hirschmann went to Turkey, and his intervention with the Rumanian minister in Turkey resulted in Antonescu's issuance of a decree whereby the Jews in Transnistria were saved.

days after my departure. All this was fraught with grave consequences.

During these days, Bandi Grosz displayed a restless activity. I was no longer able to control him. I lost count of the number of people he met each day. Everything he did was done with the greatest secrecy, but one day he came to me and declared emphatically, "Joel, I have found a solution at last. We will both go to Aleppo and then to Jerusalem, where we will get in direct touch with the Allies. There's no point in talking with these local Sochnuth delegates. You must come along with me."

I was taken aback. Eichmann had forbidden me to do anything without Bandi Grosz, yet I did not wish to go either to Aleppo or to Jerusalem. There was no time to waste. Eichmann would not wait, and every day large transports were wending their way to the Oswiecim annihilation camps. But Bandi Grosz was not one of us. He felt no responsibility toward the hundred thousand people who had sent me on my mission. I appealed to his conscience, but in vain. He had already obtained from the British a travel permit to Jerusalem.

"I have good relationships with the Allies, Joel, and the British and American attachés have definitely advised me to go to Syria. If there is anywhere that the fate of our mission will be decided, that is the place. There's no sense in your going back to Budapest. If we don't achieve anything here, Eichmann will simply send you straight to Oswiecim. No one will be any the better off for such self-sacrifice on your part."

I appealed to the other delegates to dissuade Bandi Grosz from going, but they made only halfhearted attempts to do so.

About two days later we received disappointing news. Mosche Shertok was unable to obtain a visa to enter Turkey. I found this quite incredible, for even then I regarded Mosche Shertok as the foreign minister of the Zionist movement, and of the nascent Jewish state. The Jews were the truest allies of the Western powers and Turkey was England's friend. Why then was the representative of the Jewish Executive now refused a visa to a country that he had already visited frequently during the war?

Bandi Grosz left Constantinople on June 1, 1944, thirteen days after our arrival in Turkey. On the afternoon of this same day the delegates called a meeting to discuss the situation that had arisen as a result of the refusal of an entry visa to Shertok. I was informed only of the decision that had been reached: that I must immediately attempt to meet Shertok in Syria. If that should prove impossible, then I must go on to Jerusalem.

I protested strongly against this decision. At the time I cherished no suspicions against England and had no fear of falling into a trap, but I did not wish to take responsibility for the delay that would be thus incurred. The delegates reassured me, saying that they had discussed it with the British and the Americans. They had been promised that first priority would be given to my journey in the Near East, and that my mission was being taken very seriously. I could travel everywhere by plane and would even be given an air passage back to German-controlled territory. It was necessary that delegates of the Allied powers should be present at my conference with Shertok, and therefore I would have to go to Aleppo.

On the day before my departure, I had a private interview with Barlasz. "Herr Barlasz," I said, "our comrades here cannot appreciate the situation in Budapest as I can. Every day counts and I have already been away two weeks. I have reached the end of the time limit that Eichmann granted me. It will take weeks of negotiations between the Sochnuth, the Allies, the Germans, and the transit countries before a final agreement is reached, and I cannot stay that long. I now have what I need to gain time in Budapest, since for this the provisional agreement will be enough. It is annoying that Grosz has run off, but somehow or other we'll manage to get over that. The Germans themselves have an interest in the matter."

Barlasz's reply was sharp. "I simply cannot agree, Herr Brand. The organization has made the decision, and you must abide by it. We have talked with the British, and they are expecting you in Aleppo. It depends on the Allies whether or not we can accept the German proposals, and they want to hear at first hand what you have to say. It is no fault of ours. We have promised that you will go."

I made further protests, but he cast all my objections aside. "We have a definite promise that the negotiations will be completed with great speed, and that you will then be able to return to Budapest at once. Everything possible will be done to speed your journey. But it has been decided that you must meet a member of the Executive, and you must abide by the decision, Herr Brand."

I gave in.

I was to be accompanied by Echud Avriel. I signed several blank sheets of paper, which could be used by our comrades during my absence for the purpose of communicating with Budapest if they should have occasion to do so, and I also gave them the key to our code. I cabled Eichmann, informing him that I had to go further afield to meet the Allies in order to pursue the negotiations at the highest level, and I told him that the text of the interim agreement could be expected to reach Budapest within the next few days.

On the morning of June 5, 1944, that is to say on the seventeenth day after my arrival in Budapest, Echud Avriel and I boarded the Taurus Express for Aleppo. All the delegates came to the station to see us off. We shared a sleeping compartment, and Avriel told me that the Turks had sent a detective with us, lest I attempt to leave the train en route. During the whole of this forty-eight-hour journey, however, we saw no sign of the detective.

The train stopped in Ankara for about one hour, and Klarmann, the representative of the Revisionists, and Griffel, of the Agudas Israel, were waiting for us. I could see at once from their expressions that something had happened.

They took us aside and Klarmann said with great earnestness and emphasis, "We have information that Joel Brand is being lured into a trap. Shertok was not granted a visa because the British want to entice Brand onto British-controlled territory and then arrest him. I warn you both, and in particular Brand, against continuing this journey. In this matter the British are not our friends, and they do not want Brand's mission to succeed. Unless Brand goes back at once, he will not be able to return before the end of the war, for the British will put him in prison."

The conversation took only a quarter of an hour, and at the end of it I was completely bewildered. I admit that I was not familiar with the ramifications of world politics, but I could not bring myself to believe that England would now refuse to help us. I had always had grave doubts about our success in obtaining from the British, in the middle of the war, ten thousand army trucks for freeing the Jews. We, in Budapest, had never wished to provide war materials for the Germans. But it did not enter my head that the British would arrest an officer bearing a flag of truce, or that they would deprive the duly appointed representative of the Jewish underground movement in Europe of his freedom of action. Yet Griffel and Klarmann were responsible people, and I was deeply discouraged by what they had told me.

Echud Avriel was also much disturbed. After discussing the matter, I became convinced that the Revisionists were opposing all the undertakings of the Sochnuth as a matter of principle. The Sochnuth had officially authorized and ordered us to make this journey to Aleppo and Jerusalem, and the people there must be assumed to know what they were doing. Venia Pomeranz had certainly given Mosche Shertok full details of my mission, and he must be aware that my imprisonment, or even delay, would have catastrophic results in Central Europe. The more I considered the matter, the calmer I became. It depressed me somewhat, however, to observe that my companion's anxiety exceeded my own.

We crossed the Syrian frontier early next morning and were still in bed when the French control officials asked for our passports. They almost fainted when I handed them my German travel permit. They turned it over and over and conversed among themselves with great animation. But everything was in order and the pass had a perfectly authentic British visa, so finally they had no choice but to put the entry stamp on it. They did not touch my luggage. Half

an hour later we arrived at the British control point. I could
see immediately that they knew who I was. I gave them my
pass, but they did not even glance at it; instead they gave
me a penetrating stare and handed it back to me without a
word. It was almost painful, and Echud became more and
more anxious.

"Joel," he said, "if we should unexpectedly be parted,
you must follow these instructions implicitly. Don't allow
yourself to be questioned except in the presence of a representative of the Sochnuth. You must request that Mosche
Shertok be informed, and you must answer no questions
whatsoever before his arrival."

We expected some of our comrades to be waiting for
us at the station, since there was a local representative of
the Sochnuth in Aleppo, but we saw no one whom we recognized.

We got our baggage ready and Echud went to fetch a
porter. I gazed out of the window while he ran down the
platform nervously. He found a porter at last and sent him
to my compartment, while he searched for the Sochnuth
representative. I gave my luggage to the porter and was
about to follow him onto the platform when an Englishman,
wearing civilian clothes, entered the compartment and addressed me in his own language.

"Mr. Brand?"

"Oh, yes."

"This way, please."

I wanted to follow the porter, but the Englishman
barred the way and pointed in the other direction. At this
moment more men arrived and forced me to go that way.
It had all happened so quickly that I had no time to collect my wits. A jeep was waiting by the compartment door,

with its engine running. The Englishmen forced me into it. Only now did I attempt to resist, and, turning around, I shouted for Echud, but he was nowhere to be seen. The jeep shot off; we left the town behind us at great speed. We pulled up in front of an empty barracks. There was no one about—no guards and no other soldiers. I was taken into a large dormitory where some British sergeants were seated around a table, reading newspapers. They hardly glanced at me and greeted my companions with a very unmilitary, "Hello, boys!"

I had the choice of a dozen beds that lined the walls. No one addressed a word to me. My luggage was brought in by a soldier, who put it by the side of my bed and departed without speaking. A little later I was invited to join the noncommissioned officers at their table, where I was given an excellent breakfast. The Englishmen spoke about the weather, but no one even attempted to discover who I was. Their manners were truly remarkable. I was quite unable to make out whether or not I had been arrested, but I was certainly not at liberty. I imagined that my papers were being examined, and that I would then be taken to Mosche Shertok.

On the following day I was at last brought before an officer, who politely asked me my name. I plucked up sufficient courage to reply, "I am not permitted to answer any questions. I am a Jewish emissary, and I am not allowed to make any statement except in the presence of a representative of the Jewish Agency."

The officer accepted this statement with equanimity and asked me whether I had any information to impart to the British authorities. I said I had not, and he then left me. He returned after a time, with good news. "We have decided to grant your request, and tomorrow morning you will be able to see Mr. Shertok, and speak to him in our presence."

This granting of my request and the politeness with which the Englishmen treated me did much to reassure me. I had already convinced myself that my detention did not mean I had been arrested. After all, I had come from an enemy country with a German pass, and it was only natural that a nation at war should interrogate such a person, if only to extract information from him.

After breakfast next morning, I was taken in a jeep to an Arab villa. I entered a room that was heavily furnished in the Oriental style. Some British officers and several civilians were seated there. As I came in, a tall, middle-aged man rose and walked toward me. This was Mosche Shertok. He greeted me most cordially, offered me a drink, and then opened the conversation. The Englishmen remained silent throughout, but followed with close attention what we said to each other. In addition to Mosche Shertok there were present, I believe, two representatives of the Sochnuth named Zwi Jechieli and Ruven Zaslany. Mosche Shertok spoke first.

"Comrade Brand, I know your story but shall ask you now to give me exact details. You can speak quite openly. Our British friends here are most interested in your report, and we have nothing to hide from them. Can you speak English fluently?"

"I can understand English very well, but I have not spoken it for many years. I can express myself much better in German."

"In that case, of course, speak in German."

I spoke for ten or twelve hours. I gave a clear picture

of our misery and distress and of the catastrophe that had overtaken our brothers in Poland and the Baltic states. I gave the history of our organization, of our illegal work, of the infiltration of the Hungarian and German secret services by our agents, of Gisi Fleischmann's negotiations in Bratislava, of the first days of the German invasion, and of our talks with Wisliceny and Eichmann. Even the Englishmen were deeply stirred, although they spoke no word and the only sound was the scratching of the stenographers' pencils. Now and then Mosche Shertok would interrupt me with a question, or to say that on such and such a point he was already sufficiently informed and I was not to waste time on it. On several occasions we broke off the session in order to have some refreshment. However, I still had not come to the crucial question: what answer should I give the Germans and what counterproposal should I take back to them?

Then Mosche Shertok interrupted me.

"Comrade Brand, I want to put three questions to you. Please consider your answers most carefully. First: What will be the result, in Budapest, if you return with an affirmative reply? Secondly: What will be the result if you return with a negative reply? Thirdly: What will happen if you do not return at all?"

I thought for a long time before replying, and I know now that I thought too long.

"Comrade Shertok, a week ago I would have answered your first question clearly and unambiguously and my answer would have been this: If we accept Eichmann's offer, he will destroy the gas chambers in the concentration camps, stop the deportations, and send one hundred thousand Jews across the Spanish frontier. Now, however, Bandi

Grosz has made me feel somewhat less certain. It may be that the Germans have intertwined our journey with other plans of theirs. It may be that the establishment of contact with the Allies is more important to them than are these negotiations of ours."

Mosche Shertok made no comment, and I passed to his second question. Here I was able to give an emphatic reply, "This second possibility does not exist for me. If I return to Budapest, I will never admit that my mission has failed and that you have refused Eichmann's offer without making some counterproposal. For that would be both murder and suicide. It would mean a terrible catastrophe for the remaining Jews in Central Europe."

To the third question I made an equally sharp reply. "In the case I don't return to Budapest, Eichmann would at once arrest my wife, my relatives, and all the leaders of the Waada. Every day twelve thousand people would be deported to Oswiecim, and in two months the survivors would number no more than the few persons who escaped from the Warsaw ghetto."

Looking back now, I must admit that I painted the picture in too dark a color. I had underestimated the courage and the skill of my comrades in the Waada and also the effect of the rivalries in the leading circles of the SS. After my arrest hundreds of thousands went to the gas chambers, but hundreds of thousands, and particularly the Jews living in the capital, were saved. Our work, and the sacrifice of our best people, had not been entirely in vain.

The Englishmen were obviously impressed, but it soon became apparent that their official position prevented them from expressing their own opinions. Mosche Shertok withdrew into a corner with them, and they talked softly but vehemently together. Then he came back to me and laid a hand on my shoulder.

"Dear Joel, I have something very bitter to tell you. You must now go on further south. The British insist on it. I have done all I can to make them alter their decision, but it is an order from the highest authority and I cannot change it."

For a few seconds I was completely at a loss to understand the meaning of his words. When at last I realized that I was to be arrested, my nerves snapped.

"Don't you understand what you're doing?" I shouted. "This is plain murder! Mass murder! If I don't go back, our best people will be slaughtered! My wife! My mother! My children! They will be the first to go. You've got to let me return. I have come here under a flag of truce, on a special mission. You can agree or not as you will, but you have no right to seize an emissary. I am not even an emissary from the enemy. The Germans are my enemies just as much as they are the enemies of the Allies, and far more bitter enemies, too. I am here as the delegate of a million people condemned to death. Their lives depend on my return. Who gives you the right to lay hands on me? What harm have I done to England? So far as has been within our power, we have helped the Allies, albeit we had enough to do to save our own lives. We have done what damage we could to the Nazis. What do you want from us? What do you want from me?"

I begged, I threatened, I wept. The fate of my children was before my eyes, and this gave me eloquence. The Englishmen remained silent, but I felt that I had spoken straight to their hearts.

My words made a deep impression on Mosche Shertok

and the other two Sochnuth representatives, and they argued passionately with the Englishmen. The latter, however, had received their orders and were not in a position to reach any other decision. I had now become quite hysterical, and Mosche Shertok tried to calm me.

"Joel, this is just as hard for me as it is for you. I will not rest until you are free once more. I will fly direct to London and have the matter taken up at the highest level. I am sure you will be set free and will be able to continue the negotiations. We will see that matters are put right. But now, at this moment, we are powerless and must do what we are told, you as much as I."

Mosche Shertok expressed his readiness personally to take me in his car to the Allied officials in Jerusalem, but the English officers refused to allow this. I cannot remember the manner in which I took my leave of Shertok and the other two comrades. I know only that I was brought directly to the station, where I was given a sleeper, and that I was accompanied by a young British officer.

This officer treated me with the utmost courtesy and never let me feel that I was his prisoner. I had money and was free to go to the buffets of the stations at which we stopped. I even considered the possibility of escape. But only those who have belonged to a party held together by the strongest ties of ideology will understand my attitude at that time. I was a Zionist, a party member, and my leaders were the party Executive. I was bound by party discipline and I did not dare rebel against it. The thought often crossed my mind that it was my duty to escape, to return illegally to German territory, and to try to save whatever there was left to save in Budapest. Perhaps that is what I really should have done. But I felt so small, so insignificant

—a man thrown by chance into the boiling caldron of history—that I did not dare take on my own shoulders the responsibility for the fate of a hundred thousand people. I lacked the courage to defy discipline, and therein lay my true guilt.

We spent the night in Beirut and next afternoon went on by train to Haifa. In the early hours of the morning we were on the soil of Palestine. I sat on the carriage steps and gazed out into the distance, breathing the air of this land of our dreams. My British companion feared I might jump from the train, but after exchanging a few words with me, he apparently understood my sentiments and left me alone.

We had a long wait in Haifa, so we left our luggage at the station and strolled into the newly built quarter around the harbor. My companion had some business with Barclay's Bank, and he left me outside the building. Once more my thoughts turned to escape. I was now among my own people, and there would be men here who would help me hide. A man in his thirties, with a large dog, was standing on the other side of the street. I remembered that I had an acquaintance in Haifa called Alfred Marchand, whom I had not seen for fifteen years, and whom I would hardly recognize again. But I had heard in Budapest that he bred dogs, and I now felt sure that this man with the dog must be my old friend. I went across to him, but immediately realized I was mistaken. Nevertheless I spoke to him.

"I do not know who you are and you do not know me, but you have got to help me. I have come direct from Budapest and am a delegate of the illegal Zionist organization there. I have important news for the Sochnuth. But the British arrested me in Aleppo and are taking me to Cairo. The officer who is guarding me is at this moment in the bank. Please hurry to the Sochnuth and inform them that I am leaving for Cairo on the afternoon train. They must at all costs spirit me away."

No one had observed us. Some minutes later my officer came out of the bank, and I was convinced that he had seen nothing, for he made no comment. Nevertheless months later in Cairo prison, this same officer asked me who the man was with whom I had spoken in Haifa.

Chapter VII

THE BRITISH SECRET SERVICE

WE REACHED Cairo in the early hours. No one came to meet us and we took a cab into the town, where we stopped in front of a small house. My companion got out and kept me waiting for over an hour. I was just about to run away when he reappeared. His expression had completely altered, and I got the impression that he no longer cared to look me straight in the face. He addressed a few words to the driver and then got in the cab without speaking to me. We drove straight out of town and finally pulled up in front of a fortress-like building. There were no guards visible and practically no one about. An iron door swung open, revealing a courtyard in which about a dozen Abyssinian soldiers were standing with fixed bayonets.

We were received by a British noncom who asked my name.

"Joel Brand."

"Your passport gives a different name."

"The passport is a false one. I am not a German, and I have never been called Eugen Band."

He took no notice of this but simply copied down the particulars in my passport. When he had done this, he handed me the paper to sign. I refused. "I am not making any false declarations while I am in Allied territory," I said. "My real name is Joel Brand. I have no reason now to keep it secret."

"But I cannot put a name down on this document different from the one in your passport."

"That is your affair. As far as I'm concerned, I am only signing my correct name."

We made a compromise. He left his document unaltered while I signed with my true name, and we left it to the British administration to sort out this paradox.

A friendly corporal led me to my cell, which in fact was a large and well-furnished room. He left the door open, but always remained near at hand. If someone passed by, he would temporarily lock me in. This made me aware that I was now indeed a prisoner, and I decided to make a formal protest. My guard had apparently been instructed what to say should I do this.

"How can you say you're a prisoner, sir? A prison doesn't look like this. You have only been brought here for a few days in your own interest. I don't myself know the reason for this, but be patient. Everything will be explained in time, and you will eventually be able to go wherever you want. There's a war on."

I was treated as a person of importance. The food was excellent, and an Arab waiter laid the table with great at-

tention and asked me what wine I would care to drink. He
served me the choicest foods, and far more than I was able
to eat. A bowl of fresh fruit stood on a table in my room,
and twice a day the Arab servant washed the floor to keep
the place cool. No one entered the room without first knock-
ing on the door. I was allowed books, and my suitcase had
been given to me untouched. My hat and coat, however, I
had left in the hall, and this was the cause of my meeting an
old friend, Samu Springmann.

Samu had left Hungary early in 1944 on a legal emigration certificate. His nerves had not been strong enough
to stand the strain of those last few weeks. The police were
on his track, and Constantinople had suggested he leave
Budapest and come there. We had given him strict instructions not to go to Palestine but to remain in Constantinople, for we particularly wanted to have a representative in
the Sochnuth delegation there. Samu Springmann had from
the very beginning been active in building our own organization, had a firsthand knowledge of the illegal conditions
under which we worked, and would be able to explain to
the members in Constantinople the meaning of our half-
coded letters.

We had written many times from Budapest to Barlasz and others, asking them to help Springmann remain in
Constantinople. However, as I was to learn later, they had
not done this, and in the end the Turks had ordered him to
leave the country. His appeal against the expulsion order
was turned down. At the last meeting of the Sochnuth he
attended, he stormed angrily into the room and shouted,
"Thank you very much, comrades, for all your help."

No one answered and he left the session and also Constantinople. He was arrested in Aleppo and was taken to

this same Cairo prison, six weeks before my arrival there.[1]

All this I learned much later. At that time I had no idea that Samu Springmann was so close to me. He, however, recognized my hat and coat in the hall, and the day after I arrived I suddenly heard Hungarian songs being sung in the courtyard. Then I heard someone whistle in a way that only Samu Springmann could whistle, and I rushed to the window. Samu raised his head, and we recognized each other.

At first my joy knew no bounds. But when I came to analyze the situation I was extremely depressed. The comrades in Constantinople must have been only too well aware that Samu had been arrested by the British. Why, then, had they not warned me? What was back of all this? What possible advantage did England derive from injuring us in this way? We were surely trustworthy confederates in the struggle against Hitler, and the Western powers were carrying on this struggle in the name of humanity. Why then should they wish to let these helpless people be destroyed by the Nazis, when there was still a chance of saving them?

I could understand nothing any more.

Next day we devised a system of whistles and songs by which we were able to talk to each other, although it was not until five months later, in Jerusalem, that I learned the whole story of what had happened to him.

I was left completely alone for three days, but then a British officer came into my cell and sharply ordered that my suitcase be taken out. I protested against this, and a

---

[1] It was explained to me later by the people in Constantinople that their efforts to obtain a residence permit for Springmann had been abortive.

heated argument ensued, during the course of which I made strong objections to my imprisonment. Unfortunately this officer had not had time to read through my dossier, but his tone became more polite when he saw that I was not going to let myself be intimidated.

The following day he called me into a room used for interrogation, where he sat on a raised platform about eight inches higher than the floor. He was now politeness itself and apologized for having to question me from such a position, but explained that that was the regulation.

"You understand, don't you, Doctor?" I interrupted him to say that I was not a doctor, and that my name was Joel Brand.

"You must realize, Mr. Brand, that everything we are doing here is done in your own interest. You may rest assured that you have not been imprisoned. We have no right to do that. You have not been charged with any offense, and you have only been brought here for reasons prescribed by military necessity."

"I don't understand you, Captain."

"Mr. Brand, you will shortly return to Hungary, and it is possible that the Germans will use all the means in their power to get you to describe what you have seen in the British war theater. In that event it would be best if you were able to assert that you had seen nothing, since you were kept in prison. Otherwise you may be forced by torture to make statements."

That Englishman probably has no idea, even today, how consoling I found his answer. I wanted to believe him, and so I did believe: England was the home of freedom and our ally. It was unbearable for me to renounce this belief, and I therefore drove all doubts from my mind.

The Englishman continued to address me repeatedly as "Doctor" and apologized each time for doing so. At last he said, "I have read through your dossier and it has impressed me very much. You may be sure that your affairs will be taken very seriously and dealt with at the highest level. Mr. Shertok has been summoned to London by my government in connection with this matter. I myself have been entrusted with the duty of obtaining from you all the relevant information, and cabling to London a daily report of our conversations."

There now began an interrogation the purpose of which remains hidden from me even to this day.

In Aleppo, in the presence of Mosche Shertok, I had already given the British officers an exact account of our situation in Hungary. I had spoken there for twelve hours, and I believed that we had completely exhausted the subject. Nevertheless, here in Cairo, this man interrogated me for eight hours a day, for months on end. I do not know how I was able, after even one week, to tell him anything new, or how he could have expected me to do so. If a name were mentioned—and there are many names in my story, important and unimportant—he would at once demand the life story of the unfortunate person and the history of his family and of the people with whom he associated. It is possible that he mistrusted me and hoped by cross-examination to discover contradictions in my story. But I do not believe this was the case, for after a few days I got the impression that he was convinced of my trustworthiness. In addition, there was nothing I wished to conceal. During the whole time I was completely convinced that England and ourselves had common interests and that it could be only because of a misunderstanding that we should face each other in the roles of prosecutor and accused.

In the first three interrogations, he let me do practically all the talking; he hardly expressed an opinion. He was endeavoring to form a picture for himself of how our Budapest organization had been built up. I had the feeling that the problems that touched me most deeply were for him of only secondary importance. He did not seem to regard the last-minute rescue of a race condemned to death as of any consequence in comparison with the collection of material that might some time or other be of use to the British intelligence service. During the fourth interrogation, however, we came up against the real problem.

"Do you believe," he asked, "that the Germans intended this offer to be taken seriously?"

"Completely seriously."

"Do you think the whole business is a private deal on the part of Eichmann, Wisliceny, and Krumey, or has it got the backing of the German government?"

"I do not know whether the German government is behind it, but I am sure that these people are acting with the authority of Reichsführer SS Himmler."

"What makes you believe that?"

"The whole security service in Budapest, Vienna, and Bratislava are involved. Herr von Klages seemed to me to be a very important person in the German hierarchy, and he was told about it and gave it his support. I was provided with a German passport and a German courier airplane. Although I am a Jew, I was officially allowed to leave German-occupied territory in the middle of the war. The German Embassy in Constantinople was also informed. These SS officers are a pack of murderers, but they aren't children. They know that if the agreement were concluded, the transport of one hundred thousand men could never remain the private concern of a few SS men. I always had the feeling during our negotiations that they were in continuous touch with Himmler in Berlin."

"So you are convinced, Mr. Brand, that the Germans will give the remaining Jews their freedom, if their offer is accepted?"

"If one can believe Eichmann, not all the remaining Jews. There are probably about one and a half million Jews still living in German-occupied territory and he says he will free one million."

"And all for ten thousand army trucks?"

"For less. For a few million dollars. I am absolutely convinced of that."

"Then would you mind explaining, Mr. Brand, how you reach that conclusion? These people have provoked the hostility of the entire world by their mad project of exterminating the Jews. They have already destroyed five million of them, and yet now, for a few million dollars, they are ready to let the remainder go free. What would even a hundred million dollars amount to, when compared with their daily war expenses? What possible sense is there in such a policy?"

"I have my own opinions on the matter, but I have not come here to theorize about the Germans. I am certain that their offer should be accepted, or at least that I should be allowed to continue to negotiate with them. What does England stand to lose by this? Maybe in the end the Nazis will kill me, and in that case instead of five million Jews destroyed there will be just one victim more."

"Before we discuss that, we must first try to discover what the Nazis are hoping to achieve by this offer."

"You could find that out by inviting them to send delegates to a neutral country to negotiate this deal. The Sochnuth should include among their representatives an observer from the Allies."

"That will certainly be done, Mr. Brand, but it is not a matter that I can deal with. My task is to discover what your opinions are, so don't be afraid, please, to give my your theories on the attitude of the Nazis in this affair."

"It is all much more complicated than you think. It is a mistake to regard the German power apparatus as a monolithic block, for it consists in fact of many different groups and cliques, all struggling against each other. So long as everything went well with the Nazis, these rivalries were hushed up, but now the internal dissensions are becoming much sharper. Let me enumerate the reasons that could have led these SS officers to act as they are doing. First: These people foresee the impending catastrophe and are trying to fabricate excuses for their past acts of lawlessness. They have countless crimes to answer for, committed against all the peoples of Europe, but none lies so heavy as the crime they have committed against the Jews. In this connection there is one fact that must be understood. They think the Jews possess immense power. They are haunted by the fairy tales of the Protocols of Zion, and of a secret global ruling class. If what Bandi Grosz has said is true, they are hoping that we shall enable them to establish some sort of contact with the Allies. When I was driven secretly to that farmhouse on the outskirts of Budapest, I did not take the theories of Herr Laufer very seriously. Now, however, I keep remembering many things that I had forgotten, and it is becoming more and more clear to me that Himmler wants to try to conclude a separate peace with the Allies, possibly by sacrificing Hitler himself. He probably has the idea that he can come to some sort of arrangement with the Western powers directed against Russia, and thus obtain a general pardon for his people. But all that is high-level politics and no concern of mine. I have a definite mission to fulfill. I am here to ransom a million Jews."

"You spoke of several possible Nazi motives."

"The clique with whom I have been negotiating wants to earn money and also to be exonerated individually."

"But why should these people want trucks? They surely don't intend to keep them for their own use after the war?"

"It is possible that they only want them in order to be able to persuade Hitler that he must stop the murder of the Jews. Hitler is a maniac. This idea of the total extermination of the Jews is his *idée fixe*. They have, therefore, had to advance military arguments to restrain him, even though the situation is quite different now from what it was in 1942."

"In what way, Mr. Brand?"

"When the German government at the end of 1941, after America's entry into the war, decided on the liquidation of the Jews, they still hoped they would win and be able to set up their New Order in Europe. At that time they wanted to free the whole of Europe, not just Germany, of Jews. They regarded us Jews as people afflicted with an infectious mental disease that endangered the rest of the people. They wanted to eliminate us in the countries they controlled. Now, however, after recent Allied victories, they do not expect, when peace is made, to retain anything more than their native land. The prospect, therefore, of our infecting the enemy countries with our disease can only be viewed by them with pleasure. Take Eichmann for example. He has always wanted to enforce the mass emigration of the Jews, for he believed this would weaken Germany's enemies. It is possible, however, that there is another motive behind his present actions."

"What do you mean?"

"He may believe that you will refuse his offer. It would then be easy for him to lay the blame for the mass murders on you, or at least make you his accessories in crime."

"How do you mean, Mr. Brand? When the Germans gas the Jews, they don't do it on our orders."

"No, the Nazis are murderers by choice. In the court of world history no one will ever be able to disguise their guilt. But they would be able to say; 'We wanted to be rid of the Jews, to expel them, but the others wouldn't accept them. So we had to exterminate them.' "

"That seems to me a most peculiar form of logic, yet I almost get the impression that you agree with this train of thought, Mr. Brand.'

"You do me an injustice, Captain. For me, a murderer is a murderer. But an onlooker who does not intervene when murder is being committed must also bear his share of the guilt."

"But we have intervened. We were the first to do so, and we do not intend to give up the struggle until the Nazis have completely surrendered."

"For us your victory will come too late. You cannot resurrect the dead victims of German fascism. You can, however, still secure those who are left, if you would send me back with full authority to negotiate, instead of keeping me locked up here."

"You are not in prison, Mr. Brand."

"That is a quibble. I am not allowed to return to the one place where I can do something."

"Do you really imagine that we would deliver ten thousand trucks to the Germans in the middle of the war?"

"I have already said a dozen times that we don't want any of your trucks. Give us a promise that you will never have to carry out, and on the strength of that alone I can save a hundred thousand lives."

"But how so, Mr. Brand? You surely don't expect the Allies to give an official promise and then not keep it, do you?"

"We are not asking the Allies to do any such thing. It will be enough if the agreement with the Germans is signed by the Sochnuth. In this way a hundred thousand people will be freed, and later the Sochnuth can dishonor the agreement and deliver nothing to the Germans. There is no need to keep one's word with murderers."

"But the Allies will have to take over these hundred thousand people at some neutral frontier, and then put them on ships. Have you any idea what such an operation would entail in time of war, or how much shipping space would be required for such a mass transportation?"

"The Germans are poorer than you, but they managed to collect sufficient railroad cars to take millions of people to the gas chambers in eastern Poland. They moved them clear across Germany, and in the middle of a war, when their railway system was already overstrained by the requirements of their Eastern Front. Yet you say that now, with the enemy already beaten to his knees, you are unable to find enough ships to move a hundred thousand people who have narrowly escaped from hell."

"I am saying no such thing, Mr. Brand. Probably our government will find a solution. I only want to tell you that such an operation could not be based on a private agreement between Eichmann and the Sochnuth. To bring these people to the Spanish frontier would necessitate agreement with several countries. If we should join in them, we could not then go back on our word."

"All you have to do is to start the ball rolling. The negotiations will go on for months. More months will be needed to work out the question of transport. And in the meantime Germany will have collapsed. Don't you see that it's a question of gaining time and nothing more? The moment you open negotiations, Eichmann will stop the deportations and blow up the gas chambers. They will never be rebuilt, not even if the negotiations come to nothing, for by then it will be too late. In any case I am absolutely convinced that we shall manage without the trucks, and that these people will accept money instead."

"Now tell me one other thing, Mr. Brand. If the German government really is behind this offer, why don't they communicate it officially to the Allies through some neutral country?"

"I have already told you that up to now Himmler is probably the only person behind this proposal, and that the SS leaders are hoping to win Hitler and Goebbels over to their scheme later. But there is yet another reason why the Germans chose this method of approach."

"And what is that?"

"The Germans cannot open international negotiations, via a neutral country, by saying: give us ten thousand army trucks, or else we will gas one and a half million people. The Nazis have never admitted that they have gassed the Jews and that they are still doing so. We Jews know it, of course, but even in their dealings with us the Nazis have usually described their actions in euphemistic terms. Furthermore, as I have said, they believe that we possess enormous power and that our Sochnuth has much secret influence among the Allied governments. They are quite unaware of the powerlessness of the Sochnuth, of which I had experience in Constantinople. And I hope to God they never find out about it, or our people in Budapest will undoubtedly be lost. They will realize the true situation, though, if you keep me here much longer."

"I can assure you, Mr. Brand, that you will not be here much longer. Mr. Shertok is now in London with Mr. Eden, and a decision will soon be reached."

All my arguments were repeated dozens of times and the interrogations were becoming monotonous. Each day I gave the same answers to identical questions, and grew more and more impatient. However, a week after my arrival I at least received exciting news. My interrogator informed me that a delegate from the U.S.A. was there to see me and that my affairs would soon be put in order. I was taken to a private house on the banks of the Nile, which apparently belonged to a British officer. There were over a dozen people in the room, and also some stenographers. I was introduced to a slim man, of medium height, in his early thirties.

"I am Ira Hirschmann," he said. "President Roosevelt has sent me here to talk to you, Mr. Brand. I flew from New York to Constantinople, but got there too late. So I followed you to Aleppo and missed you again, both there and in Jerusalem. Finally I came on here to see you."

Later on I learned of the difficulties that the British had put in his way. He has described them in his book *Life Line to a Promised Land:*

> . . . I went immediately to the Embassy to see Ambassador Steinhardt . . . and asked him about the two Hungarians [Bandi Grosz and myself, J. B.]. "The British have captured them and spirited them over the border into Syria," said the Ambassador. "They are now out of my jurisdiction."
>
> "Where in Syria?" I asked.
>
> "Nobody seems to know."
>
> "I have instructions to interview these men at all costs," I said, "and we will have to ask the British to return them to Turkey; otherwise I shall have to go after them."
>
> The next day, at a meeting we had with British Minister Bennett, I pressed for specific information on the whereabouts of the two mysterious figures. After an hour's stubborn insistence I wrung out of him the admission that they had been taken to Cairo, that they were under the surveillance of the British Intelligence, and that the entire matter had now been placed in the hands of Lord Moyne, Cabinet member and Deputy Minister of State in the Middle East.
>
> There was nothing for me to do but to fly back to Cairo. . . . There was difficulty in meeting Lord Moyne. . . . When I arrived at the American Legation, Minister Tuck had a message for me from John Hamilton, assistant to Lord Moyne, to the effect that I was invited by Anthony Eden to leave at once for London by special plane; that the matter for which I had come to Cairo was to be taken up on the "highest levels" in London, and that there was no need for me to see Lord Moyne nor the German agents in Cairo.
>
> Instinct and complete physical exhaustion both in-

dicated that another plane trip at this point was a wrong
move. . . . I decided not to permit the British to change
my instructions. . . . I insisted that arrangements be
made at once for me to see Lord Moyne. . . .

Promptly at twelve o'clock the door opened and I was
ushered before a tall, thin, angular man of sixty-five to
seventy years of age. The entire atmosphere surrounding
him seemed gray. His eyes were cold and unemotional. . . .

In spite of the formal setting, I was intent enough on
my purpose and sufficiently resistant to the official British
atmosphere to be cooler than I had expected to be in this
situation. . . . Lord Moyne talked quietly, sagaciously,
reservedly . . . for about twenty minutes without com-
mitting himself to anything. . . . The statement was intended to dispose of the matter by shipping me to London
to meet Eden on the subject. . . .

. . . I quickly disposed of Giorgy [Bandi Grosz, J. B.]
by stating that so far as our Government was concerned,
the British could keep him in prison—I did not wish to
see him. However, I persisted in my demand to see the
other agent, Joel Brandt.

Lord Moyne pressed me to accept Eden's invitation,
stating that the talks were going to be "centralized" in
London. I was told that Moshe Shertok, representative of
the Jewish Agency, who had come to Cairo on the same
business, had warmly accepted Eden's invitation.

"I am flattered by the invitation from Mr. Eden," I
said, "but I take my instructions from Washington. I cannot and will not take them from London."

The counterplay of pressures continued for about one
and a half hours. Finally I rose and said: "Mr. Minister, I
come from a sporting people. So do you. I will agree to take
my instructions from Mr. Eden if you will agree to take
yours from Mr. Hull. I will go to London if you will go to
Washington."

Lord Moyne apparently saw the logic in this. I then
showed him the letter from President Roosevelt support-

ing my mission. . . . He turned abruptly to Brigadier Maun-
sell and said: "Arrange for Mr. Hirschmann to meet Joel
Brandt this afternoon at 3:00 P. M."

At first Mr. Hirschmann struck me as a somewhat con-
ceited and pompous person. In the course of our conversation, however, I saw that my story had impressed him. He
asked me whether Eichmann's offer had been made in
writing. I replied that it had not. I tried to make him see
that there was no question of actually delivering any goods
to the Germans, but that it was essential to keep the negotiations from being broken off, in order to win time. In this
way we should be able to accept the hundred thousand
Jews offered us as an advance, and save the remainder from
destruction. I told him that I must return at once, or we
would lose all our maneuvering power.

He promised a great deal, and he made one remark
that has stuck in my memory: *"I beg you to believe me,
Mr. Brand, when I say that my government entirely disap-
proves of the way in which the English are handling this
matter.* I shall fly to London and shall there, and also in
Washington, demand your immediate release. You will be
given the opportunity of continuing your mission."

Yet nothing happened. The interrogations were resumed—the same questions followed by the same answers.
I began to despair.

Some days after my meeting with Ira Hirschmann I
announced to the British officers, "You have no right to
keep me here. I have come as a spokesman, and your action
is contrary to international law. You ought to be the first
to realize this. What you are doing to me is contrary both to
your interests and to ours. I will not discuss that, however.

But I tell you, here and now, that unless I am released within three days' time, I shall go on a hunger strike."

They tried to calm me, but I now refused to believe a word they said. On the fourth morning I refused to eat. At first the Englishmen took no notice. They presented me with especially appetizing dishes which, after a little time, they took away again. My interrogator talked to me in friendly but serious tones.

"Mr. Brand, please believe us. Everything is being done in your own best interest. Your problem is even now being deliberated in London. In a few days' time you will be free to carry on your work on behalf of your people. If you starve yourself, you will lose your strength and will be physically unable to complete your task."

During the first three days it took all my strength to prevent myself from touching the food, but later on I ceased to feel hungry.

On the ninth day my officer brought me a letter from Echud Avriel:

JOEL,

I am taking the opportunity of writing you a few lines to tell you how the business is progressing.

You know that Shertok is in London. We continue to receive optimistic news from him. The same can be said of America, and we believe that our basic demands have been as good as met.

Venia is ready in Istanbul. We hear regularly from Hansi and now and then from Rezsö. After the initial bitterness, matters have at last reached a balance, and we have reason to believe that all is not yet lost.

Yesterday we heard from Istanbul that someone had

arrived there who had seen Hansi and the children. He reported that they were well and that life was much as usual with them.

14.7.44

Yours ever,
ECHUD

This letter changed my attitude, for it made me feel that the work was being successfully carried on in my absence. It was in good hands, and I realized that in the final analysis no one is indispensable. If they were in touch with Eichmann, then it was not absolutely necessary for me to be there too. I decided to break my hunger strike.

A week later, however, I received a severe blow. The following report from the Reuters agency appeared in the papers:[2]

We learn from reliable sources that the Germans have recently made a proposal amounting to blackmail.

They state that they are willing to spare the Hungarian Jews if the Allies will agree to a partial lifting of the blockade. It is understood that out of the 800,000 Hungarian Jews, 400,000 have already been deported to Poland, where they have been gassed by the Nazis. The same fate now awaits the remaining 400,000 Jews.

The Germans have chosen this moment to dispatch from Hungary to Turkey two emissaries with proposals that are alleged to have been put forward by the Gestapo. These proposals consist of an offer to free the remaining Hungarian Jews and to put an end to the policy of liquidation, in exchange for certain concessions, namely, the

---

[2] See photostatic copy of *Times* article, documentary appendix.

*lifting of the blockade to allow the entry of army lorries
and other goods.*

*The two emissaries have made it known that the
policy of annihilation of the Jews will be continued if
these demands are not fulfilled. An examination of the
proposals has shown they have no serious or solid foundation and that they consist of a mixture of blackmail and
threats and are designed to sow discord among the Allies
with a view to crippling the war effort. It is quite clear
that the Allies will not be deterred by any German threats
or offers from making every effort to alleviate the fate of
the Jews, wherever and whenever possible.*

*At the time when this German proposal was made,
it had already become known that Admiral Horthy, no
doubt as the result of strong pressure from the Swedish
and Swiss governments, had ordered the slaughter of
Jews to be halted for the time being. It is as yet too early
to judge the significance of this report.*

This publicity given to our mission by the official
British news agency was shocking in the extreme. The matter was reported in the Egyptian press without comment.
Now it was all quite clear to me. These people were the
enemies of my people. The cruelest blow of all, however,
was the fact (which I only learned later) that the official
Zionist organ in Erets Israel also published the Reuters report, and without comment of any sort. The Sochnuth must
certainly have known what it all meant. Why then did
they not seize this opportunity to protest the British inter-
pretation of the affair? Why, when it was a matter that concerned the fate of the remnants of our people, did they not
mobilize the American press? I was quite unable to understand it all.

Chapter VIII

PROCRASTINATION IN EGYPT

THE ENGLISHMEN were much more friendly to me after my hunger strike. They did their best to make my stay with them as pleasant as possible. I ate with them in their mess and we talked together. Their commanding officer invited me to go to the movies with him. In short, they did what they could to make me feel that, far from being their prisoner, I was a respected personality who was only there for reasons of security.

I would often be invited to parties given in the Cairo hotels and clubs and in the homes of senior officers. But although the conversation was free and easy, I always had the feeling that it was all a rather refined form of interrogation. There was one conversation I had that stood out from the others. That was with a man who, I was afterward told, was Lord Moyne, the British Minister of State for the Near East.

It took place in the garden of the British-Egyptian Club in Cairo, where we sat drinking around a luxuriously laid table. The Englishmen offered me cocktails or long drinks. Next to me was Lord Moyne, who asked, "Did you take this offer of Eichmann's really seriously?"

"Absolutely seriously. I am completely convinced that the mass murders will be stopped if Eichmann's offer is accepted."

"But how can you imagine that we would let the Germans have ten thousand trucks in the middle of the war?"

"That isn't the point, sir. The Germans will accept some other sort of goods—maybe food, maybe just money, maybe nothing at all. It's possible that they only wish to make contact with you."

"What will happen, then, if you go back? How do you think of proceeding from here?"

"It will be much easier than you think, sir. A single order from Eichmann and the deportations will stop. Then he will ask us to draw up lists for the transport of the hundred thousand. The first transport to Spain may possibly consist of only some twenty thousand, but nevertheless these twenty thousand lives will be saved."

"But will this Eichmann let the people go without first getting a guarantee that we will deliver the goods to him?"

"He will let the advance party go just as soon as the Jewish Agency accepts the offer. Whether the Jewish Agency then decides to go back on its word, whether it gives him trucks or food or nothing at all, all that is of no further interest to me, provided we have been able to save these people."

"How many people will be in the advance party?"

"I've already told you, a hundred thousand people."

"And how many will there be altogether?"

"Eichmann spoke of a million."

"What on earth are you thinking of, Mr. Brand? *What shall I do with those million Jews? Where shall I put them?*"

That was too much for me and, rising, I said, "If there is no place for us on this planet, then there is no alternative to the gas chambers for our people."

With studied rudeness, I turned to my officer escort. "I cannot stand these endless questions any longer. I have a headache and do not feel at all well. Please take me back."

The officer got up and accompanied me outside.

This conversation was soon known in Erets Israel. Some months later Lord Moyne was shot dead in the streets of Cairo by two young Jewish terrorists. When on trial the young men refused to answer questions, and simply quoted from the Bible. They were sentenced to death and went silently to the gallows, where they sang the Jewish national hymn before being executed.

I later learned that Lord Moyne himself had often deplored the tragic fate of the Jews. The policy, however, that he had to follow was one dictated to him by a cold and impersonal administration in London. It may be that he paid with his life for the guilt of others.[1]

These parties and social functions continued. The invitations were mostly transmitted to me by the commanding officer himself. I seldom learned the names and ranks

---

[1] I have read, since then, that the man with whom I spoke on that occasion was not Lord Moyne, but another British statesman. Unfortunately, I have no means of clarifying this.

of the people who wanted to talk to me. They were mostly British generals, but sometimes important civilians. On one occasion French officers were also present. At first I used to accept every invitation with enthusiasm. I always hoped that I would be able to win these people over to our cause, and I regarded them as sufficiently influential to be able to engineer a decision in our favor. Later, however, I got the impression that I was being paraded before senior British officers, on their arrival in Cairo, as though I were a curious sort of animal. My English escorts nicknamed me "Hess number two."

Early in August my interrogator sent for me and said, "I've good news for you, Mr. Brand. It has been decided to let you travel back to Hungary. I want to thank you for all the information you have given us. We have found it very useful. I wish you luck, and I hope that you will be able to complete your mission successfully."

"What instructions have I been given and what am I to say to Eichmann? Is his offer accepted in principle?"

"I myself cannot answer these questions, but you are taking the Constantinople plane, which will stop in Jerusalem on the way. A delegate from the Sochnuth will join you on the plane there, and will give you exact instructions. The Germans will have to arrange for your journey from Constantinople to Budapest. My role in this matter is now finished."

I could not believe my luck, and the next few days flashed by as in a dream. Every day I went to parties in the Cairo hotels and clubs, at which the British officers drank my health, wished me luck, and paid me the most extravagant compliments. They regarded me as a hero, because I dared to return into the lion's den. I myself knew that there was nothing particularly heroic about what I was doing, since I was certain that I would be able to come to some practicable agreement with Eichmann.

My suitcase was returned to me on the day I was due to leave. My clothes had been washed and my suit pressed, and my money was handed back to me. I was now ready to leave. I asked the commanding officer to allow me to go into town to buy a few small things for my wife and children, and he placed his car at my disposal. I bought a Turkish coffee machine for my wife, and toys for my children.

In the evening a farewell party in my honor was held in the officers' mess. I gave the officers the books I had brought with me from Istanbul. The atmosphere was one of gaiety and excitement.

I was due to leave at half-past five next morning. I was not able to sleep a wink and at three o'clock I got up and made ready. Half-past five came, but no one fetched me. I heard a clock strike seven, then eight, then nine, but still no one appeared. At half-past nine an officer entered my room and said, "Mr. Brand, I am very sorry. We have just received a cable from Jerusalem. The Sochnuth want us to postpone your departure."

I was almost struck dumb. "What do you mean? The Sochnuth? I don't understand."

"Don't get upset, Mr. Brand; it says here 'postpone.' That only means a short delay. We'll probably get another cable today, and then you'll be off."

I was in despair. I had no faith in the British officers' assurances. They were decent fellows who only wanted to calm me down. I no longer knew what to believe. Did the

British really want me to go? Or was the cable an invention? And how could the Sochnuth postpone my departure? My comrades had always declared that they wanted to help me, but that they were dependent on the British. Were the parts each played now reversed? I was completely bewildered. I actually contemplated suicide, but the Englishmen must have read my thoughts, for in the days that followed they never left me alone for five minutes. Then I was put into another cell, where I was never left by myself.

I decided to go on hunger strike again and I refused all food. After several days the commanding officer came to me and said, "Mr. Brand, you have been invited to lunch today with the delegates of the Jewish Agency at Shepheard's Hotel. They are your own people and they will explain everything. You will be able to arrange about your journey with them."

I breathed again. At last I would be able to break out of the invisible ring in which they had encircled me. I was taken to Shepheard's Hotel, where I was received by Teddy Kollek and his associates. Kollek was a colleague of Ben Gurion, who of course was to be Israel's prime minister. Ben Gurion was at that time chairman of the Sochnuth Executive and Kollek was his right-hand man. Kollek now holds the position of Director General in the Presidium of Ministers.

My English escort introduced me, was told by Kollek to come back for me that evening, and departed. We had the whole afternoon to ourselves, and we spoke our minds. I soon found I was beating my head against a brick wall, even though the bricks were soft and resilient. No one contradicted me, and everyone was convinced of the importance of my mission. But nothing concrete or decisive was said.

"Comrade Joel, you have undertaken a great task, and we are with you to the very end. The deportations have been stopped, and negotiations are under way. The Hungarian Jews will be saved."

"Please tell me what is happening. Why have I been held captive here? The British wanted to let me go on Friday. Why did you cable them to postpone my departure? Have you all gone crazy?"

"It was a question of a few days' postponement, that's all. The request came from Constantinople. I myself do not know the contents of the last telegrams they received there from Budapest, but it seems your colleagues in Budapest wanted your return postponed."

I was extremely upset by what he said and I did not believe that Budapest wanted to delay my return. I could contain myself no longer. "What has been going on here? Why haven't I been kept informed? Why am I not allowed to go back? I am not saying that I am the best person to undertake these negotiations, but I wanted at least to take a hand in them. Also I am convinced that we have no one in Jerusalem or in Constantinople who is sufficiently aware of the ins and outs of it all. Why have I been held prisoner? Am I a criminal?"

"Don't get so excited, Joel, and have a little trust in us. Jewish lives are just as sacred to us as they are to you. Just a few more days, and you'll be free to go."

"I don't care about myself, but I know that while I am sitting around here, our one big chance may be lost. I am convinced that thousands are being deported and gassed each day, and I simply do not believe that without me you would be able to take the extreme measures that are necessary to stop these murderers."

"You do not do us justice, Joel. I can promise you that the deportations have ceased. Negotiations are under way."

He said this with such insistence that I became calmer. At this time I was completely convinced of the necessity of my taking a personal part in the negotiations, but this was of subsidiary importance compared to the negotiations themselves.

"I can also tell you this, Joel. Your arrival here with these German proposals, and your counterproposals, have at last forced the Allies to face the question squarely. Thanks to you, we have succeeded in accomplishing what we were unable to do before. The conscience of the world has been aroused, and in all quarters of the globe people are now intervening on behalf of those Jews who are still alive. Have a little patience, Joel. You have embarked on a noble undertaking. It must be brought to fruition, and I am sure it will be."

I had no reason to doubt his words, and I believe even today that he spoke in all sincerity. But the news that he and Zwi Jechieli (whom I was to see later) brought to me during the next few weeks was, if not actually false, decked out in the best possible colors. They recognized how nervous I was, and they wanted to do their best to spare me anxiety.

I was not officially on a hunger strike now, but I simply refused all food in the hope that the British would thereby be forced to let me go. Nevertheless, during these weeks I had almost a dozen meetings with the Sochnuth delegates at various Cairo hotels. Naturally I had something to eat at these meetings, and I hoped it would not be known to the British. I see now how naïve I was then. They knew all about it, and that was why they took me, as often as possible, to visit my comrades at Shepheard's Hotel and at the Metropole. At this time I shared a cell with an Englishman who was alleged to have been arrested as a deserter. This man used to tell the most fantastic tales. I now believe that he had been put there by the prison authorities to keep an eye on me. There soon ceased to be any point in my hunger strike, so I gave it up.

Nothing new came of my conversations with the Sochnuth. I was repeatedly upbraiding them, and they replied by giving me optimistic news. I believed a part of what they told me, just because I wanted to believe. They told me a lot about my wife's heroism. They said that Kastner had taken over the negotiations with Eichmann and Wisliceny, and that everything was going well. But they never once gave me an explanation of why I was being kept there.

One day I was taken to see Zwi Jechieli, the Sochnuth's official representative in Cairo, at the Hotel Metropole. He immediately offered me a fascinating solution to my problem.

Without any preamble, he began: "Joel, I command a detachment of Jewish parachutists. We are training men for that sort of work, not far from Cairo. Can you suggest places in Hungary where we should be dropped?"

I thought for a moment before replying: "Before I answer, Comrade Zwi, I would like to ask you a question."

"You speak like a good Jew. What is it?"

I rose and said, "I should like to be dropped with you."

"That is not a decision that I myself can make, but I

see no reason against it. I'll let you know the answer next time we meet. Meanwhile sit down and tell me about suitable landing areas."

"If I'm going to be dropped with the others, then I think it's best that we should jump near Siofok on the shore of Lake Balaton. We've a house there and some reliable Christian comrades. We could be in Budapest in one hour."

"Do you think our men ought to wear English uniforms? It would protect them from being shot out of hand."

"But they couldn't do much in uniform anyway. They'd be stopped on the roads at once."

"They'll be dropped at night, and when they've reached a certain point they could change into civilian clothes."

"I don't see any sense in that, and as far as I'm concerned there would be no question of it. I would report at once to Eichmann, although naturally if I'm dropped with the others I'll wait until I've seen that they're safe."

But it was all just so much eyewash. They only wanted to cheer me up, to keep me quiet. And in this they succeeded. They postponed my departure not only for weeks, but for months on end. It was always only three more days, and I hovered perpetually between hope and despair.

Bandi Grosz had also been arrested by the British and brought to Cairo. My interrogater proposed to confront him with me. "The man is lying to us," he said. "Give him a good talking to and get him to tell us the truth."

I was sitting in an easy chair, when they brought Bandi in. He looked ill and weak, and I saw at once that he had been treated very differently from me. I tried to encourage him, but he just shook his head and indicated that he did not wish to speak in the presence of the interrogator. The latter noticed this and arranged that Grosz and I should have a private meeting.

I was taken to the military prison in Cairo, where Bandi was kept. He was in an ordinary cell, poorly furnished and without a chair. He lay on a wooden pallet. I was almost ashamed when I thought how much better I had been treated. This man, after all, had committed no crime against either us or the Allies. He was a boastful, scheming fellow, and he did everything for money, but he was not a criminal, and he had been of great help to us. Without him we should never have been able to organize the network of agents who secured us our contacts abroad and later enabled us to negotiate with the Germans at the highest level. What did they want of the poor fellow?

He seemed confused, and I got the impression that he had almost lost his powers of reason. He prophesied the most terrible misfortunes for our people.

"They should have let us go back," he said. "Now it is too late. The Hungarian Jews will be slaughtered to the last man."

"But Bandi, when you were in Constantinople, you said you couldn't return at any price, and that your only desire was to reach British territory."

"That's not true. I had to go to Aleppo to confer with the Allies. How was I to know that I'd be locked up in jail instead? They treat me like a criminal. They starve me and swindle me in every way. There'll be a bloody revenge for this one day. You've no idea what a lot I've done for the Allies and what a lot I could still do. But these British don't understand anything, and the Sochnuth people are plain idiots who swallow all the lies the British tell them."

I did my best to calm him, but I myself left the prison in a very depressed state of minu.

At the beginning of September my officer said to me, "Our business with you is now finished, and we are no longer interested in keeping you here. Whether or not you return to Hungary is a matter you must arrange with the Sochnuth. We are going to send you to an army camp, where you will have complete freedom. You will have the rank and pay of a lieutenant in the British Army. We would ask you, however, to keep your name and history a secret while you are there. Until further notice you are now Lieutenant Jacobsen. I would like to thank you for the trouble you have taken on our behalf and to wish you good luck for the future. All the best, Lieutenant Jacobsen."

I was driven in a car to a place not far from the pyramids. The camp was a comfortable one, housing about thirty people. Most of these were agents of the British intelligence service who were awaiting a new assignment, and included people who would be entering enemy territory by parachute or submarine. There were men of many nationalities in this camp—Englishmen, Germans, Frenchmen, Indians, and so on. All of them had carried out dangerous assignments in enemy territory and by various incredible means had somehow managed to get back. There were two pretty girls there as well; ostensibly wives, they too were actually secret agents.

We were completely free, and the guards were only there to see that no stranger entered the camp. We could go out when we wished, but we had to promise not to go to Cairo. We visited the neighboring villages and inspected the pyramids. We ate magnificently, but were forbidden alcohol. Nevertheless, I have never drunk as much as I did in this place, for every inmate considered it his moral duty to smuggle in as much liquor as he could.

After I had waited for ten days, during which nothing happened, no one called, and I received no letters, I decided to send an official communication to the Sochnuth. I could have posted this without further to-do in some Egyptian village, but I wanted it to go through the camp censorship. I wrote more or less as follows:

> To the Executive of the Sochnuth
>
> *It has hitherto been my belief that my detention has been brought about by friends of our people, acting in the interests of our common cause. The long months of my imprisonment have, however, at last convinced me that this is not so, and that I am dealing with enemies. In these circumstances I am compelled to inform you that I no longer feel bound by the obligations imposed on me by Mosche Shertok in Aleppo. If I am not set free within eight days, I shall, regardless of British bayonets, seek all possible means to escape and by illegal means shall return to my comrades in Budapest. I hold you responsible for all the consequences that may arise as the result of my conduct.*
>
> *With comradely greetings,*
>
> Joel Brand

Three days later an officer came to the camp and handed me back my letter.

"We cannot forward such a letter," he said. "We want to have absolutely nothing more to do with your affairs. We have decided to send you in a few days to the Sochnuth in Jerusalem. You will be able to complete your business there with your own people. You had better get ready for the journey."

I was taken from the camp on October 5, the day on which my ultimatum would have expired. In Cairo, in the same house in front of which, on my arrival four months before, I had had to wait so long, I was informed that I would be going to Jerusalem by the night train. I would be accompanied by an officer, and I must continue to call myself Lieutenant Jacobsen.

To my surprise I met Bandi Grosz's wife on the train. She had also been allowed to go, but she had heard nothing of her husband.

We reached Jerusalem next morning.

Chapter IX

JERUSALEM

I WAS taken by my English companion to the head-quarters of the British intelligence service in the King David Hotel. I was left standing in the corridor while he went into an office. After a few minutes the passage was filled with British officers, who came out of every door to stare at me as though I were some strange animal.

I was then conducted through various rooms to see various officials, all of whom exchanged a few friendly words with me, until finally I was presented to a high-ranking officer who said, "Mr. Brand, you are now free to do whatever you want. You can go to Constantinople, or Budapest, or Zurich, or wherever you wish. Talk it over with the Sochnuth. You will find that we are ready to help you to the best of our ability, but I would advise you to rest for a while, and discuss with your friends how you can best complete your work. I wish you the best of luck."

"Thank you, Major, but I think your people in Cairo have given me a long enough rest. In any case I don't require any more, and all I want is to get on with the job as soon as possible."

I was taken by an officer to police headquarters, where I was received by an inspector who, in spite of this thoroughly English appearance, bore the Hebrew name of Chaluz.

"Mr. Brand," he said, "we are getting your documents ready. If you come back this afternoon, we can give you your identity card. Have you enough money, or do you wish us to give you some?"

I told him that I still had almost all of the two thousand dollars with which I had arrived in Aleppo, and that I had also received pay while I was in prison.

"I will telephone the Sochnuth now, Brand, and arrange an appointment for you."

To my astonishment the police officer rang up Teddy Kollek and told him I was there. Kollek was amazed when he heard my voice on the telephone.

"Is that Joel Brand? Are you really here? Have they set you free? Take a taxi at once and come along here as quickly as you can."

The Arab taxi driver gazed at me stupidly when I shouted the word Sochnuth at him. Nor had he ever heard of the Jewish Agency. Finally he drove me by a devious route to King George Street, where Teddy Kollek was waiting for me in front of the door of the Sochnuth building. The house was empty, for it was the eve of the Feast of the Tabernacles.

"This is really exciting, Joel, your arriving here. We had no idea. You must see Ben Gurion at once. The old man is waiting for you."

Now at last I was face to face with one of the chief leaders of Jewry. Ben Gurion was president of the Executive and president also of my own party, the Mapei. During our conversation, I poured out all the bitterness that had accumulated inside me during the long months of imprisonment.

"You mustn't take it so hard, Joel. Everything is progressing all right. We have started negotiations, and will pursue them to a satisfactory conclusion."

"Who is negotiating on our behalf?"

"Sally Mayer, the Swiss representative of the Joint. He is a very experienced man."

I now became really angry. "You can say that quite calmly, Comrade Ben Gurion? Have you any idea what Sally Mayer stands for? He is an old man, and is simply incapable of handling negotiations such as these. Sally Mayer, indeed. He is a national misfortune."

Too late I noticed Ben Gurion's own white hairs, too late to take back my tactless remark.

"There are some tasks that one old man can perform better than three young ones," Ben Gurion pointed out to me.

I was not, however, ready to leave it at that. "What has been going on in Hungary all these months?"

"Matters are going better than you think, and a great deal has been accomplished. Hundreds of thousands will be saved in the end."

"I must go back at once. You've got to let me go now. My place is over there."

"Teddy Kollek will arrange everything. You must speak to him. We will help you."

Teddy Kollek got me a room in the hotel, and the next few days were a time of bewildering confusion. As I saw it, I now had two tasks. The first was to inform myself of all that had taken place in Hungary during my months in prison. The second was to discover the reasons for all the mistakes and omissions of the last half year. But I sought in vain for the man who could give me the picture in full; there was no one person who knew all the ins and outs of what had happened. Nor was there any single office in the Zionist Executive or in the Jewish Agency or in the Central Trade Union that controlled the work of the Hazalah. There were innumerable offices whose functions overlapped. The reports that were received from Budapest were passed on to various organizations and individuals, who failed to keep each other informed. Day after day I hurried from office to office until I gradually began to see that I was in fact squandering my energies chasing a phantom.

I went to a department of the Jewish Agency there called Waada Ezra we Hazalah—the Council for Rescue and Relief. It bore, in fact, the same name as our committee in Budapest. It was the central office for rescue work and all the branches, such as those in Constantinople, Budapest, Bratislava, and other places, were subordinate to it. I naturally expected to find a general staff there dealing with secret rescue work. How bitterly disappointed I was!

Jizchak Grünbaum ran this office. This former member of the Polish Sejm granted me only a few minutes' conversation about the matters that lay nearest my heart. I naturally assumed that, having access to all our reports, he would have studied our problem from every angle, but a few weeks later I realized that he had never really appreciated what had happened and was happening in Hungary.

He said to me once, "Why haven't you rescued my son, Herr Brand? You should have been able to get him out of Poland into Hungary."

I replied: "We have not usually undertaken the rescue of individuals."

"But you ought to have thought of my son, Herr Brand. It was your duty to do so."

I respected his gray hairs, and I said no more. I did not say how often we had, in fact, strained every nerve to rescue individuals. We had employed our best people, and all our resources, to bring to safety the surviving leaders of the revolt in the Warsaw ghetto. They had, however, refused to leave their posts. Jizchak Grünbaum's son was unknown to us, and had not rendered any special services to the movement.

I also called on Eliahu Dobkin, the head of the Jewish Agency's immigration department. This man was much better informed than the others and wielded considerable influence behind the scenes. He had been selected at this stage to accompany Dr. Joe Schwarz, the director of the Joint, to Portugal to meet Kastner and Colonel Becher, the German representative. It had been arranged that the negotiations we had begun with the SS in Budapest should be completed in Portugal.

Dobkin talked to me for a long time, and expressed his belief that it would be well if I accompanied him to Portugal, but he did not believe that the British would give me the necessary travel permit.

After repeated applications the British finally did give

me a travel document in the name of Eugen Band, the name that Eichmann had bestowed upon me. In the end, however, it was found impracticable for the meeting to take place in Portugal, and the venue was transferred to Switzerland. The Swiss consulate was prepared to issue me a visa, provided I was vouched for by two members of the Sochnuth. Dobkin refused to agree to this.

"You will understand, Joel," he said, "that I cannot vouch for a man called Eugen Band, when your name is Joel Brand."

"Are you aware, Eliahu, that many Jews in Central Europe have been sent to the gas chambers simply because officials have refused to sign documents that were not absolutely correct?"

The central office for the illegal work was the Moszad Alijah Beth (Department of Illegal Immigration). Strictly speaking, this office was subordinate to the Trade Union Organization, but in fact it ran all the illegal work of the entire movement. It was engaged in an unceasing struggle with the British and did its best to frustrate the intentions of their white paper. These people of the Alijah Beth were kindred souls. They were young people who recognized the desperate necessities of the times and were prepared to use every means in their power to carry out their jobs.

After the festival, Teddy Kollek accompanied me to Tel Aviv. We went to a half derelict house near the newly constructed congressional building of the Trade Union Organization. There was a conspiratorial air about our arrival as we entered and walked up a concealed staircase. The Alijah Beth had their headquarters in this house, and they conducted their business in an atmosphere of great secrecy. Almost every piece of furniture had its secret drawer, and I was reminded very much of our illegal offices in Budapest.

The members crowded about me, eager to hear what I had to say. We sat informally in a large office room, drinking tea and coffee. After an hour of free and open conversation we went over to the trade union building, where about a hundred people had gathered in a large hall.

The meeting was opened by Josef Sprinzak, who was later to be president of the Israeli Parliament: "I welcome here today our comrade Joel Brand, the leader of the Jewish workers' movement in Hungary. He has brought with him the greetings of Hungarian Jewry. . . ."

The tone of this speech, which reminded me of Social Democratic meetings before the war, seemed to me monstrous. I wondered where this Hungarian Jewry was, whose greetings I was now supposed to be delivering. Before my eyes there floated the picture of unfortunate men and women being hounded into trucks, and I thought of the Oswiecim transports in which so many died even before they reached the gas chambers.

No doubt I was expected to make a polite reply to this speech, but I had had enough of such talk, and I spoke from my heart.

"Comrades, I have no greetings to bring you from Hungarian Jewry, and I must politely refuse your ceremonial welcome. I came to Constantinople in order to save the last remnants of our race in Central Europe from annihilation. You were the last hope of hundreds of thousands condemned to death. You have failed them. I was those people's emissary, yet you have left me to sit in a Cairo prison, while they were being done to death in the gas

chambers of Oswiecim. You have kept on the right side of
the law. You have refused to declare a general strike. If
there was no other way, then you should have used force to
get me out of prison. I have got to go back to Hungary, so
that I can save what still remains to be saved. You have
given me no help and therefore have betrayed those who
sent me here."

The festive atmosphere vanished and an awkward silence descended on the assembly.

Two members of the Alijah Beth, Saul Meyeroff and
Zwi Jechieli, took me aside. "Joel, you mustn't talk like
that here. We don't know who is in the hall, and someone
might go and tell the British. We could get into great
trouble." They hurried up to the reporters who were present and begged them to hush up the matter.

The tension was at last broken by Eliahu Galamb.
Galamb was at that time chief of the secret military organization, Haganah, and one of the organizers of the Jewish
Brigade in the British Army. He was a sober-minded man
who was held in high esteem, and he spoke quietly and
carefully:

"You are doing us an injustice, Joel. Mistakes have
been made, as they always will be, but it is not true to say
that all is lost. There are in Hungary hundreds of thousands who are still alive, and we are doing everything in
our power to enable them to survive the war. You are doing
yourself an injustice, Joel Brand, if you don't see that. Your
coming here has helped us to breach the walls of silence,
and we are no longer alone. The conscience of the world,
which has slept for so long, has at last been awakened.
President Roosevelt, the Pope, and the King of Sweden
have all intervened on our behalf. We arranged this in Lon-

don and in New York, but in the final analysis it has been
your mission that started the ball rolling, and you have a
right to be proud of that. If we have acted too late, then we
regret it bitterly. But it is unjust to reproach us with having done nothing, and it is an injustice to yourself to believe that your mission has been a failure. I am glad that
you are here with us today, Joel. There is much that we do
not understand in the reports that our members send us
from Central Europe. You will be able to help us decipher
this information. We shall do our best to see that you play a
part in the negotiations that must now be conducted with
the enemy. Don't be impatient, Joel, and don't be embit-
tered, but instead be glad that you can once again take up
your task."

These thoughtful and gracious words did me good.
Melech Neustadt, the head of the World Union of Jewish
Labor Parties, proposed that a commission be set up to examine my accusations and suggestions, and this was agreed
to unanimously. The commission was duly convened but
after a solitary session was heard of no more.

At the time of my release Mosche Shertok was in London. On his return a few weeks later he was to speak at a
large gathering in Haifa, and I went there to hear him. I
arrived late and the hall was already overflowing with people, but when Mosche Shertok recognized me from the
rostrum, he interrupted his speech to say:

"Comrades, someone has just come into the hall who
has been the cause of my making several journeys to London. This man has given us a great task to perform, which
to my sorrow I have only been able to accomplish in part.
The Allies were not prepared to cooperate in the way this

man requested. Had they done so, hundreds of thousands of our brothers would be alive today.

"They did not give us what we asked, but instead they gave us the Jewish Brigade of the British Army. You well know, comrades, how dear to my heart was the organization of the Jewish Brigade. Nevertheless, I declare now, before the whole world, that I would have sacrificed the Jewish Brigade if I could thereby have accomplished more of what this man requested."

I was already aware of the trouble Mosche Shertok had taken to found the Jewish Brigade, so I was able to appreciate the value of his words. I was beginning to grasp the fact that destiny, and the mighty of this earth, were stronger than the leaders of our movement and that our influence in the world was very slight. The truth of the matter was very different from what it appeared to the diseased minds of the German Nazis and "world rule by the Elders of Zion" existed only in the pages of *Der Stürmer*.

When I returned from Tel Aviv, I wrote to Professor Chaim Weizmann, president of the Zionist World Organization and of the Jewish Agency, and after a fortnight I received his reply. The president regretted that he was too busy to receive me but said he hoped to do so in the near future. Two weeks later his secretary, Fraülein Itkin, telephoned and arranged for me to see him on the following day.

Weizmann received me in a friendly manner, and I repeated my complaints, to which he listened in silence. He agreed with much that I said and told me to set my views down in a memorandum. He also promised to help me return to Europe.

I prepared the memorandum and for the sixth time I

repeated what I had already said in my other reports. Weizmann read it and placed it in the file. I never heard any more about it.

Afterward I wrote to the Jewish Agency, to the Executive of the Labor Party, and to most of the leading personalities, but all my complaints and demands fell on deaf ears.

I was dealing with an impersonal organization, and it was quite impossible to fix the blame on any individual. Although no one denied mistakes had been made, no one took any steps to repair some of the damage. All my efforts to return to Hungary, or at least to Europe, came to nothing, and all my activities at this time seemed to be regarded as those of an impracticable visionary. At length I grew resigned to the situation.

There was a moment in March of 1945 when my hopes revived. I was visited by Griffel, a representative of the orthodox party Agudas Israel, who said to me, "Joel, it was true what I told you in Constantinople, and now you can see that I was right. You never listened to me but went on to Aleppo and got involved in all these misfortunes. Now I come to you once more. I know the fight you are putting up, and how you are giving yourself no rest in the matter, but you will never get anywhere with the Mapei. I am making you a proposition. Why don't you come to us? I can arrange for a French warship to take you illegally to Marseilles, and then you will be able to get to Switzerland. Our people there are now trying to get these negotiations with the Germans taken out of Sally Mayer's hands, and you can help. It is your last chance."

I spent a sleepless night considering his suggestion, but I found I lacked the strength to forsake the party and the labor movement in which my whole life had been spent. I would have felt a traitor.

I once more experienced the urge to take part in the work of the Budapest Waada, and I redoubled my efforts to find out exactly what had been happening in Hungary during my months of imprisonment. I studied all the material that I had collected from the various offices, and I plowed through the dispatches that reached us from Constantinople and Switzerland. These reports would end up in many offices which had no contact with one another and which were sometimes even located in different towns. The Sochnuth was in Jerusalem and the Alijah Beth in Tel Aviv, but the ships with the refugees and the letters from Constantinople arrived in Haifa.

On their arrival the immigrants would be taken by the British into a sealed camp at Atlit, and I was only able to enter the camp in the guise of a latrine cleaner. I took fruit and cigarettes to these people who had come from Hitler's territory, in order to get them to talk to me. Often I would make the journey from Tel Aviv to Jerusalem twice in a day, to collect the latest dispatches.

The officials were tired of seeing me in their offices and regarded me as a monomaniac. The petty bureaucrats and secretaries adopted a haughty and condescending attitude toward me, and many times I would have to wait a whole hour before I was allowed to see a telegram; occasionally I was not allowed to read it even then. In the end I organized my own information service, and every week I sent dozens of telegrams to Zurich, to Constantinople, and indirectly to Budapest.

My money ran out, and I had to get forty-three hundred Turkish pounds sent to me from Constantinople against a deposit I had left behind in Budapest. I used the greater part of this money for obtaining the reports and information I needed. I no longer believed that I could do anything to influence the course of events, but I could never free myself from the desire to know all that was going on in my country.

With the help of hundreds of separate items of information and details in reports, I succeeded in reconstructing the story of the Hungarian Jews during the last year of the war.

PART II

IN THE WAKE OF THE MISSION

The preceding chapters have been based principally upon Joel Brand's own recollections.

The events that are dealt with in the following parts of this book did not fall within Joel Brand's personal experience, and his own statements do not give a complete picture of them. We have, therefore, been obliged to have recourse to other contemporary records. The most important of these are Dr. Israel Kastner's report, Otto Komoly's diary, the notes made by Herr von Freudiger and Engineer Andor Biss, the recollections of Hansi Brand, Perez Revesz, and Shulem Offenbach; to a lesser degree we have made use of the reports of Colonel Kurt Becher, the man who in the final stages of the war was Himmler's representative in the ransom negotiations.

ALEX WEISSBERG

Chapter X

THE TERROR CONTINUES

IN THE outlying districts of Hungary, in Russian Carpathia, and in the northern part of Transylvania, the great massacre had begun. On May 13, 1944, three hundred and twenty thousand Jews in these areas were shut up in makeshift ghettos, and a few days later the wholesale deportations began. The Germans felt they had no time to lose, and so a process that had taken several months to complete in the small towns of Poland was now greatly accelerated. The inhabitants of the ghettos were crammed into cattle cars. Each car held nearly a hundred people and was supplied with two buckets, one for water and the other for use as a latrine. The cars were then sealed.

There was no resistance to these deportations. The ghettos were usually located in open country, in abandoned brick factories on a branch line of the railway; and the living conditions in these improvised assembly camps were so disgusting that the inmates were only too glad to leave them behind. Large numbers of these people had been tortured by the Hungarian police in an attempt to make them reveal where they had hidden their possessions, and so most of them felt only relief when they saw the trains arrive. They were certain that they were going to be taken to some small town in Hungary proper, and the Germans themselves did their best to foster this illusion. The Budapest Waada, in which Brand was a leader, made every effort to explain the real situation to these people, and called upon them to flee or to resist. But the warnings were not heeded: the people would not willingly contemplate their own imminent destruction.

The Waada sent Hanna Ganz, Saje Rathsprecher, Hansi Brand, Fritz Knoll, Menachem Klein, Engineer Kirschner, and many others to the camps, but their admonitions went unheeded. A German engineer of the I.G. Farben, who had been sent to Mukachevo, carried out his task so thoroughly that, although he himself was shot, the Jews there did in fact revolt. But the Waada was always severely handicapped by the lack of able-bodied young men, all of whom had been conscripted into the labor force.

The Germans made good use of the experience they had gained when they annihilated between three and four million Polish Jews. First came the posters calling upon the people to leave their homes and proceed to some central assembly point. This cut at the very roots of resistance, for left in their home districts the Jews would have been able to find many means of self-defense. The Hungarian and German police were by now far too weak to search out and deport thousands of isolated individuals. So the intimidated people were forced, on pain of death, to report to the deportation points. If there was to be resistance, it should have come then, when the Germans made their first attempt to separate them from their non-Jewish neighbors. But only a few realized that to register with the Jewish Council or to wear a Star of David was the first irrevocable step on the way to the Oswiecim gas chambers. By the time they recalled the terrible lesson of the Polish Jews, it was already too late.

The destruction of the Jews in the country districts of Hungary was a simple business. It proceeded with such speed that even the most skillful resistance organization would have been hard put to find any effective countermeasures.

Philipp von Freudiger has described the terror of those days:

. . . Incidents similar to those described here took place at almost all deportation centers.

> *The victims were driven to the embarkation points with the maximum brutality, and in a manner devoid of any vestige of humanity. All their belongings were taken from them and even writing materials, documents, and identity papers would be snatched by the police. Women were publicly stripped and subjected to a physical examination by a midwife. This was done in the presence of the police, who often amused themselves by taking a hand in it.*
>
> *Sick people, people who had recently undergone operations, mothers in childbirth, those in pain, and those who were mad were all crammed, in the literal sense of the word, into the trains.*

In Nyiregyháza, for example, they were driven, out of pure sadism, through streets broken up by the recent torrential rains. Children over a year old had to march at the same pace as the others, and this was enforced with whips.

In Satoraljaujhely many people lay across the railroad tracks to stop the trains. They were all shot on the spot.

In Tata a young mother who was unable to move, having just given birth to twins, was taken by her hands and feet and hurled into the car, and each of her newborn children was flung in after her.

In Kosice the eighty-four-year-old mother of a distinguished citizen, who had just had her foot amputated, was dragged from the operating room to the train. Her son, who was standing by, tried to shoot himself, but the weapon was knocked out of his hand and half his face was shot away. Unconscious and streaming with blood, he too was thrown into the car.

Members of the conscripted labor force, who were traveling with their military passes on duty or on leave, were the subject of especial persecution.

In Oradea, Hatvan, and many other stations, the police would snatch these men out of the cars and put them on the next deportation train. Such cases became so numerous that the Defense Minister was compelled to issue orders prohibiting labor conscripts from leaving the barracks without a military escort.

The floors of the freight cars measured 215 square feet, and seventy-five people were herded into this space. Each car had one two-gallon bucket for water and a similar one for excrement. In many transports no food was supplied at all. *In some towns there was an issue of half a pound of bread a person, and in others it was as much as four pounds. Since normally so many people would not even be able to stand in the cars, it was necessary for the police to pack them in tightly, using clubs and bayonets. Often they achieved this simply by firing their rifles at the front row. The tightly packed cars were then sealed and the windows nailed shut.*

Thus did these trains set off on their tragic journeys. From all parts of Hungary came reports of these convoys as they waited in the railway stations, while their human cargo, thirsty and starving, screamed for help. Those who died were left in the cars, and so long as the trains were still in Hungary the doors remained sealed or, at the most, were only opened for a matter of minutes every few days. In such conditions, these trains can only have arrived at their destination bearing a load of dead and dying human refuse.

It was reported that the German deportation command, now headed by Wisliceny with one hundred and fifty SS men at his disposal, had agreed with Eichmann to the dispatch of at least one, if not two, of these trainloads every day. A train consisted of forty-five carriages, containing an average total of about thirty-two hundred people.

This, however, was not enough for Hungarian Secretary of State Endre[1], who demanded that six trainloads should be dispatched each day. With Eichmann's approval, a compromise figure of four trainloads a day was finally arrived at. In order to carry out the deportations

---

[1] Secretary of State Endre was the spokesman for the extreme anti-Semitic wing of the Hungarian government.

at this speed, Endre mobilized a force of five thousand policemen to be used solely for this purpose.

Every day twelve hundred people were moved from the country districts of Hungary in these crowded trains. Many died before reaching Oswiecim. On their arrival, the transports were in most cases driven straight to the gas chambers. The prisoners of Oswiecim were filled with horror as they watched the machines swallowing up their huge human meals.

Hansi Brand and Rezsö Kastner hurried in a frenzy to Eichmann and pleaded that the deportations be stopped at once.

Eichmann abruptly declined. "It's up to you and your people in Constantinople to have everything settled quickly. If I stop the deportations, you'll all take me for a weakling, and you'll make no effort at all to have the negotiations started."

On the same day Kastner sent this telegram to Istanbul: "Deportations have been resumed."

The pogrom in the border districts led many people to flee to Rumania. A group of eighteen Polish and Slovak refugees were arrested by the Hungarian police while they attempted to cross the Rumanian frontier, and were brought to Budapest. These young Chaluzim were tortured in an effort to discover who had supplied them with money and false documents. The majority remained silent, but one of them betrayed the name of the printer. The printer, a Hungarian, was arrested and told everything, including the name of the person who had given him the work to do.

On the following day, Saturday, May 27, three detectives of the Hungarian secret police arrived at the Waada's illegal office in Budapest, 15 Semsely Andor Street. They seized the foreign money and many of the Waada's secret documents and arrested Brand's wife, Rezsö Kastner, Shulem Offenbach, and their wives.

They interrogated Hansi Brand first of all and confronted her with the printer, who had been so badly beaten up that she did not recognize him. He stated that it was she who had paid him to print the forged documents. Hansi Brand decided to take all the blame so that the others would be freed. But the police had heard vague rumors about Joel Brand's journey to Istanbul, and they wanted to know the nature of the mission on which the Germans had sent him. On this matter, however, his wife remained silent, in spite of the most fearful tortures: she firmly believed that the success of his mission depended on its being kept a "state secret." The police bastinadoed her feet, and for weeks on end she was unable to walk.

The SS heard about this the next day and Eichmann intervened, requesting the Hungarian police to transfer all the prisoners to the Germans. Before they had been in the hands of the Gestapo for an hour, they were set free.

How had this happened?

Krumey and Klages had immediately called on Hain, the head of the Hungarian secret police. Hain had laid the forged documents on the table, some of which bore the letter heading of the German Embassy, and refused to surrender his prisoners. The Germans, however, feared that if the prisoners were kept for long in a Hungarian prison, and subjected to constant interrogation, the "state secret" would inevitably be disclosed. This would have been ex-

tremely embarrassing for them. Minister Wesemeyer, who
was Germany's senior representative in Hungary, went to
see the Hungarian Prime Minister, President Sztójay, who
had at once telephoned Hain and ordered him to hand our
people over to the Germans.

On June 3 Brand's telegram with the news of the interim agreement arrived in Budapest. Kastner went
straight to Eichmann and requested that he stop the deportations.

Eichmann abruptly refused. "I have no intention of
doing any such thing. On the contrary, I shall order them
to put on more steam. A telegram can be sent by anyone.
Brand must come back and bring the text of the agreement with him."

Eichmann was, however, prepared to consider a further request. He would allow the eight hundred holders of
certificates (already referred to) to travel through Germany and thence to countries abroad. He took the list of
names and, in Kastner's presence, issued the order for
these people to be taken from their ghettoes in the provinces and brought to Budapest. Soon afterward he canceled
this order behind Kastner's back, and most of the unevac-
uated country ghettos were emptied without any attempt
to segregate those people who had already been selected
to go abroad. Cluj was the only large Jewish community in
Transylvania that had so far escaped.

Kastner hurried to Eichmann, who declared: "I cannot allow any Jews to be brought to Budapest at this time.
I am on my way to see Jaross, the Hungarian Minister for
Internal Affairs, who is certain to ask me what kind of a
bargain the SS made with Baron Weiss's family. They've
heard about that deal. Jaross will make me suffer for that

dirty business. Me of all people. What do you think about that? If Jews were now brought from Transylvania to Budapest, I would certainly be asked by Endre what new deals we're thinking of making. No, I'm not going to play your game."

Kastner answered, "But you gave us your promise, and you've always said you keep your word. You sent a telegram to Cluj on the lines of our agreement."

Eichmann replied, "I sent a telegram yesterday canceling that order. Is that clear? I've got no more time for you."

Kastner then went to Krumey and together they sought out Klages, who promised to intervene with his chief. A conference between all the interested parties was held in Eichmann's office. The following account of it is given in Kastner's report:

> At eleven o'clock Eichmann returns to his office. I ask to see him at once. The secretary replies that Eichmann is too busy to see me. I wait in the corridor. Half an hour later Eichmann calls me in. His personal staff, Krumey, Wisliceny, Huntsche, and Novak, are standing behind him. Klages has just left the room.
>
> "You may sit down, Kastner."
>
> Eichmann begins to roar at me. I keep silent. One must first let his frenzy subside. It is clear to me what is now at stake. It is not just a question of saving the few hundred Jews in the provinces. If Eichmann cannot here and now be made to alter his decision, then this roulette game, with the men's lives as the stake, will have been lost. The Waada backed the German number. If they should now lose, they will simply be following in the foot-

steps of all those other naïve gamblers of occupied Europe. The handing over of millions will then look like an act of madness. Furthermore the loser in this case will also be branded as a traitor.

Eichmann at last asks, "What is it exactly you want?"

"I must insist that our agreements be kept. Will you bring the people whose names we have given you from the provinces to Budapest?"

"When I have once said no, I do not change my mind."

"In that case there is no point in continuing these negotiations."

I made as though to get up and go.

"Your nerve is going, Kastner. I'll send you to Terezin for a cure. Or would you prefer Oswiecim?"

"You would gain nothing from that. There is no one else to take my place."

"Now, get this straight once and for all. I've got to clear this Jewish filth out of the provinces. No arguments and no tears can alter that."

"In that case our arguments in Istanbul will be equally useless."

"Why do you attach so much importance to this handful of Jews?"

"It's not just them. Our negotiations in Istanbul are breaking down because of your insistence on these deportations. You've got to give some proof that your offer is meant seriously. Anyhow, why do You attach such importance to this handful of Jews?"

So it goes on, for one whole hour. The others present listen in silence. Huntsche and Novak grow irritable and impatient; Krumey and Wisliceny remain impassive.

Sometimes it seems to me that Eichmann is about to give in, and then he is suddenly overcome by frenzy again. He bangs his fist on the table and says he will hear no more.

After about an hour he makes a completely unexpected proposal.

"I'll tell you what I'll do. I'll send a hundred or two Jews from Cluj to Terezin. We'll arrange for them to be placed in five extra cars which will be coupled onto a deportation train. These cars will then be uncoupled in Slovokia. They won't go on to Oswiecim."

I turn down this proposal at once, without even considering it.

"You don't believe me then?"

"I do not see how it would be possible to arrange for an emigration transport of Hungarians from Terezin."

"But try to understand that I cannot be responsible for what the Hungarian government does. I cannot play the part of a Jew-saver. I have promised László Endre that not one single living Jew will ever return to this country."

Wisliceny, who has been standing with his back to us till now, joins the conversation.

"I don't think, Adolf, that you'll have any trouble with the Hungarians. I have told Lieutenant Colonel Ferenczy that we are on the track of a dangerous Zionist conspiracy, and that we are following up various clues in the provincial ghettos. I've told him these conspirators cannot be left to mix with the others, as they might create unrest and hinder the war effort."

"What did Ferenczy say to that? Did he swallow it?"

"Yes, he swallowed it. Baky and Endre are also in the picture."

"They really swallowed that!" Eichmann repeats.

He smiles, and one can read on his face his sublime satisfaction at this latest proof of the master race's genius for diplomacy. He considers the matter for a short time and then says: "Good. In that case the people from Cluj will be brought to Budapest."

Then we start to haggle over numbers. Eichmann offers fifty individuals. I demand fifty families, on the grounds that we ought to be compensated for people who were not removed from the other ghettos before he destroyed them.

"If we're going to have a conspiracy, it might as well be a large one."

Eichmann raises the number to one hundred and finally agrees to "about two hundred."

He summons a noncommissioned officer and orders him to go to Cluj. The noncom takes the list of names that I had handed to Eichmann. It is hastily agreed that the people from Cluj will not have to travel in sealed cars and will even be allowed to bring their luggage.

"But where are you going to put them?" Eichmann asks. "I don't want any scandal or sensations in Budapest."

I explain to him that we have had a camp prepared, but that it will have to be guarded. Krumey is ordered to supply SS guards.

The conversation lasts for more than two hours. I can now leave Eichmann's office.

In the corridor I come across the noncom who had been told to take Eichmann's order to Cluj. He had seen me seated before his dreaded commanding officer. Now he lets me whisper in his ear that he can count on a good reward should the people in Cluj take a broad-minded

view of the numbers to be sent. "About two hundred"
could be interpreted to mean considerably more.

To begin with, the SS leaders had been willing to allow between six hundred and eight hundred holders of
certificates to go abroad. This figure was finally increased
to seventeen hundred. The selection of these people presented the leaders of the Waada with a serious problem of
conscience. Who should be saved? The majority of the
community having been marked for slaughter, the choice
of those who would survive was equivalent to sentencing
the remainder to death.

At a later date, Rezsö Kastner was unfairly blamed for
having devoted too much energy to the rescue of these seventeen hundred—the so-called Bergen-Belsen transport—
and for having thereby neglected the interests of the remaining hundreds of thousands. Another and more serious
allegation was that he had included all his friends and relatives in the Cluj group, which went to Bergen-Belsen. If
it was a mistake, then it was a very human mistake.

Whatever Kastner's personal reasons for devoting so
much time and energy to the Bergen-Belsen transport, he
had another and far more important motive. Since the Allies and the Jewish authorities abroad had at that time no
evidence whatsoever that the Germans seriously intended
to keep Eichmann's bargain if it were accepted, the arrival
of almost two thousand Nazi prisoners was bound to create
a sensation. It would provide conspicuous evidence that
the Waada was right, that it was in fact possible to buy off
these bandits who had already murdered five million Jews.

Now the Waada had two aims: to snatch the victims
from the murderers' clutches, and to break through the

wall of silence in the outside world. About a quarter of the Hungarian Jews survived the war—a percentage greater than that in any other country under German control. This achievement was due in no small measure to the work of the Budapest Waada. If Kastner, as the leader of the Waada after Brand's departure, must be held responsible for all mistakes and omissions, then it is only right that he should also be credited with the success of this work. And the charge that he collaborated with the Germans solely to insure the departure of the Bergen-Belsen transport, and that by saving a few hundred he sacrificed hundreds of thousands, is a shameless calumny.

The Waada built a special camp in Columbus Street for the reception of the three hundred people from Cluj who had been intended for the Bergen-Belsen transport. Devecséri, the architect, managed in a very short time to run up several large barracks. The camp was organized by Zsigmond Léb, the president of the Cluj orthodox community. The Cluj people arrived on July 10. The camp was guarded by five SS guards who had orders to treat the inmates humanely. They did so with the same slavish obedience that they would have shown if they had been ordered to do the opposite. Columbus Street was to become—grotesque though it may seem—an asylum for the hunted, an island of safety in a sea of devastation.

Meanwhile Eichmann, with growing impatience, was demanding Brand's return from Istanbul. Kastner sent a telegram to say that he should be sent back by force if he lacked the courage to come of his own free will. The people in Budapest had at that time no idea of what had happened in Aleppo. Eichmann was expecting daily to receive the text of the interim agreement. He said to Kastner, "If Brand doesn't return in three days' time, I will set the mills of Oswiecim grinding once more."

The Waada called a meeting and decided to raise a million dollars in Budapest itself, to be offered as a token payment until the arrival of the interim agreement. Kastner went to Eichmann and requested him to hold back one hundred thousand of those earmarked for deportation, so that they could be handed over as soon as the Allies' acceptance of the offer was received. These hundred thousand would be surety, and he could therefore pay the advance at once. Then, after the agreement was signed, they should be sent to the Spanish frontier. The Waada, Kastner announced, was meanwhile prepared to hand over five million Swiss francs against the larger advance.

Eichmann asked, "Where do you expect to get so much foreign currency?"

"Principally from abroad," said Kastner. "It is a payment in advance."

Eichmann promised to consider the matter. On June 14 he sent for Kastner again.

"I'll accept your offer, but the figure of a hundred thousand is impossibly high. I am prepared to move a dozen deportation trains with, let's say, thirty thousand Hungarian Jews to Austria, and keep them on ice there. But we cannot take these thirty thousand from Carpathia or Transylvania. Those Jews are ethnically more valuable and better breeders. I have no intention of keeping that kind alive. We will take the thirty thousand from Hungary proper. As for the money, you must give me the five million francs now, at once."

Haggling began. It was eventually agreed that fifteen thousand Jews from the provinces and fifteen thousand from Budapest should be moved to Austria.

A few days later, on the basis of this agreement, six trainloads comprising about eighteen thousand people, primarily from Debrecen, Szeged, Szolnok, and Balassagyarmat, were moved to Austria. These people lived for the rest of the war in special camps, mostly in Strasshof. The Germans never received the five million francs that the Waada should have paid for them. It is true that the money was collected from the Budapest Jews in the form of jewels, gold, and notes and handed over to Lieutenant Colonel Becher, the SS treasurer. But it was credited to a general account of Jewish "disbursements," and was later pooled with the payments made for the release into Switzerland of the sixteen hundred and eighty-four Bergen-Belseners.[2]

Brand's delay in returning to Budapest, so inexplicable to his comrades there, became finally a serious menace. Eichmann was delighted, for he had always been secretly opposed to any sort of agreement with the Jews, and had only made his offer under pressure from his superiors in the SS. His hands were free now, and the speed of the deportations was redoubled. The gruesome machine of mass destruction worked day and night. While Brand suffered agonies in Constantinople, arguing with a group of people

---

[2] Becher was not fully informed about Eichmann's transaction. He took the whole sum as payment for the Bergen-Belseners and forgot about the people at Strasshof. Nazi administration in the occupied countries was famous for its mixture of brutality and corruption. The right hand never knew exactly what the left hand was doing, and in many cases preferred not to know.

who could never grasp the problem, and speaking later to deaf ears in Aleppo and Cairo, the German talent for organization was celebrating its greatest triumph. Never had so many people been put to death in so short a time as during those June days of 1944 in the provincial towns of Hungary.

Brand's comrades of the Budapest Waada sent horrified appeals for help to Constantinople. At long last the delegation there decided to do something. They explained that Brand was indispensable in their negotiations with the Allies, and said that Menachem Bader, the financial expert of the Constantinople delegation, would be returning to Budapest in his place. They requested a visa for Bader, and Eichmann sent this to the German Embassy in Constantinople.

But suddenly Menachem Bader began to make excuses. He refused to set foot inside the German Embassy. Eichmann, who wished to prove to the other SS leaders that the promises made by the Jews were mere bluff, gave instructions to the German Embassy to visit Menachem Bader. A secretary from the Embassy telephoned Bader and arranged a meeting in a neutral place. The two men finally met in a bookshop.

"Herr Menachem Bader, if I am not mistaken?" said the diplomat. "We have received instructions to supply you with a visa. We have in addition arranged a seat for you on our courier plane."

"I am sorry, but I cannot go. I am a citizen of Palestine, and the British will not grant me an exit permit."

"We could give you a German passport, but after all that has happened I can quite understand your refusing it."

"There can be no question of that, so far as I am concerned."

"There might be a way out. Perhaps you could acquire the necessary documents from a neutral country?"

But it all led to nothing. A few days later Bader received two telegrams, signed by Mosche Shertok and Ben Gurion, which forbade him as a citizen of Palestine to make the journey. It had been decided to transfer the negotiations to neutral soil. The people in Constantinople felt that the cancellation of Bader's journey would harm the already catastrophic situation in Budapest. They therefore finally decided that the interim agreement, which had been in their possession for over a month since Brand's departure and imprisonment, should be sent to Budapest in the diplomatic bag of a neutral country. This tragic procrastination had cost several hundreds of thousands of lives.

The interim agreement arrived in Budapest on July 7.

Kastner and Hansi Brand hurried at once to the SS headquarters, where Becher declared, "Himmler will accept this. I will go to Berlin and put it through."

Eichmann ordered Kastner to send a telegram to Constantinople immediately, saying: "We are ready to negotiate. Nominate your representatives."

The arrival of the interim agreement had succeeded in canceling the worst effects of Bader's refusal to go.

Chaim Barlasz, the head of the Sochnuth in Constantinople, answered Kastner's telegram. He proposed a conference in Portugal between the Jewish representatives and the Nazis. Joe Schwarz, the director of the Joint, and Eliahu Dobkin, a member of the Zionist Executive, were nominated on behalf of the Jews. The Germans accepted.

Himmler authorized Becher to head the delegation.

Kastner was to accompany him to Lisbon. Everything seemed to be going well, the deportations had been stopped and Budapest breathed again. Then the blow fell. On July 19, 1944, the British government broadcast a declaration that the Eichmann offer would be refused as a piece of shameless blackmail.[3] Everyone feared the worst.

But on the following day, Count Stauffenburg's bomb exploded in Hitler's headquarters. The shock made the Nazi leaders more amenable. Becher, in particular, saw the end of German power approaching and was ready to draw the necessary conclusions. The fact of Brand's imprisonment also became known in Budapest.

In Budapest all the necessary preparations had been made for the conference in Portugal, when the second blow fell. At the last moment, Joe Schwarz and Eliahu Dobkin refused to go. As citizens of Allied countries, they had been forbidden by their governments to take part in the negotiations. By a stroke of good fortune their withdrawal coincided with Becher's. After hearing of Brand's imprisonment, Becher was afraid to set foot on Allied territory, and had proposed to transfer the negotiations to France, with Biarritz as the meeting place. But the rapid change in the military situation, which took place after the Allied invasion of France, made it impossible for the SS leader to go there. It was finally agreed that the conference should take place in Switzerland, and the Jews chose as their representative the most unsuitable person imaginable: the Swiss representative of the Joint, Sally Mayer.

---

[3] See photostatic copy of London *Times* report in Appendix.

Chapter XI

PARACHUTISTS FROM ISRAEL

EARLY IN 1944 Dr. Mosche Schweiger had received a
letter from Constantinople appointing him the leader of
those secret military operations called the Haganah undertaking. In the letter he was informed that three parachutists from Israel would be dropped over Yugoslavian territory. Their task would be to reach Budapest and assist
him in the organization of military operations. The people
in Constantinople requested Schweiger to supply details of
a suitable place at which to cross the frontier, together with
addresses in Budapest. Schweiger compiled with both requests.

Soon after the Germans occupied Budapest, Schweiger was arrested. The Waada heard no more of the proposed parachute operation, and they believed it had been
abandoned. However, the Sochnuth had placed many

young volunteers at the disposal of the British Army for commando tasks behind the enemy lines.

One particular group of volunteers had been trained as paratroops by the British Army. The tasks entrusted to them were primarily of a military nature, such as helping British airmen, who had bailed out after bombing the Rumanian oil fields, make their way back to their own lines.

Ruven Daphne was in command of this group, which consisted of Hannah Szenes, Perez Goldstein, and Joel Nussbecher-Palgi. Hannah Szenes was dropped into Yugoslavia on March 18, 1944, and Perez Goldstein and Joel Nussbecher-Palgi followed her seven weeks later.

The Yugoslav partisans gave Hannah and her comrades a great welcome. The mere sight of a beautiful girl and two brave men from an Israeli kolkhoz, all clad as British officers, was enough to awaken the enthusiasm of the Yugoslav partisans. However, the road to Budapest had become extremely dangerous and difficult, for the Germans had occupied Hungary on March 19, and the border was now tightly sealed.

Hannah, however, would let nothing deter her. She came from a middle-class Budapest family, and had left her mother in order to go to Israel, where she had joined a *kibuz* and tilled the soil of the Holy Land. Her romantic spirit was forever seeking an ideal worthy of self-sacrifice. When she was accepted by the British Army, and given the most dangerous tasks to undertake, it seemed that at long last her desire would be satisfied. Everyone warned her against making an attempt to cross the frontier just then, but she paid no attention. Her friends refused to help her and so did the British, including her commander Ruven Daphne. So she decided to cross the frontier on her own.

She next got in touch with some escaped French prisoners of war, who had joined Tito's partisans. Her charm, her excellent education, and her linguistic talents won the hearts of these Frenchmen. They looked everywhere for a guide to take her over the border, and finally they got in touch with a Hungarian official who was reputed to be friendly to the Allies and on good terms with some smugglers. Thus Hannah was able to start on her journey. Ruven Daphne, who was full of forebodings, accompanied her as far as the frontier.

After crossing into Hungary, Hannah hid her radio transmitter. Soon the whole group was arrested by the Hungarian border police. A short fight took place, during which one of Hannah's companions was killed, and she and the two others were taken prisoner. They were brought before Hungarian security forces. The frontier police very soon found Hannah's radio set. The officer who interrogated them told her that her companions would be shot.

Hannah, in an effort to save them, declared, "They are innocent. The radio is mine. I brought it over with me."

There were many puzzling features about their arrest, but what followed was truly mysterious. Hannah was immediately taken to Budapest, and on June 17 was confronted with her mother at the headquarters of the Hungarian security service in the Hadik Barracks. At that time the Waada in Budapest was unaware of Hannah's existence or of the landing in Yugoslavia of parachutists from Israel. She had crossed the frontier with forged papers, which she had obtained in Yugoslavia, and not with those that Mosche Schweiger had duly sent to Constantinople. Had she been betrayed by the Hungarian official? Had Hannah confided in him the purpose of her mission? Had she been under observation by German or Hungarian agents even while she was still in Yugoslavia? To this day the answers to these questions are not known.

Hannah's friends Perez Goldstein and Joel Nuss-becher-Palgi knew nothing of her arrest. They were, however, very worried about her, and eventually decided to follow her. They were more cautious and left their radio equipment behind in Yugoslavia. The partisans promised to send it on to them in Hungary. They were taken across the frontier by a Major Stipa of Tito's army, but at a spot different from that chosen by Hannah. They succeeded in getting across without incident, but as they changed trains at Pecs station, it seemed they were being watched. However, they reached Budapest and, after arranging a meeting place, parted at the station. They had Kastner's address and also Brand's; but they had already been told in Yugoslavia that Brand's address was no longer usable, and were given instead the address of the Jewish community where the Chaluzim group had their illegal headquarters. They decided to meet at Kastner's address, a boarding house in Vaci Street.

Kastner had known them both in the Cluj youth movement and gave them a hearty welcome. There were many people waiting to see Kastner, so their conversation was short and they said nothing about Hannah or about the military tasks that they had been sent to carry out. They established the fact that Kastner was ignorant of Hannah's existence. A meeting was arranged for the following morning, and the two young men then left Kastner and went to their hotel room.

Brand's wife, Hansi, was present next morning when

Joel Palgi arrived. He was alone, for Perez Goldstein had gone to the Chaluzim's office in the community house. Later Hansi and Joel Palgi joined him there, but almost at once it was observed that Hungarian police spies were mingling with the crowd surrounding the building. Hansi took fright and handed the two Palestinians over to Shulem Offenbach, who succeeded by devious and adventurous means in smuggling them out of the house. The three then separated and arranged to meet the same evening at the lodgings of their comrade, Dr. Erzsi Kurz.

Immediately after they had separated, Perez Goldstein vanished. He did not turn up at the evening meeting as arranged, nor did he keep an earlier appointment with Palgi. The more eminent leaders of the Chaluzim group were already waiting at Erzsi Kurz's place. Kastner arrived somewhat later and took fright when he heard of Goldstein's disappearance. He led Palgi aside and discussed the situation with him. Palgi was afraid that the nineteen-year-old Perez might give way under Nazi torture. Kastner thereupon decided to be completely open with Joel Palgi, whom he had known ever since he was a boy. He gave him a full description of the Jewish situation in Hungary, and told him about the negotiations with the Germans, of Brand's mission, and of the possibility of rescuing hundreds of thousands of our people.

"Nussi," he said (this was the name by which Palgi had been known in the youth movement), "Nussi, you must realize that this is serious. Just how serious you will understand when I tell you that in the next few days a train will leave for abroad, carrying between fifteen hundred and two thousand Hungarian Jews. And that is only, so to speak, an advance delivery. We are in fact concerned with the rescue of all those Jews who are still alive. But if Perez has really been arrested and is made to talk, then the whole thing will fall through. A little while ago the Hungarians arrested all the Waada leaders, and the Germans had us set free because of their interest in these negotiations. But nothing can now help us if we are compromised through Perez Goldstein's arrest. The Germans will regard the whole matter as no longer a Jewish affair, but simply as British espionage. And then everything will be lost. I cannot see any solution."

Joel Palgi was deeply impressed, but nevertheless he said nothing to Kastner about Hannah Szenes's crossing of the frontier. He has stated in a book, and before a court of law, that his reason for not doing so was that he had taken an oath of secrecy as a British officer. His silence was to prove fatal. If the Waada people had known about Hannah Szenes in time, they could have made all the necessary preparations to ward off catastrophe.

Kastner pondered for some time and then proposed a way out of the difficulty to Palgi. "It is important," he said, "that the Germans should be convinced that you are here on Jewish business. We can tell them that the people in Constantinople sent you here to find out whether Eichmann's offer is to be taken seriously or whether it is all a fantasy of Brand's. But the Germans will want to see you. Are you prepared for that? Alternatively, we can always find some way of getting you out of the country, or we can hide you in some safe place where no one will find you."

Joel Palgi at once declared himself ready to run any risk to help his comrades and the Waada. Hansi Brand and Sulem Offenbach were brought into the discussions, and it was finally decided to speak to Captain Klages, who was head of SS security service in Budapest. He had hitherto been so helpful and unmercenary in all cases of arrest or imprisonment that Kastner and Brand's wife were convinced he was secretly an opponent of Hitler. Hansi was authorized to call on Klages next day.

Klages seemed very pleased when Hansi told him the whole story. "It's a good thing you came to me straightaway," he said. "I regard it as a good sign that your Sochnuth has sent two representatives here to test the authenticity of our intentions. Send them both along to me at once. I assure you they will be quite safe."

Palgi took the risk and arrived at the SS headquarters on the Schwabenberg. Klages was not able to receive him owing to an air-raid alarm, and he told his adjutant, Kraus, to speak to the two Palestinians. Kraus received Palgi most politely; meanwhile Hansi waited outside in a state of such extreme agitation that she could not stop biting her fingernails. Palgi later reported this conversation as follows:

> KRAUS: "I am very glad to meet you and I admit I am impressed by you. How exactly did you reach this country? Weren't you afraid to come to see us here?"
>
> PALGI: "Why should I be? Your people have made certain proposals to my superiors, and I have been sent here to ascertain how far we can rely on them. I am a sort of unofficial emissary, and under these circumstances I have never considered my task a dangerous one."

Kraus wanted particularly to know by what means Palgi had entered the country. Joel told him some fictitious tale to the effect that he had only left Jerusalem a few days earlier.

> KRAUS: *"But I understood that you had a companion. Why isn't he here with you?"*
>
> PALGI: *"I don't know. He simply disappeared. I had a feeling that we were being followed. Perhaps he's been arrested. I would be glad if you would take steps to find him and to have him released if he's in prison."*

(Palgi did not mention Hannah Szenes. At that time he still hoped she might have gone back to Ruven Daphne in Yugoslavia.)

> KRAUS: *"If everything is found to be in order, that will certainly be done. I can set your mind at rest on that score. It's not my business to discuss your mission with you. My chief will have a talk with you as soon as he is free."*
>
> PALGI: *"Can you give me an identity card, so that I won't be arrested in the streets?"*
>
> KRAUS: *"We'll talk about that later. For the moment it will be enough if you make a note of this telephone number. If anything should happen to you, ring up and we'll come and get you out of trouble."*

When Hansi saw Palgi come out, she felt enormously relieved. She brought him to Offenbach, who had prepared a hiding place for him. Palgi insisted, however, on staying at Brand's old lodgings in Buljovsky Street, and nothing would dissuade him from this. Much later he explained why. He hoped that Hannah Szenes might turn up there, if she were in fact still in Hungary. They had given her this address in Palestine, and Palgi was not quite sure whether she had been informed that the address was no longer to be used.

That same evening the Waada received the good news that Perez Goldstein had reappeared. Tension relaxed, and the worst difficulties seemed over.

But on June 29 disaster struck. Offenbach had just sent a girl to try once again to persuade Joel Palgi to move to a really safe address. Palgi had again refused, and at that very moment men of the Hungarian security service appeared and arrested him. The girl who had acted as Offenbach's messenger was later seized. It is true that she did not know much, but the little she did know she refused to divulge, in spite of the cruelest torture.

The remaining members of the Waada were in a fever of anxiety. Would the emigrants' transport leave next day, or would it be held back because of the arrest of the British parachutists?

On June 30, 1944, the train left the station in Budapest with sixteen hundred and seventy-six Jews and began its eventful journey to a neutral land. Perez Goldstein had refused to let himself be included in this transport, and he remained in hiding in the Columbus Street camp.

At four o'clock the following morning, officials of the Hungarian security service raided Engineer Biss's lodgings in Semsely Andor Street, which were secretly used by the central office. They arrested the Waada members Dr. Kastner, Engineer Biss, and their wives, and Hansi Brand. Kastner remained behind with a detective called Halasz, but the others were taken to the Hadik Barracks.

Hansi was severely interrogated but remained silent. Toward ten o'clock Kastner was also brought to the Hadik Barracks. The interrogator shouted at him, "Bring us the other person, or Nussbecher will be shot in ten minutes."

Kastner was in despair. He feared for the safety of the trainload of emigrants that had just left. He wanted time to think. So he said, "Let me talk to my people."

As a result Kastner and Brand's wife were briefly set free, and the others were kept as hostages. After considering the situation, the Waada decided to send Hansi, Dr. Kastner, and Sulem Offenbach to the camp to talk with Perez Goldstein. Sulem Offenbach was the spokesman.

"Perez," he explained, "this problem has become too difficult for us. We must leave the decision to you. There are a few secret exits from this camp. You can escape through the back and be free. We will then hide you. On the other hand, if you leave the camp by the front gate, you will be arrested by the Hungarian police, who are waiting there. You know what this is all about, and you know how much is at stake. You must decide for yourself."

Perez Goldstein's parents were among those in the transport, and he took no time in reaching a decision.

"I will give myself up," he said.

Kastner did not try to dissuade him.[1]

---

[1] All my efforts to reconstruct the exact circumstances surrounding this tragic incident have proved vain. The evidence given by the survivors has never been more contradictory than it was in this case. There seemed to me no alternative, particularly since Joel Brand himself is convinced that this version is correct, but to give this version, which is based on the assertions made by Kastner and his friends, Hansi Brand and Sulem Offenbach, although of course Kastner himself was deeply involved.

During the legal proceedings against Grünwald, Kastner was accused of being responsible for the fate of this young parachutist, and of course Kastner must have known that his appeal to Goldstein's spirit of self-sacrifice was, in fact, a command. He well knew the heroism of these young men from the *kibuzim*. Did he think it right that one should be sacrificed in order that thousands might be saved? I do not believe so. Kastner is, above all else, a self-confident man. Because of his relations with the Hungarian security service and with Herr von Klages, he thought it would

He was convinced that with Klages's help he would be able to get the two young men released in a day or two. He knew the leaders of the Hungarian security service personally, and he felt he had only to telephone Lieutenant Colonel Garcoly to have everything put right. It did not turn out that way, however.

Hannah Szenes, Perez Goldstein, and Joel Nussbecher-Palgi remained in prison. The people of the Waada made repeated efforts to obtain the release of the two officers. They knew nothing of Hannah Szenes's plight. On June 1, Hannah had already been confronted with her mother and had taken this opportunity of telling her to ask the Zionists for help. Frau Szenes was soon released, but she herself, as a thoroughly assimilated Jewess, had no connections with the Zionist organization. However, through her daughter she knew the Palestine Office and its secretary, Mosche Kraus. She tried to speak to Kraus, but only managed to see his assistant Sany Grossmann. She asked the latter to put her in touch with Kastner, but Grossmann did nothing but try to calm her with empty promises. It seems that she did not tell him why she wished to see Kastner.

It was impossible for the Waada to approach the Sztójay government in the matter of the parachutists. Only after Horthy's change of front and General Lakatos's appointment as premier were the Waada representatives able to intervene in the matter. On October 14, 1944, Kastner spoke to ministerial Counselor Otan, the War Minister's

---

be a trifle to have these two young men set free. But a few weeks later, Klages was dead, shot by Hungarian officers, and a few months after that Horthy was overthrown and the leaders of the Hungarian security service arrested. The Crossed Arrows party seized power and the Waada's influence dropped to nil. Goldstein was sent to an extermination camp. A.W.

personal secretary. Also present at this meeting were Friedrich Born, the representative of the International Red Cross, Lieutenant Colonel Garcoly, the head of the Far Eastern department of the Hungarian Defense Ministry, and Major Hatz, the Hungarian military attaché in Turkey.

The attitude of the senior Hungarian officials toward the Jews had undergone a fundamental change. They spoke openly with Komoly and Kastner and Stern of Hungary's impending breach with the Axis powers. At this meeting on October 14, the Minister for War promised to release the imprisoned parachute officers.

At eleven o'clock on the following morning, Horthy announced Hungary's capitulation, and it is possible that during the next few hours Hannah and her friends might have been able to escape from prison. But the moment passed and the three remained in jail. The SS *Putsch* came, and a few hours later Horthy was arrested. The Crossed Arrows government was then set up. All hope had now disappeared.

The two Jewish officers were deported, but Joel Nussbecher-Palgi managed to escape from the train by sawing through the window bars. He reached the capital and continued the fight in the ranks of the Chaluzim. He is now one of the directors of the Israel airplane company El Al. Of Perez Goldstein nothing more was ever heard.

Hannah Szenes was tried as a British spy and sentenced to be shot. She was proud of being a Jew, and she hung the Star of David in her cell window to show her community with the other Jews imprisoned there, who, unlike her, were compelled to wear this badge. When she was asked if she wished to appeal, she said, "I do not ask grace of murderers."

Hannah's mother knew nothing of her daughter's death sentence. She had made many attempts to get permission to visit her in prison, and at last, on the afternoon of November 6, she was taken to the judge's office. She was greeted with the words, "Your daughter was a heroine; you and all your race can be proud of her."

That same morning Hannah had been executed in the courtyard of Budapest prison.

Chapter XII

THE HUNGARIANS WAVER

SINCE THE Allies were not prepared to accept Eichmann's offer, Joel Brand was unable to fulfill the immediate purpose of his journey to Constantinople. Their objections were based not so much on the delivery of trucks or other goods to the Germans but on their reluctance, at that late stage of the war, to accept one million human beings and look after them abroad. Nor were they prepared to make any counterproposal. This was probably due to the fear that the Germans might declare themselves willing to accept money or food, for in this case world public opinion might have forced the Allies to agree. It seemed to Brand, when he was released in Cairo, that his mission had been a failure; but a later study of events in Budapest led him to take a more encouraging view.

Mosche Shertok had flown to London several times to

solicit aid from the Allies. But they refused to make any concessions, and flatly turned down the Eichmann proposal. Nevertheless, they felt compelled to do something on behalf of the Jews. And so, for the first time, those interventions were now made which had been awaited in vain ever since the first Polish Jews, three years earlier, had been taken to the extermination camps.

Horthy received protests from all the Christian churches. The Pope intervened. The aged King of Sweden wrote a letter to Horthy. Finally President Roosevelt made a vigorous *démarche* to the Regent through the Swiss ambassador. King Gustav made the first concrete offer. He said that Hungarian refugees would be allowed to enter Sweden. Subsequently, both Sweden and Switzerland offered safe-conducts to the Budapest Jews. All this happened during the month after Brand's arrest at Aleppo.

Other considerations were also beginning to influence the Hungarian government. On June 6 the Allies landed in Normandy and during the course of the summer overran the whole of France. The Rumanian government capitulated, and opened the frontiers to the Red Army. Russian troops soon appeared on Hungary's eastern border, and in the Carpathians. The Vitebsk offensive brought the Red Army, after a swift advance, to the very gates of Warsaw. In Germany itself, the senior army officers regarded the war as already lost and attempted to overthrow Hitler in the July 20 revolt. Horthy and his people, faced with the example of Rumania and Bulgaria, began to prepare for a break with the Axis powers. It was true that Hungary was occupied by the Germans, but Horthy was still commander in chief of the Hungarian army and the administration of the country was in the hands of his ministers. The contacts between the Budapest Waada and the Hungarian government, which had been established by Engineer Otto Komoly, now began to bear fruit. Komoly initiated discussions with the Papal Nuncio and the Prince Primate of Hungary, and he succeeded in getting the church dignitaries to make a strong protest to Horthy about the deportations. The Papal Nuncio, Angelo Rotta, had already informed Sztójay, the Prime Minister, on May 15 that the world was watching closely the terrible events then taking place in the provincial towns of Hungary. Now he decided on renewed action. Meanwhile the head of the Protestant Church, Bishop Ladislaus Ravasz, called upon the Prince Primate of Hungary to make a joint *démarche*. The leaders of the two churches threatened the government with having a pastoral letter on the subject read from every pulpit in the country. The chief presbyter of the Reformed Church, Albert Berecky, was persuaded by Kastner to speak up on behalf of the Jews, and this he did with great personal courage. The president of the International Red Cross, Professor Huber, also used his influence with the Hungarian government on our behalf.

In view of Roosevelt's *démarche*, Horthy summoned a Council of Ministers on June 26, 1944, as a result of which the Prime Minister, Sztójay, was instructed to put an immediate stop to the deportations. On the same day Eichmann had summoned the chief of the Hungarian police, Ferenczy, and the Secretary of State for Internal Affairs, László Endre, to a meeting to work out a detailed plan for the transportation of some two hundred thousand Budapest Jews. At this meeting it was decided to transport the Budapest Jews to Oswiecim in a single week, between July 5 and 12, 1944. Eichmann's extermination group, the so-called *Judenkommando*, and their Hungarian lackeys, Endre and Ferenczy, resolved to move all the Jews into twelve

hundred houses, which would be marked with the yellow
star. Sztójay did not dare openly to oppose Eichmann by
carrying out the Council's decree of June 26.

Eichmann was jubilant and said to Kastner, "I am
rooting the Jews out of Budapest. There will then be only
about thirty thousand Jews left, in eastern Hungary, and I
understand that from an ethnic point of view they are not
worth much. If you want me to, I can move the lot to Austria. They will be kept ready for this deal with the Sochnuth, which you are constantly promising me is being arranged in Istanbul, although I myself don't believe a word
of it."

The resistance of the Hungarians, however, was growing stronger by the hour, and even the head of the Hungarian police showed a certain reluctance to provide guards
for the deportations. Horthy could give no direct orders;
but, under his influence and that of his son, powerful
groups within the government were working for a break
with the Axis powers and were doing their best to sabotage
the actions of Eichmann's *Judenkommando*. Matters
reached the point where Eichmann had to carry out a part
of his deportations illegally. Even as late as July 14, long
after the deportations had been forbidden by the Hungarian government, Eichmann in collaboration with Baky,
another anti-Semitic secretary in the Ministry for Internal
Affairs, was attempting, to smuggle secretly out of the
country fifteen hundred Jews from the internment camp in
Kistarcza. The Jewish Council immediately informed
Horthy's cabinet secretariat of this, and the train was ordered to return from Hatvany to Kistarcza. This victory,
however, was more apparent than real. Some days later
Eichmann invited the leaders of the Jewish Council to his

headquarters and kept them with him until late in the evening, during which time he succeeded in having the whole
Kistarcza camp transported. The camp at Szarvas was liquidated on the same day, by similar underhanded methods.

The Prime Minister, Sztójay, was between the devil
and the deep blue sea. He was more afraid of Eichmann
than of the Regent. But at this time Eichmann was up
against the growing resistance of the Hungarians. He became even more demanding, and asked that the Jews in the
Hungarian labor service be handed over to him, under the
pretense that they would be employed on important military work in Germany. He was met by a solid wall of opposition. Csatay, the Hungarian minister responsible, refused even to consider the matter. As soon as he heard of
Eichmann's plan to start deportations from the capital on
July 5, he immediately conscripted all Jewish men up to
the age of forty-eight into the labor service, thus saving
them from the clutches of the Germans. Eichmann was
forced to seek his victims elsewhere. During the first part
of July, he "cleaned up" western Hungary; there had been
thirty thousand Jews there. He then tried to move in on the
capital, and he succeeded in getting his hands on Ujpest,
Kispest, and Pestszenterzsebet in the suburbs. The Jews
from these places were taken to the brickworks at Buda-
kalasz and Monor.

At the same time he tried, with the help of the state
secretaries Baky and Endre and of some leading police officers, to stage a small, private *Putsch* in an effort to overthrow the Horthy regime. The *Putsch* was to be carried out
by the police, without the help of the SS, so that it would
appear to be an internal Hungarian affair. Horthy was to be

taken prisoner, and by those same policemen who were to assist in the deportation of the Jews from Budapest. László Endre was designated for the post of Prime Minister. But the Regent's adherents learned of this plan in good time, the army was alerted, and part of the police barracks was occupied. A tank and an infantry regiment were brought from the provinces to the capital, and on July 8 the police were ordered to leave Budapest.

This day marked the turning point. The text of the interim agreement, which had been held back by the people in Constantinople for over a month, at last arrived in Budapest. The Waada at once sent their representatives to Eichmann and Becher requesting that the deportations be stopped forthwith, and Eichmann was compelled to give in. Becher used the Jewish proposals contained in the interim agreement in an attempt to persuade Himmler to put an end, at least for the time being, to the gassing of the Jews.

Everything now combined to create a favorable atmosphere for the negotiations, which were to take place in Switzerland between the representatives of world Jewry and of the German SS. Nevertheless, however highly the value of the interventions by neutral countries may be rated, one indisputable fact remained: up to July 8, 1944, an unbroken sequence of trains had passed along the lines to Oswiecim, and on that day the last official deportation train left the country. During the period from May 15, 1944, to July 8, 1944, four hundred and thirty-four thousand Hungarian Jews were deported to Oswiecim and there were murdered.

Roughly the same number of Jews still remained in the country, and it was for these that the Waada fought their last, desperate battle.

Chapter XIII

NEGOTIATIONS ON THE SWISS FRONTIER

IN BUDAPEST events followed each other with increasing speed. The military situation was changing from day to day, and each day brought new dangers. The fate of Germany was already sealed; but though the Reich was practically defenseless against the crushing blows of the Allies, its waning power was still great enough to drag the last remnants of the Jews down with it, into the grave. When the shock of the July 20 revolt against Hitler had subsided, Eichmann once more took up the cudgels with the Hungarian government to get the deportations from the capital going again. In Bratislava, after the outbreak of the partisan revolt in Slovakia, he succeeded in having the rest of the Slovak Jews destroyed.

In these conditions the one last hope lay in the nego-

tiations between the SS and the representatives of the Jewish world organizations. It was absurd but true that, in spite
of their desperate military situation, the Germans devoted
a large part of their energy and resources to finishing their
war against the Jews. Even more absurd, yet also true, they
were ready to undertake the most complicated negotiations
in order to make a little money selling the remaining Jews.

To study the actions of the Germans at this time, to
read the documents and talk to the surviving SS leaders,
can lead to only one conclusion: that the Germans really
were ready, or to be more exact Himmler was ready, to sell
the Jews, and for a low price. The Allies could in fact have
bought them. From a military point of view, the price
would have been totally insignificant and could not have
prolonged the life of the German war machine by a single
day or even by one hour.

If the leaders of the Western democracies had too
many cares on their shoulders at this time to worry about
the fate of the remaining Jews, such was not the case with
the Jewish leaders, for whom the matter was one of ex-
tremest urgency. The way of getting the Jews out of the
clutches of these bandits was by bargaining with them.
Yet it was more than three months before the negotiators
first met: Brand arrived in Constantinople on May 19, but
not until August 21 did Sally Mayer meet Colonel Becher,
Himmler's representative, on the bridge over the Rhine at
Sankt Margrethen.

The way this meeting was organized was typical of the
entire negotiations. It had already been discussed for
months on end. There had been ample time to have everything prepared. It might have been thought that in a matter that directly concerned hundreds of thousands of lives,

the Sochnuth would have considered carefully every eventuality and would have given their representatives the most complete instructions. But this is what happened.

Kastner told Becher that everything was ready for the agreement to be signed. Then, when Becher tried to get to Switzerland to meet Sally Mayer, it was found that his Jewish opposite number had failed to obtain a visa for him. Sally Mayer and Kurt Becher therefore had to meet on the middle of the bridge. Becher suggested that the discussions be continued in the Swiss Customs shed, but the Swiss would not allow him across the frontier. He then invited Sally Mayer to come into the German Customs building but Mayer refused even to take ten steps on German territory. They had to conduct the negotiations while they stood on the bridge.

The difficulties soon became apparent.

Becher said, "I am the authorized representative of the SS Reichsführer. I have been given full authority to sign a temporary agreement with you, which will become legally valid as soon as it is confirmed by the SS Reichsführer. Are you prepared to accept the German demands conveyed to you by Herr Joel Brand?"

Sally Mayer replied, "I am not here as the representative of the Joint, but as the president of a Swiss organization for helping the Jews. I know nothing of your demands or of the proposals that you say Herr Joel Brand has brought. So far as the Budapest Jews are concerned, there are no two ways about it. The Germans have got to stop this damned gassing right away."

Becher said, "I shall propose to the Reichsführer that the gassings be stopped. We have already shown our good will in this matter by allowing a group of three hundred and eighteen Jews to leave Bergen-Belsen and come to Switzerland. The rest of this Budapest transport will also leave German territory very shortly. First, however, I want to hear what you have to offer in return."

"Would money do to begin with?" asked Sally Mayer.

"No. We want goods."

Sally Mayer tried an appeal to the conscience of this representative of the SS. Finally he said, "I have no power whatsoever to promise you goods, and I must get in touch with the appropriate authorities."

This infuriated Becher, and he turned on Kastner, who had accompanied him. "You have had three months to prepare for this conference. You entice me to the frontier and keep me standing in the rain while we talk. Then this man proceeds to preach a humanitarian sermon, as though I were personally responsible for all that has happened, when you know that I've disapproved of it all as strongly as you have. I'll give you one week to get everything properly organized. At the end of that time I shall expect you to bring me concrete proposals."

However, events of far-reaching importance occurred during this week. Rumania capitulated. The Hungarian government had already sent the Germans a note requesting the withdrawal of the *Judenkommando*. At eight o'clock on the evening of August 25, Wisliceny telephoned Kastner to come to see him.

"You have won, Herr Kastner," he said. "Our staff is leaving."

Himmler was forced to heed the Hungarian government's demands in order not to run the risk of having Hungary break with the Axis at this critical moment. He ordered the withdrawal of the *Judenkommando*, but left the

Gestapo in Budapest. In view of the impending collapse, Wisliceny was anxious to show his helpfulness. He asked Kastner for the addresses of Jewish contacts with whom, in his new role, he could discuss the problem of further delaying tactics in the Jewish question.

The *Judenkommando* left their offices in the Schwabenberg, and Eichmann retired to an estate in the provinces, where he bided his time. Behind the scenes, Wesemeyer was already plotting to overthrow the Horthy regime and to bring Szálasy, who represented the Crossed Arrows party, into power.

The news of the withdrawal of the *Judenkommando* spread like wildfire among the Jews in the capital, and everyone breathed freely once more.

On September 1, Kastner and Dr. Billitz, a baptized Jew and a director of the Manfred Weiss group, went to the Swiss border a second time. Becher himself had refused to take part in a further conference on the frontier bridge, but had sent his adjutant, Captain Grüson, to accompany the German representatives onto the bridge. Sally Mayer arrived from the Swiss side accompanied by his lawyer, Dr. Wyler. Once again, however, he was unable to put forward any concrete proposals.

Dr. Wyler explained: "We have nothing positive to say to you. We have only been authorized by the American authorities not to say no."

Grüson turned to Sally Mayer and said, "Herr Mayer, even if you have no definite offer to make, give me at least some sort of promise that my chief, Herr Becher, can use. Otherwise it will be impossible for him to intervene with the Reichsführer on behalf of the Jews, and the deporta-

tions will start again. Surely you can make some sort of a
promise; it's only a matter of words. It will give you time,
and so much can happen before you have to carry out any
promises you may make."

"A citizen of Switzerland only gives promises that he
knows he can keep," answered Sally Mayer.

When his adjutant reported this conversation to him,
Becher said, "I am sorry, gentlemen, but I cannot do any
more on behalf of the Jews than Herr Mayer allows me to."

Billitz and Kastner tried to calm Becher down. "There
is nothing more to be discussed," Becher said finally. "I
will wait in Budapest for an unequivocal yes or no from
Sally Mayer. Until I receive a telegram with his answer,
there is nothing I can do. If the answer should be in the
affirmative, I will obtain a Swiss visa and sit at a proper
table with the Jewish delegates. I am not going to let myself in for a third session of pointless talk."

Becher's attitude was greatly influenced by the change
in the military situation. A year earlier he would probably
not have spoken like this, but now he had two very good
reasons for trying to come to an agreement. He was, after
all, an officer of the SS, and it therefore behooved him to
make a favorable agreement that would result in the saving
of hundreds of thousands of Jews. Only then would he be
in a good position once his country had lost the war. Furthermore, he had confidently assured Himmler that the
negotiations would have a successful outcome and that
army trucks and other war materials would be duly delivered. It would be awkward for him to have to admit that
Eichmann had been right and that the whole matter was
only Jewish bluff. Faced with this dilemma, he did everything in his power to prevent the discussions from breaking

down. His subordinates have maintained that he even risked his neck by knowingly giving the Reichsführer false information to win time and to prevent the deportations from being resumed. It is, however, hard to say how much truth there is in this.

The revolt of the Slovak partisans took place at this time, and many Jews seized the opportunity to take up arms against their oppressors. Eichmann at once requested permission to have the whole of the Jewish population in Slovakia liquidated. Gisi Fleischmann and her friends went in a panic to Kastner, who in his turn saw Becher.

Becher, however, refused to intervene with Himmler on their behalf. "I achieved absolutely nothing when I went to the Swiss frontier. Now I have no influence with Himmler. I can only suggest that you go to Bratislava with my adjutant, and see if you can get something done on the spot."

Kastner went to Bratislava, and the Waada there decided to collect money and goods on their own initiative. These they offered to Becher if he could, in exchange, have the deportations stopped. Becher said that he could only accept the Bratislava offer after he had received Sally Mayer's long-awaited telegram. The telegram, however, did not arrive in time, and when it did arrive, it was not positive enough. The Slovak Jews were exterminated.

A third conference was held at the frontier on September 28. It was no more successful than the other two. Sally Mayer was annoyed at being "drawn into this damned Slovakian business." He was not going to let himself be blackmailed. In the end he promised Becher money.

Meanwhile a change had taken place in the political

climate of Budapest. Horthy had dismissed Prime Minister
Sztójay, who was perpetually vacillating between the Germans and the Hungarians. He had entrusted the government to the liberal General Lakatos. Lakatos was preparing to go over to the side of the Allies. Horthy and he
behaved like the conspirators of the July 20 *Putsch*. Without any conspiratorial foresight or imagination, they simply
tried to maneuver the Germans out of Hungary. Horthy
invited delegations of the left-wing parties to the Castle in
Budapest to discuss the formation of a coalition democratic government. Lakatos sent General Faragó, the head of
the Hungarian police, who had once been military attaché
in Moscow, to the Russians with an offer of surrender. All
these actions were common knowledge in Budapest, and
the Germans, warned by their experience with Bulgaria
and Rumania, had time to take the necessary countermeasures.

The position of the Jews also altered at this time, in a
remarkable way. Engineer Komoly almost lived in the various Hungarian ministries, and the state secretaries discussed with him the prospects of the intended capitulation.
Kastner was asked to cross the Russian lines under a white
flag, accompanied by a Russian-speaking Hungarian Communist. This came to nothing. The relations between the
Waada and the Hungarian Communists grew much closer.
The Waada supplied them with money, false documents,
secret lodgings, and even with weapons and ammunition.
The Chaluzim prepared for the possibility of an armed
rising.

All of a sudden Jews became socially acceptable in
Hungary, and the president of the Jewish Association of
Communes, Councilor Samuel Stern, was invited to the

Castle for an audience with Horthy. Engineer Komoly spent many hours closeted with the younger Horthy.

At this time Kastner, with dogged tenacity, was trying to get the Bergen-Belsen transport under way. Eichmann had demanded a ransom of two hundred dollars a person, but Becher, who was always anxious to demonstrate to his chief how much he could get out of the Jews, raised this to two thousand dollars. The Waada offered one hundred dollars, and the SS leader forwarded this offer to Himmler. A week later he received a reply, signed by Himmler himself, which read:

> *Our opponents appear to be out of their minds. It costs a European 1,000 dollars to get to America. It will cost a Jew 1,000 dollars to get out of Europe.* HIMMLER.

Horthy had intended to bring Hungarian troops into the city from the provinces and then to announce Hungary's capitulation. The Germans knew of this plan, however, and decided to provoke Horthy into acting prematurely. The Regent's son was lured into a trap. He was led to believe that he would be meeting representatives of Marshal Tito, but on arrival at the rendezvous he was met by Gestapo officials. A struggle ensued during which SS Captain Klages received a fatal bullet in the stomach. The young Nicholas von Horthy was arrested.

This incident led the Regent to act prematurely, and at eleven o'clock on the morning of Sunday, October 15, he had his proclamation of surrender broadcast over the Hungarian radio. He took this opportunity to declare that the Hungarian nation had only cooperated in the persecution of the Jews at the behest of the Germans. At one o'-clock in the afternoon the Germans reacted. Their troops occupied all the key positions in the capital, and the Regent was taken prisoner. It was announced over the Hungarian radio that a new government had been formed by the Crossed Arrows party, under Ferenc Szálasy's leadership.

This gutter government of Szálasy's was quite incapable of maintaining any kind of order. The Crossed Arrows men, now freed of all restraint, murdered and looted at will, and the Jews in the capital were their first victims.

Eichmann returned to Budapest two days later and summoned Kastner to his office.

"I am back," he said. "You probably imagined that the Rumanian and Bulgarian story would be repeated here. Apparently you forgot that Hungary lies in Germany's shadow, and that our arm is still long enough to reach the Jews in Budapest. Now mark my words. This government does what we tell it to do. I am getting in touch with Minister Kovarcz at once. The Budapest Jews will be transported, and this time they will have to go on foot. We need our trains for other purposes. Or does this idea not appeal to you? You're getting worried, are you? Don't come to me with any more of your American fairy tales. We are going to act promptly and efficiently, see?"

Eichmann once more held the whip hand.

Kastner hurriedly approached Becher, but the latter would not make any attempt to stem the new current of events. "There's nothing I can do," he said. "Your friends could not even get me a Swiss visa, so how can I believe that these international negotiations will ever lead to anything?"

Kastner and Billitz sent telegram after telegram to

Switzerland, until at last, on October 25, a visa was obtained for Becher.

On October 29, Kastner and Billitz met Sally Mayer in St. Gallen, and Becher joined them there on November 2. He told Kastner that "things were moving" and that Himmler had given orders for the Bergen-Belsen group to start.

Sally Mayer again proved unequal to the task. He was completely unworldly, and only exasperated the German delegates with his humanitarian homilies. No progress was made until a man of a very different caliber appeared. This was the American, Roswell McClelland, who represented Roosevelt's War Refugees Board.

McClelland was a cultivated and level-headed young diplomat, a Quaker and humanist, and also a man who knew how to do business. He did not consider it part of his mission to preach morality to the representatives of Nazi Germany. He wished to take practical measures to alleviate the fate of the stricken Jews, for whom he felt pity.

"I am not here to give you my view about a régime that has given cold-blooded murder the status of government policy," he said to Becher. "I am here to help. I am ready to agree that twenty million francs shall be deposited in Switzerland. This money can be found by the Joint. You ask for goods. But you cannot expect the Joint to procure them for you. Germany herself must make those arrangements. I reserve the right to keep a check on the goods that are bought, and also on what the Germans give in return. It is of course a matter for the Swiss government to decide whether or not export permits will be granted for these goods. But under the circumstances, I am ready to approach the federal government on your behalf."

Then came a discussion over what the Germans should provide in exchange. The Waada and the Joint had already prepared a document containing twelve separate demands. McClelland, however, with a princely gesture, pushed these aside and made one single demand: that the Germans should respect human life, and should protect all civilians, without distinction of race or creed.

According to Kastner, Becher was deeply impressed by the behavior of this American. For the first time he found himself face to face with the representative of a nation that knew how to combine freedom with power. Becher promised to submit McClelland's demands to the SS Reichsführer, who, he was certain, would give them very careful consideration. He ordered his companion, Kettlitz, to remain in Switzerland in order to organize the purchase of goods.

When Becher was shown a telegram that Sally Mayer had received from Cordell Hull, the United States Secretary of State, authorizing the transfer of five million dollars to the Joint for these purposes, he was thoroughly happy. Now at last he could send his chief the long-awaited news that the negotiations had been successfully started. He emphasized in his telegram to Himmler that he had been in personal touch with Roosevelt's special representative.

It was left to Sally Mayer to destroy this new-found optimism next day. He was asked by Kettlitz, "When are you going to bring the chest along, Herr Mayer?"

"What chest?"

"The one with the money in it, of course."

"What are you thinking of? Do you imagine we're going to throw our money away?" Mayer asked and banged his fist on the table.

There was silence for a few seconds, Kastner records, and then Becher, who had grown very pale, said, "Herr Mayer seems to have very weak nerves."

The discussions were never resumed.

When they returned to German territory, Becher at once took away Kastner's passport.

Chapter XIV

THE HIMMLER DECREE

WHILE BECHER tried to get Himmler to agree to Mc-Clelland's demands, Eichmann raged in Budapest. This was the worst period for the Jews in the Hungarian capital. On November 8 the deportations were started again, and this time the deportees had to go on foot. Guarded by soldiers and Crossed Arrows men, ten thousand people, most of them women, were driven along the road from Budapest to Vienna. Those who were unable to keep up were shot out of hand. The nights were spent in the open. After several hours' march, the exhausted people threw away their last pieces of baggage and staggered on like living corpses. Two SS officers, Colonel General Jüttner of the Waffen-SS and SS Lieutenant Colonel Höss, the commandant of Oswiecim, were traveling from Vienna to Budapest at the time and witnessed this death march of Eich-

mann's. They were so disgusted that even the butcher of
Oswiecim communicated indignantly with Becher. Höss
had come straight from Himmler's headquarters, where a
new policy had just been laid down as a result of Becher's
meeting with McClelland. On November 17, Jüttner ordered the Budapest *Judenkommando* to put an immediate
stop to the forced march.

Those who were still on the road were sent back to
Budapest. The cancellation of the march was the first successful result of the Swiss negotiations. But on the next day,
Becher received a telegram from Kettlitz in Switzerland,
and once more everything was in jeopardy. It read: "Money
not yet received. Fresh objections raised. Am convinced
they either will not or cannot produce full amount offered."

This infuriated Becher, and in his rage he wanted to
go straight to Himmler to decline any further responsibility for the matter. But he could no longer retrace his steps.
He had promised a successful outcome to the negotiations,
and he feared a breakdown even more than Kastner did.
He managed to convince himself that the reasons for the
delay were only of a technical financial nature.

His enemy was Eichmann, to whom the extermination of the Jews was more important than victory itself.

To begin with, Eichmann wanted, as much as Becher,
to see the conclusion of an agreement that would enable
them simultaneously to get rid of a million Jews and to acquire war materials. But when Joel Brand failed to return,
he must have realized that this prospect was an illusion,
so he turned his hand once more to mass murder. His private spies abroad kept him informed about the situation in
Switzerland. On November 21, he ordered a repetition of
the forced march, whereupon Kastner redoubled his efforts

and bombarded Becher with requests that he go at once to
Himmler. The situation at the fronts indicated that German resistance would collapse very soon. Becher no longer
bothered about the bargaining going on in Switzerland. He
went to Berlin, where he had several fierce arguments with
the SS Reichsführer. In the end he won his point. On November 25, Himmler gave the decisive order. The gas
chambers were to be destroyed and the annihilation of the
Jews to be stopped forthwith. He made the commandants
of the concentration camps personally responsible for insuring that "from now on the lives of Jews will be respected."

Himmler's decree, the authenticity of which is beyond
dispute, was the culminating achievement of those efforts
begun so long before, when Gisi Fleischmann, the heroine
of Bratislava, ransomed twenty-five thousand Slovakian
Jews from the SS leader Dieter von Wisliceny. It was the
ultimate justification of the Waada policy.

But this "Himmler decree" was not the automatic result of the change in the military situation. Himmler was
attacked to the last by those circles within the SS who
wanted to see Hitler's policy of total annihilation carried
out. The decree threw Kaltenbrunner, who was responsible for all the Nazi concentration camps, into a towering
rage. He and his henchmen, Eichmann and Müller, did
everything in their power to sabotage this new policy. To a
certain extent they succeeded, especially by pointing out
that the promises made by our delegates in Switzerland
had never been kept. Whether Sally Mayer deliberately
sabotaged the conclusion of an agreement so that he would
not have to hand over the money, whether his attitude was
dictated by some higher authority, whether he hoped the

transaction would be accomplished without his having to give anything in return, or whether he just showed a plain lack of skill—his actions caused the negotiations to break down.

On November 27, two days after Himmler had promulgated his decree, Kettlitz sent a further telegram to Becher: "Have been unable contact Sally Mayer for ten days. He will not speak on telephone. Pointless to remain in Switzerland. Request recall."

This telegram put Becher into a fearful panic, since after his talks with McClelland he had given Himmler a guarantee that the Jews would carry out their part of the bargain. He feared for his head. This was Eichmann's triumph.

At a meeting that was attended by Kastner, Eichmann said, "I tell you, I saw all this coming. I warned Becher repeatedly not to let himself be led by the nose. I have only one thing to say to you, Kastner. I will give you forty-eight hours to get everything buttoned up in Switzerland, and if I don't have a positive answer within that time, I'll have the whole Jewish dunghill in Budapest carted away."

Becher, who was now in a very dangerous position, did not dare to tell Himmler the truth. He decided to send Kastner to Switzerland again, accompanied by his adjutant, Captain Krell, who was to present an ultimatum from Becher himself, demanding that by December 2 he be sent cabled confirmation that the sum of twenty million francs had actually been received.

Becher said to Krell, "The Bergen-Belsen group will leave the camp during the next few days and move to the Swiss border. I want you to stay at the frontier, and to bring them back if the money is not forthcoming."

Toward the end of November Kastner and Krell arrived in Switzerland, where they found everything in hopeless confusion. Stettinius had canceled the permission given by Cordell Hull for twenty million Swiss francs to be placed at the disposal of the negotiators, and had forbidden all contact with the Nazis. Kastner entreated Sally Mayer to do something to avert the catastrophe, but Mayer had only four million francs at his disposal. Becher's adjutants, Krell and Kettlitz, wanted to telegraph Becher and tell him about the situation, but Dr. Billitz and Kastner managed to convince them that, in view of the "Himmler decree," doing this would cost Becher his life.

"It's your duty to help your chief win time," Kastner said.

"But we'll be risking our own necks if we send false information by telegram," said Krell.

The two SS officers considered the matter for a long time. They both knew that the collapse of Germany was imminent. They had a great personal stake in the outcome. They agreed to take even greater risks.

Five days later the Bergen-Belsen transport arrived in Bregenz. Krumey was in charge. Krell had been given definite orders by Becher in Budapest to turn the transport about if it appeared that Sally Mayer was not going to keep his promises. Notwithstanding this, Krell decided to let the transport proceed and persuaded Krumey and Kettlitz to agree to this. Kastner received permission to visit the thirteen hundred and sixty-eight Jews who had left Budapest months before, and he was able to see his friends, his wife, and his father-in-law. He could not help but notice that none of Brand's family was there. Shortly before the train's departure Eichmann had ordered Krumey to keep Brand's aged mother and his three sisters in the camp. No amount of pleading would move him to allow at least the mother, who was blind, to go. She and Brand's sisters remained in the camp, and Joel never saw his mother again. She fell sick of spotted typhus, brought on by starvation, and died a few days after being released by the Russians. She was buried with five others in a common grave.

A chapter in the history of the work of the Waada was brought to a close with the arrival of the Bergen-Belsen transport in Switzerland. The Budapest Waada's first undertaking had been the rescue of refugees from Poland, and its final efforts were devoted to the unfortunate people in the German concentration camps.

Without forgetting its main objective, the Waada managed at a certain stage of the struggle to get subsidiary concessions from the Germans, namely permission for the stepping up of legal emigration. There were good reasons for doing this. The emigrants with their Palestine certificates formed the only link between the Waada's isolated positions and the homesteads in Erets Israel. This link must not be broken: the arrival in Palestine of one live witness was worth far more than ten carefully written reports brought to the Sochnuth there by secret couriers. In addition, the appearance in foreign countries of seventeen hundred Jews, freed by the Nazis, provided a visible justification for Waada policy. No one had believed that our people could be ransomed, but the arrival of this "installment" in Switzerland demonstrated that it could be done.

The progress of the Swiss negotiations was a classic example of the disunity that prevailed among our political representatives. The orthodox and the Revisionist groups stepped in and wanted to negotiate with Himmler, independently of Sally Mayer, through the Swiss federal Councilor, Musy. The promises made to the Germans were never kept. Becher saw as little of the twenty million francs as he did of the five million. His only achievement was to place a few orders in Switzerland, and only a small part of the goods actually arrived in Germany.

At another time one might have had nothing but praise for the skill shown by the representatives of the Joint, and for the careful way in which they administered the Jewish funds. But at that moment men's lives were at stake, and every delay meant death for thousands. The Slovak Jews went to the wall because even Becher was no longer willing to take the risk of trying to save them. The initiation by the Waada of these discussions with the Nazis saved a great part of the Budapest Jews. While Kastner was bargaining in Switzerland, the Red Army surrounded Budapest. Although he tried up to the last to get back to the capital, Kastner was too late. Neither his temperament nor his conscience would permit this purposeful man to remain safely in Switzerland while the lives of what remained of his people were in extreme jeopardy. He decided to return to Germany and persuade Becher to take measures that would save the lives of the remaining Jews in German territory. A committee headed by Engineer Andor Biss was formed in Budapest to carry on Kastner's work. Becher and his people, who had originally been concerned only with exchanging Jewish lives for war materials, now gave their unqualified support to Kastner. Becher indeed made saving Jewish lives his own concern, and although as time went on the accounting staff of the SS were forced to give up all hope of ever receiving any payment from the Allies, he still continued to negotiate.

Becher was no longer interested in what the Germans were going to get out of the Jews. His one concern now was that his name should be connected with the rescue of the scattered survivors. During those last months of the war, when the end was in sight, he talked Himmler into doing everything he wanted. He was put in control of the concentration camps, and he made Himmler issue an order to all the commandants to hand over their camps to the Allies without a fight. This was no longer a matter that concerned the Jews alone. The political prisoners of all the European nations were anticipating with mixed feelings the imminent end of the war. Rumors were abroad that the Germans were resolved not to leave behind them any living witness to their crimes. These rumors were not without foundation. A portion of the SS, headed by Eichmann, Kaltenbrunner, and Müller, was definitely in favor of such action. Becher, under constant pressure from Kastner, went from one concentration camp to another, seeing that Himmler's orders were carried out. He handed over the Bergen-Belsen concentration camp to the British even against the wishes of the military authorities.

He then turned to the camp at Mauthausen. Here the commandant was preparing the mass murder of three thousand Jews who were to be loaded into ancient barges on the Danube, which were then to be sunk. He had also installed explosive charges in the shafts of the nearby mines. The prisoners, not all of whom were Jews, were to be driven into the mines, and then the entrances were to be blown up. An angry scene took place between the commandant and

Becher, during the course of which the commandant declared that Kaltenbrunner had assumed command of the
southern sector and therefore Himmler's orders had no
authority. Becher, however, went to Kaltenbrunner and
succeeded in getting him to spare the Jews—whereupon
the commandant proposed to fill the Danube barges with
political prisoners of other nationalities. But in this too he
was thwarted at the last minute by Becher. There was now
not enough time left for Becher to see that Himmler's orders were carried out in all the other concentration camps,
but he sent Kastner, with Krumey, to Terezin and elsewhere in order to insure that the prisoners should be
handed over to the advancing Russians without a fight.

Becher's last action had its comic side. On April 15 he
said to Kastner, "I am going to bring you your Dr. Schweiger from Mauthausen. This will be my personal gift to
you."

Dr. Mosche Schweiger had been arrested in Budapest
on the day of the German occupation. His crime had been
to speculate in a book on the question why no one had
murdered Hitler; for this he was taken by the Nazis to
Mauthausen, where he remained until the end of the war,
but he was treated quite decently because of the Waada's
repeated interventions on his behalf.

Becher arrived at Mauthausen on April 20, 1945, and
ordered the commandant to fetch Schweiger. Schweiger
was convinced that his last hour had come and that he was
going to be killed by an injection of gasoline, a popular
coup de grace in those last days. After taking leave of his
friends, he went to the commandant's office and snapped
smartly to attention before the Colonel.

"You are Herr Dr. Schweiger? Please sit down, Doctor. My name is Kurt Becher. I hope you have heard of me."

Schweiger had never heard of Becher. He did not dare sit down, and he believed that the SS people were getting some last fun out of him before finishing him off.

"You are shortly to be set free, Doctor," Becher continued. "Until then you will be given a separate room and receive special food. You need no longer salute anyone here, and you may smoke and move about the camp freely. Nor are you required to attend any further roll calls."

Schweiger felt faint and tried to go, but Becher called him back.

"Your wardrobe, Doctor, has become somewhat shabby. I would advise you to have a new suit of clothes made for yourself."

The camp tailor took Schweiger's measurements. When the suit was delivered, the tailor received a severe reprimand from the commandant because one of the buttons had not been sewn on correctly.

On May 4 Becher arrived and took Schweiger away in his car. Becher first attended to some business on one of the Danube steamers, which had been turned into an SS headquarters. As poor Schweiger waited on the deck, the SS man on watch shouted at him, "Who are you and what are you doing here?"

Schweiger sprang to attention, his thumbs along the seams of his trousers, and rattled off his convict serial number and cell block number.

The soldier was going for him when Becher reappeared. "Is that how you treat visitors?" Becher roared. "Leaving them standing out in the cold? Fetch hot coffee, at once."

The soldier fled.

They continued their journey in Becher's own car to Weissenbach, near Bad Ischl. Becher requisitioned a room for Dr. Schweiger in a hunting lodge, and they lived there together for a few days until the American troops arrived in Ischl.

On this day Becher said to Schweiger, in the presence of a Jewish witness, "I shall no doubt be arrested during the next few days. I will have to account for all that has happened, but I believe I shall be able to do that satisfactorily. First of all, though, I want to deal with a matter that has been preying on my mind. These six strongboxes contain valuables that are the property of the Budapest Jews. They were handed over to my staff in payment for the transport of seventeen hundred people from Bergen-Belsen to Switzerland. I want you to take these boxes and, when you have discussed it with Dr. Kastner and Herr Sally Mayer, give the contents back to those who contributed them. If they are no longer alive, then give them to the Jewish Agency and the Joint."[1]

The boxes were opened and their glittering contents poured onto the table before the astonished eyes of Dr. Schweiger and the others. They were then repacked, and it was arranged for an inventory to be taken next day. But on that day the Americans arrived, and Becher was arrested.

---

[1] In the summer of 1955, in the course of our research, Alexander Weissberg-Cybulski and I visited Becher in Bremen. Our conversations lasted for two weeks, during which time we put many hundreds of questions to him. We asked him why he had not delivered those valuables to the SS Reichsführer in the first place, and his reply was, "They remained officially in my possession because my staff was to have used them to pay for goods ordered from abroad. I always had the intention, however, of keeping them for the Jews and later I said so to Kastner."

Schweiger remained at the hunting lodge. These were
times of violence, and he did not dare even to leave his
room lest the vast treasure be stolen.

He wrote to the Sochnuth in Israel, to officers of the
Jewish Brigade in Italy, and to others, asking that they help
him take the treasure away to a safe place. He received no
answer.

Brand, in Tel Aviv, noticed Schweiger's report among
the mass of incoming documents. A special meeting of the
Executive was in session at the time, and he forced his way
into the assembly hall.

"What can you be thinking of?" Brand cried. "How can
you leave a letter like this unanswered? Mosche Schweiger is no child, and when he writes in these terms he's
telling the truth. He sends you a report about the treasures
of the Jewish people, and you sit there and do nothing about
it!"

Eventually Dr. Nahum Goldmann was authorized to
go to Europe and investigate the matter and to provide for
the safekeeping of the valuables.

Dr. Schweiger, however, could endure it no longer.
Jewish soldiers of the American army took him to the office of the Counter Intelligence Corps (CIC), where a
member of the Poale Zion from Poland was working, and
Schweiger told this man the whole story. On the same night
CIC agents arrived and took over the contents of the six
boxes. They made no inventory but gave an official receipt.

A very long time passed before the Jewish authorities
acted. Then the matter was taken up in Washington, and
eventually a part of the treasure was returned, but it was

only a fraction of what had been so carefully collected years before from the Budapest Jews.[2]

---

[2] I discussed this matter with Engineer Biss and found he held a different opinion. He said to me, "It was probably all a mistake. I was there when the Germans took over and valued these articles. The jewels were mostly of no great value, but we persuaded Captain Grüson, who was in charge of the stock-taking and who wanted to help us, to put them down at a much higher value, so that we could include more people in the Bergen-Belsen transport. When everything is taken into account, the actual value was at the very most only half the nominal value."

It is conceivable therefore that the difference in value, which was apparent when the valuables were returned from the U.S.A., can be explained, wholly or in part, by this fact.

Chapter XV

THE DELIVERANCE OF BUDAPEST

TOWARD THE end of November, 1944, the Crossed Arrows government ordered a ghetto to be established for the Budapest Jews. A grotesque situation had by then developed in the capital. Certain countries, in particular Switzerland and Sweden, had provided many of these Jews with safe-conducts in order to save them from the clutches of the Hungarians and the Germans. At first these documents had a definite validity, and even the Hungarian government recognized a number of them. The rabble government, however, was not recognized by any neutral state. It now hoped to establish a *de facto* recognition, through representations of Swedish and Swiss diplomats on behalf of the Jews. It was therefore prepared to make concessions, but was always thwarted by the relentless opposition of Kovarcz, the Minister for Internal Affairs, who dominated the cabinet and whose brutal anti-Semitism put even the worst of the SS murderers in the shade.

The number of official safe-conducts rose to over fifteen thousand; and the Waada's document department forged another ten thousand and issued them to persecuted Jews. In the end almost every second Jew in Budapest possessed one of these passes, but by that time they had lost all value. The Crossed Arrows murder squads ranged through the streets and dragged every Jew, or every person who looked like a Jew, to the banks of the Danube and shot him. Every morning corpses would be found on the pavements of the city streets. At this time foreign diplomats vied with one another in their efforts to assist the Jews, but Kovarcz ignored the advice of his own foreign minister, and even the orders of his own prime minister. His gangs continued to dominate the streets of the capital. No document made any impression on them, and they respected only the weapons of the German soldiers.

Two men rendered lasting services to our people during this reign of terror: Raoul Wallenberg of the Swedish Red Cross, and the Swiss Consul, Charles Lutz.

About thirty thousand Budapest Jews had no faith in the protection afforded them by these documents from neutral countries, and they went "underground" with Aryan papers. Over eighty thousand moved into the ghetto.

On December 7 Councilor Samuel Stern received alarming news. For the last few weeks he had been hiding in the house of the editor of a Crossed Arrows newspaper. This anti-Semitic journalist came to him in a panic and informed him of what had happened at a cabinet meeting held the day before. Minister Kovarcz had proposed the immediate slaughter of all the Jews in the ghetto. Prime Minister Szálasy, who feared Russian reprisals, spoke out against this, but Kovarcz said that they should not leave a single witness when the town was occupied by the Russians, since every Jew would then exact his revenge on the Aryan population. The majority agreed with Kovarcz, and the cabinet decided on the wholesale extermination of the Budapest Jews. Samuel Stern informed the Jewish leaders, and a meeting took place in the Swiss legation. Present were Councilor Samuel Stern, president of the progressive Jewish community in Budapest (representing about eighty per cent of the Jews), Dr. Karl Wilhelm and Ludwig Stöckler of the Jewish council, and Otto Komoly and Engineer Biss representing the Waada. Mosche Kraus, from the Palestine Office, was also present.

"We have come to the end of our resources," Stern said. "Any attempt to influence the Hungarians, either by money or by diplomatic intervention, is doomed to failure. Not even Szálasy can help, even though he may want to, for the Crossed Arrows people pay no attention whatever to his orders. Our only chance is to get the Germans to intervene with Kovarcz." He turned to Komoly and Biss. "You are the only ones who can make this attempt. There is no time to lose. It is up to you to show how much your connections are worth. I myself have given up all hope."

Engineer Biss made his way through the dangerous streets of the town. He found Becher in a very bad humor. All the promises made by the Jewish representatives in Switzerland had been broken, and so far Becher had not received a solitary army truck or a single sparkling coin. He had no hope that the negotiations to which he had so openly committed himself would ever reach a successful conclusion. He feared that he would be held responsible for this failure.

But he did not realize what Himmler was actually up to: with the iron ring drawing tighter around the Germans, Reichsführer Heinrich Himmler wanted to save himself by sacrificing his *Führer*. The negotiations with the Jews had opened a very small window to the Allies, and in spite of all the setbacks, Himmler did not want to destroy this link. The actual delivery of goods was a camouflage designed to lull Hitler's suspicions.

When Biss entered his room and asked him to intervene with the Hungarians, Becher began by shouting, "What on earth do you take me for, Herr Biss? What do you expect me to do now? I've taken everything upon myself, I've risked my neck for you a dozen times, and all you've done is to deceive me and let me down. What do you imagine Eichmann will think of me? The transport has gone to Switzerland, and we've had nothing in return from Sally Mayer. No money, no goods, nothing. When Kettlitz tries to telephone him, Sally Mayer is not at home. And now you expect us not only to keep our promises, but also to protect your people from the Hungarians."

"Colonel, there is more to this than meets the eye. If the Hungarians are allowed to murder the remaining Jews, the Allies will hold the Germans responsible. All Germans, without exception. You know, sir, as well as I do, how the war is going. There is no longer any point in beating about the bush. You now have a real chance of doing something for us."

"But I'm not alone here, Herr Biss. Every step I take will be observed by others. If you had only delivered the thirty trucks from Slovakia, I would at least have had something to show. I have to cover myself."

"But the thirty trucks and the barrels are already at your disposal. We've got them from Steger."

"I don't know anything about that. Bring Steger here and let him confirm it."

Alois Steger was a German Bohemian who had often been helpful in the past. When the Allies refused permission to have trucks delivered from abroad, somehow Steger had managed to dig up thirty trucks, for which he demanded seven hundred and fifty thousand Swiss francs. The Swiss had placed this money in a Swiss bank, but later the account was blocked. Steger had yet to receive any payment.

Biss left Becher, jumped into his car, and went to raise the money. The Waada's funds were exhausted, but he managed to scrape together, from private sources, some one hundred and eighty-seven thousand Swiss francs, which he took to Steger. Steger had originally asked for an advance of three hundred and seventy-five thousand, but he now accepted this on account, with the promise that he would receive the rest in Switzerland at a later date. He went at once with Biss to Becher.

In the meantime Dr. Billitz, whose relations with Becher were almost those of a friend, had talked to the Colonel, and his anger had subsided when Biss and Steger arrived. Steger confirmed the agreement and promised immediate delivery. Then Becher rose and said to Biss, "I will not promise you anything just yet, but I will do everything I possibly can."

After they had left the house, Dr. Billitz told Biss about Becher's discussions with the Budapest SS leader, police

General Winkelmann. Both men, he said, had telephoned Himmler in Berlin, and with Himmler's agreement Winkelmann had ordered the Hungarian Minister for Internal Affairs, Kovarcz, to come to see him.

Next day Dr. Billitz reported to the Waada leaders the outcome of this interview. "Everything is going well. Winkelmann has explicitly told Kovarcz that the ghetto must be guarded. All private acts of violence are to be suppressed. No irresponsibility is to be allowed. German interests are at stake!"

The Crossed Arrows Minister for Internal Affairs issued special disciplinary orders to the Hungarian police detailed to guard the ghetto. Any group of Crossed Arrows men attempting to force its way into the ghetto was to be disarmed. The Minister's orders were strictly obeyed, since the police had become extremely apprehensive about the imminent arrival of the Russians. They were glad to be able, through their behavior, to provide an alibi for themselves, and to feel that they would be shielded by their Minister. The order given by the Germans for the protection of the ghetto had another aspect to it, however, for all the Jews living outside the ghetto were simultaneously declared outlaws. This led to further outrages in the streets of Budapest, and to an organized attack on the Columbus Street camp. At first this camp had been under German control. The Hungarians had believed that the people in it were being collected for deportation. It had lost its legal status when Horthy forbade the deportations and Eichmann's *Judenkommando* was withdrawn, immediately prior to the Szálasy *Putsch*. It was kept going by the Waada, and was used to provide shelter for thousands of refugees who would otherwise have had no home. A red and white flag was hoisted, and the place declared a Red Cross camp. With the dissolution of the Hungarian army, more and more young people, deserters from the forced labor service battalions, arrived there. A Haganah spirit began to develop, and the young men collected a store of arms while they awaited the arrival of the Russian troops.

The Levente youth organization had their barracks in the neighborhood. The instructors of this group were Hungarian officers whose sympathies at that time lay with England, and who looked forward to Germany's imminent collapse. They established contact with the young people in the camp and even hid their weapons for them.

On the night of December 2, strong groups of Crossed Arrows men and police surrounded the camp in Columbus Street with the intention of destroying it. The camp leader was a courageous man named Miklos Moskowitz. He was uncertain whether he was faced with an unorganized attack or an officially planned deportation. He ordered his followers to resist, and after an exchange of shots two Crossed Arrows men fell dead. A terrible revenge was exacted. Miklos Moskowitz, Dr. Raffael (the camp doctor) and his son, and a dozen others were taken away and shot. The rest were driven out into open country and left there to await deportation.

Engineer Biss and Brand's wife at once hurried to the German security service. Klages was now dead, and his successor had neither the will nor the ability to be helpful. On the following day Eichmann arrived.

Biss went to him and said, "Colonel, you are breaking our agreement. The arrangements are in full swing. Kastner has cabled that the money is in the bank in Switzerland. The trains from Bergen-Belsen are on the move. Everything will be wrecked if you deport thousands of people. The responsibility is on your shoulders, and your Reichsführer will be informed of what is happening here."

"What are you whining about, Herr Biss? We are keeping our side of the bargain. It is you people who are playing dirty tricks on us. Weapons have been found in the camp and a gang of able-bodied men capable of using them. What were you thinking of? You surely don't expect me to leave such people loose in a town that will shortly have to be defended."

A long discussion ensued, and finally an agreement was reached which could hardly be called satisfactory. Those men and women who were able to bear arms would have to leave Budapest, but they would be taken by train. The others would go into the ghetto. The men from Columbus Street would be brought to Bergen-Belsen, whence they would leave for Switzerland with the next transport. The women were left behind and eventually reached the Austrian frontier after a hard, long journey on foot. They managed to survive the war.

At this time the Waada took over all the functions of the dissolved Jewish council, and many other duties as well. From then on their activities were completely illegal. Preparations were made for the approaching siege, and the Waada bought food on the black market to provision the ghetto and the registered Jewish houses.

The children became the Waada's especial care. Several thousand children had lost their parents and had no one to look after them. Otto Komoly took the initiative in work to organize homes. Then Hansi Brand sought the protection of the Red Cross.

The Crossed Arrows men, with their usual disregard

of orders, would frequently break into these children's homes, and during December the situation became critical. The teachers were mostly Jews with Aryan papers—primarily Chaluzim who had refused to move with the children into the ghetto. After each raid the Crossed Arrows men would abduct the supervisors of the home and shoot them on the banks of the Danube. The children would be left, terrified and helpless.

It was not easy to provide these homes with sufficient food, but the Waada made it their special responsibility to see that the children survived. Yet even at the very end many tragic and shameful events occurred. Fear of the Crossed Arrows men would often cause the supervisors of the homes to run away and abandon the children. Since it was impossible during the siege to bring food to the homes, many hundreds of children died of hunger. They died even after the liberation.

In the second half of December, the Red Army closed the ring around Budapest. Before they withdrew, the SS people tried to take the members of the Waada away with them. They did not succeed. The Gestapo searched everywhere for Brand's wife but did not find her. A few hours before the Germans left Budapest, they again tried to telephone her. "This is the SD. We wish to speak to Frau Brand. We need her urgently. She must come to us at once."

Hansi, who had herself answered the telephone, replied, "I am sorry, but I myself am looking for Frau Brand. As soon as I find her, I will send her along to you."

Engineer Otto Komoly, president of the Jewish Land Organization and the most esteemed of the Waada leaders, was no longer with his comrades when the city was liberated. The Crossed Arrows men had abducted him on January 1, 1945, and he was never heard of again.

A protracted battle took place for possession of the city. By January 13, 1945, the Russians had driven the Germans out of Pest and reached the gates of the ghetto. A month later they liberated Buda.

So ended the Waada's illegal work. Their leaders emerged from underground and, even during the Russian occupation, endeavored to help the former prisoners from the German concentration camps. Then they turned their energies to fresh tasks and other fields. When the State of Israel was founded many of them went there as settlers.

The terrors and anxieties of the war days have now faded, and the peaceful work of building a new country has dimmed many memories.

But Joel Brand can never forget.

DOCUMENTARY APPENDIX

ZENTRALRAT DER UNGARISCHEN JUDEN
BUDAPEST,
VII. SIP-UTCA 12

Budapest, den 16.Mai 1944.

Beglaubigungsschreiben

Der Zentralrat der Ungarischen Juden bestätigt hiemit,
dass Herr Joel Brand aus Budapest seine Auslandreise im Interesse
der gesamten ungarischen Judenheit unternimmt und ersuchen wir
sämtliche hiezu berufenen jüdischen Personen und Institutionen
seine diesbezüglichen Bemühungen weitgehendst zu unterstützen.

Angesichts der lebenswichtigen Angelegenheit,die Herr
Brand zu erledigen hat und die er persönlich vortragen wird,
bitten wir sehr,ihm jede Hilfe dringendst angedeihen zu lassen.

Wir wollen noch hervorheben,dass Herr Brand sich
durch seine bisherige hingebungsvolle,selbstlose Teilnahme am
jüdischen Hilfswerke um das Judentum sehr verdient gemacht hat
und wenn er jetzt im Interesse der übernommenen Aufgabe seine
Reise antritt,wollen wir nachdrücklichst hervorheben,dass vom
Erfolg seiner Reise das Geschick und der Bestand unserer Ge-
meinschaft abhängt.

Hochachtungsvoll
Zentralrat der Ungarischen Juden

/Hofrat Samuel Stern/
Präsident

/Philipp von Freudiger/
Mitglied des Zentralrates

Original of document translated on pages 118–119.

THE TIMES THURSDAY JULY 20 1944

Home News

A MONSTROUS "OFFER"

GERMAN BLACKMAIL

BARTERING JEWS FOR MUNITIONS

FROM OUR DIPLOMATIC CORRESPONDENT

It has long been clear that, faced with the certainty of defeat, the German authorities would intensify all their efforts to blackmail, deceive, and split the allies. In their latest effort, made known in London yesterday, they have reached a new level of fantasy and self-deception. They have put forward, or sponsored, an offer to exchange the remaining Hungarian Jews for munitions of war—which, they said, would not be used on the Western front.

The whole story is one of the most loathsome of the war. It begins with a process of deliberate extirpation and ends, to date, with attempted blackmail. The background is only too well known. As soon as the German army occupied Hungary in March of this year, anti-Jewish measures were applied with a brutality known, until then, only in Poland. At the end of last month 400,000 of the 750,000 Jews in Hungary had been " liquidated "—which means that the younger ones had been put into labour camps, where they work under conditions of appalling harshness, and the older ones were sent to the lethal camps in Poland. After reports had come that more than 100,000 had already been done to death in the gas chambers which are known to be there, both Mr. Eden and Mr. Cordell Hull expressed the horror of the civilized world and promised punishment for the guilty.

A short time ago a prominent Hungarian Jew and a German official, whose job obviously was to control his actions and movements, arrived in Turkey and managed to get a message passed to British officials. The Hungarian Jew said he had " every reason to suppose " that the German authorities were prepared to spare the lives of the remaining 350,000 Jews in Hungary, and even let them leave for abroad, if the British would send Germany important war stocks, including 10,000 army lorries. These stocks, he said, would not be used on the Western front.

THE ONLY ANSWER

Such were the terms of the offer as reported to London. The British Government know what value to set on any German or German-sponsored offer. They know that there can be no security for the Jews or the other oppressed peoples of Europe until victory is won. The allies are fighting to achieve that security ; and they know, as well as the Germans, what happens when one begins paying blackmail. The blackmailer increases his price. Such considerations provided their own answer to the proposed bargain.

Whether the German authorities seriously believed that Britain would heed the offer cannot be known at this stage. Probably even before making it they had decided for one reason or another—perhaps for transport difficulties—to drop the deportations to Poland ; yesterday, in fact, the International Red Cross announced that the Hungarian Government had agreed to put a stop to the deportations and even allow some Jews to leave. In the light of that announcement (which will be judged by events), the German " offer " seems to be simply a fantastic attempt to sow suspicion among the allies.

Fantastic though it was, London made sure that Moscow and Washington were quickly in possession of all the facts.

Budapest, July 22, 1944

MEMORANDUM

With reference to today's discussion with Hauptsturm-führer Grüson, we herewith outline our requests in the following points, adding the reasons for them:

1. We urgently request the speedy expediting to the Spanish border of the complete train which was released from the preferred camps in Budapest on June 30. The inmates of this train are at present in Bergen-Belsen, near Hanover, and it is extremely important that all of them reach foreign soil simultaneously with the arrival of your representative and ours. This will provide the psychological basis for a quick and favorable conclusion to the negotiations.

II. We request that a date be set for the trip to Lisbon, so that we may notify our friends in Lisbon, Madrid, and Constantinople, whose telegrams we presented yesterday and today. At the same time we request your assistance in acquiring for our representative the necessary passports and visas.

III. We want, if possible, to send Dr. R. Kastner as our representative to Lisbon, but we need your active assistance in locating him. He was forcibly abducted about three days ago by elements who apparently want to disturb or prevent the conclusion of our agreements, and we still do not know his whereabouts as of this moment. Of course the disappearance of Dr. Kastner must not be allowed to halt the course of the negotiations for even one day, and thus we reserve the right, if need be, to nominate another representative in his stead.

IV. As the most important preliminary condition to a successful agreement in Lisbon, we regard it as essential that, as we have mentioned previously on various occasions, the deportation of Jews from Hungary be suspended until—after an agreement has been reached—an emigration, arranged with our cooperation, of the last remaining Jews in Hungary takes the place of deportation.

V. We mention here as the foremost and most natural request our continuous, fervent petition to save from further annihilation the Jews already deported from Hungary, either as individuals or even as a group, since, on the one hand, the persons capable of working represent a real value for the German economy and, on the other, those incapable of work are scheduled, within the framework of the agreement to be concluded between us, to be the first to be exchanged. Thus these people—children under twelve, old men, and mothers unable to work—represent, even if for a short time they require certain unproductive expenditures, a latent economic value which will become realizable within a very short time.

Furthermore we are ready, to an even greater extent than before, to facilitate the provisioning of these deported Jews with food bought up in Hungary, and otherwise to care for their needs. In connection with this point we wish to reiterate that during our last negotiations with the Obersturmführers Becher and Eichmann it was established that there was more than economic value to this agreement: the value we are ready to deliver, especially in trucks, represents also a saving of German blood. Thus, through us, you indirectly receive, in exchange for Jewish persons (even the unemployable), a saving in German lives. A squandering of the Jewish material you are holding now as deportees, be it for ideological or economic reasons, would be, we believe for the reasons mentioned above, a mistake and a loss of your own people's substance.

The motivations for the five points listed above are as follows:

Ad I.   The first special train which represents, so to speak, the beginning of a large-scale political-economic transaction, was released on the basis of our preliminary negotiations and after approval from your higher authorities. To use a commercial expression, this transport is a sample shipment which you, as the seller of a larger contingent, are passing on to the buyer as a first step.

The figure of 1,600 people, compared to a total of 6-800,000, can be regarded as little more than a small sample. In principle, the total exchange value is to be delivered in the form of raw materials, goods, and especially trucks. In spite of the extremely difficult military-political obstacles which have been raised against this plan, especially in the Anglo-Saxon quarter, our friends abroad have managed to obtain the consent in principle of the other side. This is based on the information of our representative Brand. In substantiation of this are the categorical telegrams submitted to you. As for the price per head, expressed in dollars or goods, which would have to be paid for the emigrants, we have not yet arranged anything definite with you. Even *your* suggestions in this respect varied considerably. Obersturmführer Eichmann on one occasion mentioned 10 Jewish lives as the exchange value for one truck; another mention was made of a maximum of $1,000 to $1,200 per head—a price which exceeds even the capacity of our friends who are willing to make every sacrifice. From the news that has reached us, we would estimate that in Lisbon a price of between $300 and $400 per head might be established. We repeat that first of all the unemployable children below the age of twelve as well as the unemployable mothers and old men would be exchanged, while the others would be able to work in Germany until their turn comes.

Without reaching a final agreement on the per-capita quota, it had been agreed upon the release of the first train that we, out of our own resources, would deposit an exchange value in raw materials, money, and other valuables which per head would cover your highest request mentioned in the course of the negotiations. But this on-account deposit was to be applied and adjusted in the course of the liquidation of the over-all transaction on the basis of the per-head quota to be established in Lisbon.

To date we have deposited in foreign exchange, gold, diamonds, and Hungarian money an equivalent of about $1,100,-000. The exchange value of the goods already delivered or known to be in transit amounts, on the basis of the lists submitted, to about $800,000. Thus, altogether about $1,900,000 have already been paid or are in transit. Several million pengö, which J. Brand deposited earlier, are not included in this account and will be adjusted with you only after J. Brand's return.

Upon the release of the first train we notified our friends abroad that it would reach foreign soil even before the arrival of both our delegates in Lisbon since, according to the accounting above, even on the basis of the impossible demand of $1,200 per head, the exchange value of about 1,600 persons has been provided from our own resources. This amount, however, should, within the framework of the large transaction, represent coverage for three to four times that many people; but for the present, until a complete agreement is reached in Lisbon, it can serve as a security for the exchange value of the first transport. We have reported this abroad, therefore, on the basis of your assurances and in accordance with the approval of your higher authorities.

Now, after the train has left and our payments are in progress, we are informed that the transport has been held near Hanover and that a continuation of its journey to Spain can only begin after an agreement has been reached in Lisbon and the delivery of the trucks has started. This new version of your demands could have an unfavorable influence on the conclusion of a complete agreement in Lisbon and may even make it entirely out of the question. The moral credit of our reports on agreements made with you, which has already been endangered several times, could be completely destroyed.

Our foreign friends on several occasions have called us utopians—more or less with cause; for several of our reports concerning the discontinuation of Jewish deportations from Hungary, as well as the protection and preservation of persons already deported until the consummation of our transaction, proved very soon to be misinformation. Now, on the basis of your assurances and the approval received from your higher authorities, we have begun material and economic payments and we expect thereupon your generous countermove, which would consist of the promised expediting of the first transport to Spain.

Not only we, but also our foreign friends who are to become your partners in this transaction, expect this as a certainty. A failure in our expectations would, for psychological reasons, prevent a conclusion of the agreement and make it impossible for us to tap the sources of credit necessary for this transaction. We are fighting today against a certain amount of skepticism on the part of our own friends and creditors abroad, and we would lose the first round in this fight for their confidence if our reports about the expediting of the sample transport should, in spite of our efforts, not prove true.

It has been held against us that the delay in the return of J. Brand has an unfavorable influence on the expediting of the train from Hanover. We have already shown several times that this was due to passport and visa difficulties and that neither J. Brand nor we bear any responsibility for this. When the first transport was released, the question of the return of J. Brand—who was then already overdue—was tabled by mutual consent. There was no mention at all, when we began our material payments, that his urgent return was a *conditio sine qua non* for the expediting of the first transport.

We do not want to leave it unmentioned that all of us—that is, the entire Jewish population of Hungary, whether already deported to Germany or still in Hungary—remain in your power and thus represent hostages for the fulfilment of the obligations assumed by us. The initial transportation of about 1,600 persons to a foreign country only slightly changes the numbers of the remaining 6-800,000 people; but, on the other hand, it can assure the success of the entire transaction. Delay of this transport, however, could be the main reason for the failure of the negotiations.

Ad II. As can be seen from the telegrams, our friends Schwarz and Dobkin are in Lisbon as of today, and a meeting can lead to immediate agreements. We must take advantage of this opportunity right away; otherwise we might later lose too much time in bringing together the decisive factors once more.

(signed) ANDREAS BISS, LIC. ENGINEER

This memorandum was handed by the Waada to the Budapest SS leadership. It became the basis for accounting and negotiations.

Der Reichsfuhrer-SS

(1) Berlin SW 1, March 21, 1945
Prinz-Albrecht-Strasse 8

Field-Command

Dear Mr. Kersten:

Please accept first of all my thanks for your visit. I was delighted this time, as always, when you came and, in old friendship, made your great medical art available to me.

During the long years of our acquaintance we have talked about many problems, and your attitude was always that of the doctor who, far away from all politics, wants the best for the individual and for mankind as a whole.

It will interest you to learn that in the past quarter year I have realized a thought which we once discussed: in two trains, about 2,700 Jewish men, women, and children have been brought into Switzerland. Actually this has been the continuation of the course my colleagues and I have been pursuing consistently over many years, until the war and the resulting unreasonableness in the world made its realization impossible. As you know, during the years 1936, 37, 38, 39, and 40, I created, together with Jewish-American organizations, an emigration organization whose work has been very beneficial. The journey of the two trains into Switzerland, in spite of all the difficulties, is nothing but the deliberate revival of this beneficial procedure.

From a prison camp, Bergen-Belsen, there emanated in recent days the rumor that a large-scale typhoid epidemic had broken out. I immediately sent there the hygienist of the SS, Professor Dr. Mrugrowski, and his staff. As it happens, unfortunately but rather frequently in camps containing people from the East, there were cases of spotted typhoid, but with the best modern medical measures they can be regarded as under control.

It is my conviction that by eliminating demagoguery and superficialities beyond all conflicting factors, and regardless of deep wounds on all sides, wisdom and logic must win the upper hand, and with them at the same time the human heart and the will to help.

Naturally, I will always be glad to consider, as I have done in all these past years, in good and bad times, any requests which you transmit or express to me on a human level, and decide upon them, whenever possible, generously.

With my kindest regards to your dear and esteemed wife, your children, and especially to you,

(signed) in old affinity
Yours,
H. Himmler

This letter by Heinrich Himmler is typical of his attitude in 1945. The original will be found on the following pages.

Der Reichsführer-SS

(1) Berlin SW 11, den   21. März 1945.
Prinz-Albrecht-Straße 8

Feld-Kommandostelle

Lieber Herr K e r s t e n !

Nehmen Sie bitte mit diesen Zeilen zunächst
einmal meinen Dank für Ihren Besuch entgegen. Ich habe
mich diesesmal wie immer gefreut, wenn Sie kamen und
mir in alter Freundschaft Ihre grosse ärztliche Kunst
zur Verfügung stellten.

In den langen Jahren unserer Bekanntschaft
haben wir uns ja über viele Probleme unterhalten und Ih
Einstellung war immer die des Arztes, der fernab aller
Politik das Beste für den einzelnen Menschen und für di
Menschheit insgesamt will.

Es wird Sie interessieren, dass ich im Laufe
des letzten Vierteljahres einen Gedanken, über den wir
einmal sprachen, zur Verwirklichung gebracht habe. Es
wurden nämlich in zwei Zügen rund 2.700 jüdische Männer
Frauen und Kinder in die Schweiz verbracht. Es ist dies
praktisch die Fortsetzung des Weges gewesen, den meine
Mitarbeiter und ich lange Jahre hindurch konsequent ver
folgten, bis der Krieg und die mit ihm einsetzende Unve
nunft in der Welt seine Durchführung unmöglich machten.
Sie wissen ja, dass ich in den Jahren 1936, 37, 38, 39
und 40 zusammen mit jüdischen amerikanischen Vereinigun
eine Auswandererorganisation ins Leben gerufen habe, di
sehr segensreich gewirkt hat. Die Fahrt der beiden Züge
in die Schweiz ist die trotz aller Schwierigkeiten bew
vorgenommene Wiederaufnahme dieses segensreichen Ver-
fahrens.

Von einem Gefangenenlager Bergen-Belsen kam in
tzter Zeit das Gerucht, es wäre eine Typhusepedemie grös-
ren Ausmasses ausgebrochen. Ich habe den Hygieniker der ϟϟ,
ofessor Dr. M r u g r o w s k i , mit seinem Stab sofort
rthin geschickt. Es handelte sich um in Lagern mit Men-
hen aus dem Osten leider sehr oft vorkommende Flecktyphusfäl-
lle, die aber mit modernen und besten medizinischen Maß-
hmen als beherrscht anzusehen sind.

Ich habe die Überzeugung, dass unter Ausschaltung
n Demagogie und Äusserlichkeiten über alle Gegensätze
nweg und ungeachtet blutigster Wunden auf allen Seiten
isheit und Logik ebenso sehr zur Herrschaft kommen müssen
e gleichzeitig damit das menschliche Herz und das Wollen
m Helfen.

Es ist selbstverständlich, dass ich so, wie ich es
den ganzen vergangenen Jahren in guten und schlechten
iten getan habe, Wünsche, die Sie mir auf der menschlichen
ene übermitteln lassen oder mitteilen, gerne prüfen und
es nur einigermassen geht, grosszügig entscheiden werde.

Mit meinen herzlichen Grüssen an Ihre verehrte,
ebe Frau, an Ihre Kinder und besonders an Sie,

INDEX